Seekers, Saints & Scoundrels

THE COLORFUL CHARACTERS
OF RED ROCK CANYON

*Bear —
Thanks for all
the wonderful
memories.
Chuck Williams
June 2017*

by Chuck Williams, Linda McCollum,
Dan Wray, Cam Camburn,
Crystalaura Jackson, Norm Kresge
and Sharon Schaaf

D1501451

Seekers, Saints & Scoundrels: The Colorful Characters of Red Rock Canyon

978-0-9961496-0-0

Editor: Sharon Schaaf

Project coordination: Chuck Williams

Design: Carole Thickstun, Ormsby & Thickstun

This book has been financed in whole or in part with funds from the city of Las Vegas Historic Preservation Commission Centennial Legacy Grant. The contents and opinions, however, do not necessarily reflect the views or policies of the city of Las Vegas, nor does the Historic Preservation Commission guarantee the historical accuracy of the content of grant funded projects.

Profits from sales of this book will fund Friends of Red Rock Canyon programs and services benefiting Red Rock Canyon National Conservation Area.

Printed in the USA on recycled paper by Paragon Press, Salt Lake City, Utah.

DEDICATION

With our heartfelt thanks, this book is dedicated to the many organizations and individuals who were involved in the creation and protection of the Red Rock Canyon National Conservation Area. If it takes a village to raise a child, it took an army to protect this national treasure. Some of the organizations are mentioned in the book, and our hats are off to these groups who worked so hard on Red Rock Canyon's behalf. Unfortunately, it is impossible to name everyone who had a part in making Red Rock Canyon what it is today; they all deserve to be recognized. Hopefully, when they read this book, they will take renewed pride in what has been accomplished and know that Southern Nevada is a much better place because of their efforts.

Table of Contents

Foreword vii

European "Discovery" of the Las Vegas Valley 1

Travel, Settlement, Explorations, Interventions 9

History of Spring Mountain Ranch 23

Cottonwood Ranch/Blue Diamond 59

Pine Creek Canyon 81

Morgan Ranches 87

Oliver Ranch History 101

Bonnie Springs Nevada 125

Calico Basin 141

Mountain Springs 155

The Sandstone Quarry 163

One Man's Dream 177

Stone of La Madre Quarry 185

Blue Diamond Mine 189

The Smaller Mines in Red Rock Canyon 207

Others Who Left Their Mark 217

Friends of Red Rock Canyon 227

Red Rock Canyon Interpretive Association 241

Protecting the Land 247

Acknowledgments 277

Timeline 278

References 280

About the Authors 301

Foreword

By Sharon Schaaf

The Cultural Resources Committee of Friends of Red Rock Canyon conducts archeological surveys of Red Rock Canyon and other areas nearby. One of its responsibilities is to monitor and document sites, rock art and artifacts found in the conservation area. At a committee meeting three years ago, the proposal was made to write a history of the Red Rock Canyon National Conservation Area using the committee's documents and surveys as a starting point.

Longtime committee member and current Friends President Chuck Williams agreed to lead the project which began as a simple documentation of facts and dates. However, as he started talking to people who had lived in the area, Chuck realized that there was a much greater story to tell. Over the next two years he recruited six more authors to help him: Cam Camburn, Crystalaura Jackson, Norm Kresge, Linda McCollum, Sharon Schaaf and Dan Wray. Their voices tell the story of Red Rock Canyon.

Hundreds of volunteer hours have been dedicated to the creation of this book. The next nineteen chapters are the product of seven authors' devotion to the project.

Chuck Williams begins the historical account by going back to the Europeans who first came through the canyon looking for new travel routes. The routes they discovered made it possible for future travelers and traders to reach California from the east. Eventually, more adventurers came to settle in the area working as ranchers and miners.

Mountain man Bill Williams was one of the first settlers in what we now know as Spring Mountain Ranch State Park. Blue Diamond resident Linda McCollum has been doing research on the area for many years and uses her knowledge to take us through almost one hundred years of ownership on the property. First named Sandstone Ranch, then Bar Nothing Ranch and finally Spring Mountain Ranch, the land was always owned and occupied by some of the most colorful characters in Red Rock Canyon.

At about the same time, just a few miles down the road, the town of Blue Diamond was getting its start. Linda tells the story of her village using interviews, county records and other historical documents she and the Blue Diamond History Committee have gathered. Originally named Cottonwood Ranch, Blue Diamond saw many owners who farmed and ranched there. When gypsum was found in the area, Blue Diamond became a company town until 1964 when it was returned to the ownership and care of its residents.

Experienced Red Rock Canyon hiker Norm Kresge has always wanted to know more about the homestead he had seen in Pine Creek Canyon. This popular site is now part of Red Rock Canyon National Conservation Area, but ownership passed through many people in the early to mid-1900s. Norm heard that a film had been made in Red Rock Canyon, and his research led him to discover that the movie was "The Stalking Moon," filmed in Pine Creek Canyon in 1968. And so, for a few months, Pine Creek Canyon was home to Gregory Peck, Eva Marie Saint and Robert Forrester, stars of the film.

Chuck Williams picks up the story of Red Rock Canyon using personal interviews and newspaper accounts to take us back in time almost a century to visit the Morgan and Oliver Ranches. Bill and Reese Morgan were cowboys in the true sense of the word. Operating ranches in the early 1900s, they were two of the most colorful Las Vegas pioneers.

Reese eventually sold his 160 acres to CB Oliver, who kept the property as a family retreat for 55 years. Chuck's research located a copy of a 1993 interview with CB's son that provided details about the ranch. He was also able to contact and interview several individuals who lived on the ranch when their parents were caretakers of the property, along with a few friends and neighbors of Mr. Oliver. Their recollections offer insights into life in Red Rock Canyon before it became a conservation area.

Bonnie McGaugh Levinson was a neighbor of the Wilsons, Morgans, Olivers and other homesteaders in the Red Rock Canyon area. As you can imagine, the founder of Bonnie Springs Ranch has some delightful stories to tell. Dan

Wray has spent years volunteering in every area of Red Rock Canyon. As a result, he is able to make you feel as if you are sitting in a chair by the fire in Bonnie's home, in the beautiful setting of Bonnie Springs Ranch, listening to Bonnie tell her life story.

Ella Mason homesteaded in the Calico Basin before Bonnie arrived in the area. It's a shame because they probably would have become good friends. Ella sold her 160-acre Calico Basin land in 1937, and the property saw several different owners after that. Chuck Williams had the opportunity to personally interview Don Triolo who lived there in the 1950s and shares Don's narrative of life in Red Rock Canyon in those days.

At the other end of the Red Rock Canyon National Conservation Area, we find Mountain Springs, the pass connecting Las Vegas and Pahrump and part of the Spanish Trail. Ray Trousdale was a youngster when he came to Las Vegas and worked with farmer Otto Baker, rancher Paul Warner and Buster Wilson who was involved in the early history of Red Rock Canyon. In Chuck Williams' 2012 interview with him, Ray describes growing up in the Las Vegas Valley in the 1940s and 1950s.

The Red Rock Canyon National Conservation Area was home to three quarries: Sandstone, Rhea and Stone of La Madre. Judging by the number of newspaper articles from the time, Sandstone Quarry generated a lot of excitement in the early 1900s. Rhea Quarry was the dream of World War II veteran T.P. Rhea, a man who loved to study the rocks found in the canyon. One of the first interviews for this book was with T.P.'s daughter, Faye. Cultural Resource Committee member Dan Wray had the opportunity to participate in that interview as Faye, with help from her sisters Pam and Joy, shared fond memories of her father, describing how T.P. worked so hard to make the quarry profitable for his family. The owners of Stone of La Madre Quarry had to abandon the claim after the Friends of Nevada Wilderness organized a boycott of the sandstone they planned to mine.

Many men attempted to make mining a successful endeavor in Red Rock Canyon, but the largest and best known mine is the Blue Diamond Mine. Linda McCollum told the story of the Village of Blue Diamond and in this chapter she tells us about the mining company that helped build it. Using more interviews from the Blue Diamond History Committee and records from the Bureau of Mines, she takes us back to 1900 when the Blue Diamond Materials Company was formed. The Nevada deposit was found in 1923, and mining operations grew along with the town. The mine changed owners several times over the years, until the quarry closed in 2002.

As an experienced Red Rock Canyon hiker, Chuck Williams knew there had been many more mines in the conservation area. None as large as Blue Diamond, these smaller mines still had an impact on the canyon. I was surprised that there were so many mines and agreed to write the chapter about them. The men who owned LaMadra, Quo Vadis, Midnight, Smuggler, Oliver, Lucky Strike, Iron Age and White Beauty Mines were a colorful bunch coming and going into the Las Vegas Valley in the early 1900s; but none of them got rich from the deposits they found.

Red Rock Canyon had a few more stories to tell about others who left their mark there. Norm Kresge and Chuck Williams put them together in one chapter that takes us from the Naylors and moonshining, to the home of the Las Vegas Archery Club, over to a bulldozed road to nowhere, up to Inscription Rock and finishing up with the work done by the Civilian Conservation Corps in the late 1930s.

Red Rock Canyon is now in our hands. Friends of Red Rock Canyon Historian Cam Camburn takes us back to 1984 and the founding of Friends. The volunteer organization of Red Rock Canyon has grown from its 14 founding members to over 350 members today. Friends' mission is to provide trained volunteers who work non-stop to preserve, protect and enrich the conservation area. Crystalaura Jackson, board liaison for the Red Rock Canyon Interpretive Association, writes the story of the association and its establishment in 1988 to provide materials and programs promoting an understanding of the history and science of the Red Rock Canyon National Conservation Area.

The story of Red Rock Canyon doesn't really end because as long as we take good care of it, the canyon will be here for generations to come. Chuck Williams' final chapter is a reminder that the work done in the past 70 years to protect Red Rock Canyon as a national conservation area must continue in order to preserve this Southern Nevada and national treasure!

RED ROCK CANYON
NATIONAL CONSERVATION AREA

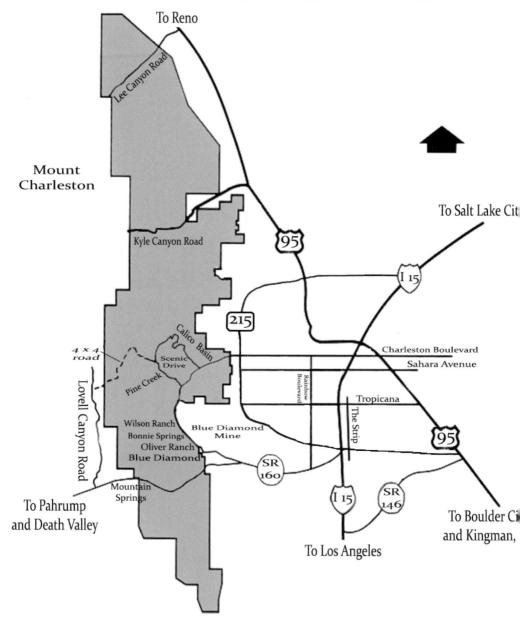

To Reno

Lee Canyon Road

Mount
Charleston

To Salt Lake Cit

Kyle Canyon Road

95

I 15

215

Calico Basin

4 x 4
road

Scenic
Drive

Charleston Boulevard

Sahara Avenue

Pine Creek

Rainbow Boulevard

Tropicana

The Strip

Lovell Canyon Road

Wilson Ranch

Bonnie Springs

Oliver Ranch

Blue Diamond

Blue Diamond
Mine

95

SR
160

Mountain
Springs

To Pahrump
and Death Valley

I 15

SR
146

To Boulder Ci
and Kingman,

To Los Angeles

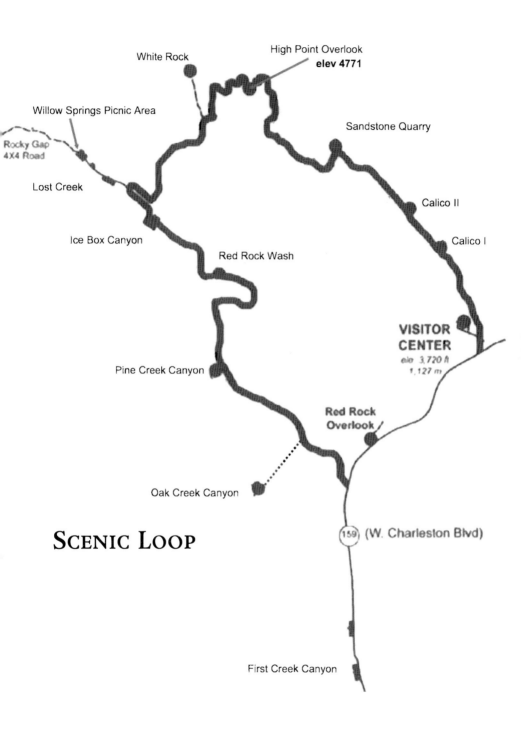

White Rock

High Point Overlook
elev 4771

Willow Springs Picnic Area

Rocky Gap
4X4 Road

Lost Creek

Sandstone Quarry

Calico II

Calico I

Ice Box Canyon

Red Rock Wash

VISITOR
CENTER
ele 3,720 ft
1,127 m

Pine Creek Canyon

Red Rock
Overlook

Oak Creek Canyon

SCENIC LOOP

159 (W. Charleston Blvd)

First Creek Canyon

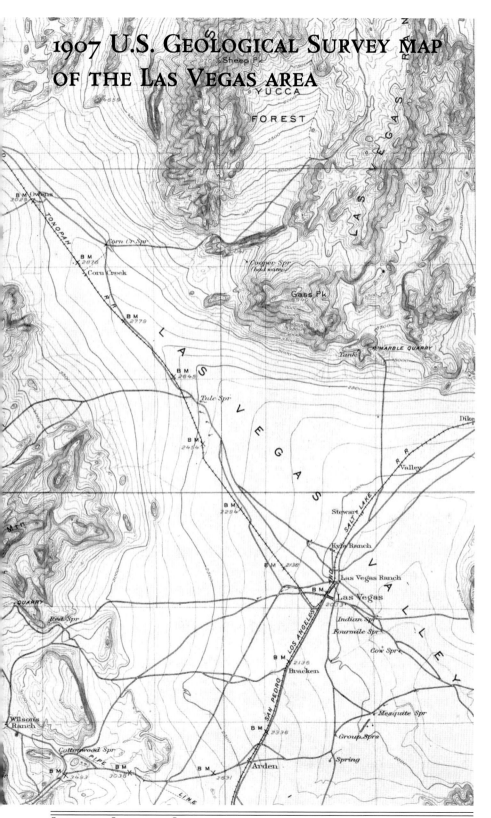

1907 U.S. Geological Survey Map of the Las Vegas area

CHAPTER 1

European "Discovery" of the Las Vegas Valley

By Chuck Williams

"It can be approached only from the south, and after entering it there is nothing to do but leave. Ours has been the first, and will doubtless be the last, party of whites to visit this profitless locality. It seems intended by nature that the Colorado River, along the greater portion of its lonely and majestic way, shall be forever unvisited and undisturbed."

> —Comments from Lt. Joseph Ives who was exploring the area around Hoover Dam and the Grand Canyon in 1857-1858 (*Humans at the Grand Canyon*, n.d.).

The European settlement of the Las Vegas area dates from the mid-1850s. The reasons are obvious. To begin with, the Las Vegas area is located off the beaten path in the driest desert in North America and the journey coming from any direction was difficult and dangerous. The early explorers who traveled through this part of the west were searching for a shorter route to California and were not looking for a place to relocate; they only wanted to pass through this area as fast as possible. When reading the reports and diaries of these early travelers, one recurring theme is the difficulty of crossing the desert and how man and beast suffered from thirst. They also make mention of the large number of bleached horse and mule skeletons that lined the trail. It was not unusual to lose half of the livestock to thirst and lack of fodder.

Illustration of Captain Cardenas at the Grand Canyon

Lastly, some early visitors were not all that impressed with what they saw, as noted by Lt. Ives' comments. Well, it wouldn't be the last time Las Vegas would be dissed.

DISCOVERY

In September 1540, Captain Garcia Lopez de Cardenas, along with Hopi guides and a small group of Spanish soldiers, traveled to the South Rim of the Grand Canyon between Desert View and Moran Point. They ventured about one third of the way into the canyon but had to turn back because of lack of water. Afterwards no Europeans visited the Grand Canyon for over two hundred years (*History of the Grand Canyon*, n.d. & Steiner, 1999). Francisco Domínguez and Silvestre Escalante, Franciscan priests, and Don Bernardo Miera y Pacheco, a cartographer, traveled with eight men from Santa Fe in an effort to find an overland route to the Spanish Missions in California in 1776. Because of many hardships they were forced to turn back, but their maps and reports assisted other nineteenth century explorers and the route traveled would eventually become part of the Old Spanish Trail (*Dominguez-Escalante Expedition*, n.d. & Steiner, 1999).

In 1826–1827 mountain man Jedediah Smith led two expeditions to Spanish California, his route following the Virgin River through present day Utah and Nevada to the Colorado. His party crossed the Colorado into Arizona and then on to California by crossing the Colorado River near today's Laughlin. His party was imprisoned by the Spanish authorities (as the expeditions were not authorized by either the American or Mexican governments) and on the second trip formerly friendly Mohave Indians killed 10 of his group. Their return trip generally followed the route of present day I-15, but it is unknown if they traveled through the Las Vegas Valley. According to Elizabeth Warren in her thesis on exploration of the region, one survivor of the Smith expedition, named Black, settled in Northern New Mexico and "He must have talked about that trip" (Dale, 1991 & Hopkins & Evans, 1991 & Warren, 1974).

Statue of Rafael Rivera

Antonio Armijo with a group of approximately 60 men and 100 mules departed Northern New Mexico on November 7, 1829. Their goal was to find a trade route to Los Angeles. The group initially followed Francisco Domínguez and Silvestre Escalante's 1776 route. On December 25 a detachment of scouts left the party to explore the next portion of the route. They returned on December 31 to the main group which was camped at the junction of the Virgin and Colorado Rivers. The next day Armijo noted in his diary, "One man is missing from yesterday's detachment—citizen Rafael Rivera." Rivera rejoined the group on January 7 and reported that he found a favorable camp site. Following Rivera's lead, the party next camped in some part of the Las Vegas Valley. Elizabeth Warren believes they came up the Las Vegas Wash to Duck Creek and camped in the area close to today's Paradise Spa. From there the group most likely followed the low pass toward California through which I-15 now passes. Armijo's diary lists their next camp as a dry lake, most probably near present day Jean. And so we celebrate Rafael Rivera as the first non-Native American to visit the Las Vegas Valley. He is remembered by a statue at his namesake Rafael Rivera Community Center and a street named in his honor (Hopkins & Evans, 1991 & Warren, 1974 & *Background on the old Spanish National Historic Trail*, n.d. & Steiner, 1999).

Many other caravans followed variations of Armijo's route but most bypassed the Las Vegas Valley. It would take another explorer to put Las Vegas on the map.

John Frémont, "The Pathfinder," served in the military and later became the first Republican candidate for President. He managed to get himself into various forms of trouble during most of these endeavors including being court-martialed. Recounting his travels, misadventures and political life would require a large

General John C. Frémont

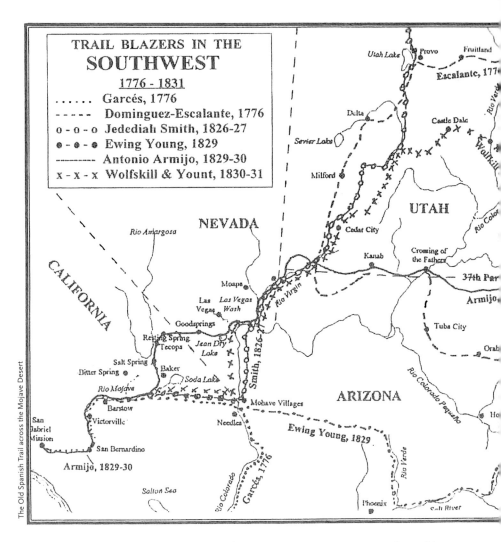

TRAIL BLAZERS IN THE
SOUTHWEST
1776 - 1831
...... Garcés, 1776
- - - - Dominguez-Escalante, 1776
o - o - o Jedediah Smith, 1826-27
● - ● - ● Ewing Young, 1829
——————— Antonio Armijo, 1829-30
x - x - x Wolfskill & Yount, 1830-31

chapter in itself (*John C. Fremont*, n.d. & *John Charles Fremont*, n.d.). Of his several expeditions, Frémont's 1843–1844 journey to Oregon, California, and Nevada with famed mountain man Kit Carson makes interesting reading and included a visit to what is now Red Rock Canyon. During the spring of 1844 the group found itself in the vicinity of Death Valley looking to meet up with the Spanish Trail in order to make their way back east. On April 18, Frémont's cartographer, Charles Preuss, wrote in his diary:

> Why do we have so many animals? One hundred and thirty-four head and twenty-one men, only seventeen of whom can be counted as animal porters! What a burden! One wonders what Frémont has in mind; it is most likely that he hopes to sell them at a good price in Missouri. He'll be fooled, as always (Preuss, 1958).

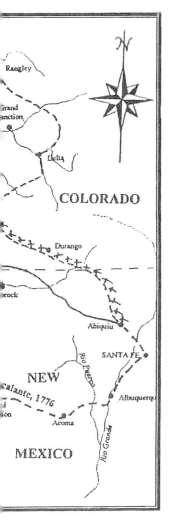

Around present day Tecopa they met a man and boy who reported that they were the only survivors of an Indian raid while their party was camping at Archilette Spring (now known as Resting Spring and Resting Spring Ranch) while traveling along the Spanish Trail. Two men had been killed and the women taken hostage along with all the group's horses. Carson and another man named Godey volunteered to pursue the trail. They returned the next day with two scalps and the missing horses; the women had not been found. There are two versions of what had transpired. According to Frémont, Carson and Godey charged into the Indian camp with guns blazing, killing two braves and chasing the rest of the village away. Carson would write that there were 30 Indians in the camp when they charged. Cartographer Preuss wrote that Carson and Godey, "sneaked, like cats as close as possible. Kit shot the Indian in the back." Preuss also noted that the rest of the Indian village consisted of women and children who escaped. When it came to the taking of scalps, Preuss had little good to say about Carson or Godey, "Are these whites not much worse than the Indians? The more noble Indian takes from the killed enemy only a piece of the scalp as large as a dollar. These two heroes, who shot the Indians creeping up on them from behind, brought along the entire scalp" (Fremont, 1845 & Remley, 2011 & Preuss, 1958).

In any case, the exploration reached Mountain Springs Pass (SR 160 on the way to Pahrump) on May 1, 1844. Frémont notes that overcoats are needed in the cold air. He writes about the plants blooming, "…which wonderfully ornaments this poor country… We encamped at a spring in the pass, which had been the site of an old village. Here we found excellent grass, but very little water" (Fremont, 1845).

Preuss writes:

Raw weather but clear, dark-blue sky. When will that eternal wind stop? We've had it almost incessantly for more than a month now. Because of these detours without grass the horses have become so weak that one after the other must be left behind. They cut off all the hair from their tails and manes [before leaving them to die—in order to make saddle girths,] which make them look ridiculous (Preuss, 1958).

Frémont writes:

> The next day [May 2] in a short but rough ride of 12 miles, we crossed the mountain; and, descending to a small valley plain, encamped at the foot of the ridge, on the bed of a creek, where we found good grass in sufficient quantity, and abundance of water in holes. The ridge is extremely rugged and broken, presenting on this side a continued precipice, and probably affords very few passes. Many digger tracks are seen around us, but no Indians were visible (Fremont, 1845).

[Note: Native Americans carried long sticks, hooked at the end, which they used to capture lizards and other small animals from their holes. Frémont used the term "digger" for the Paiute Tribe.] Preuss writes, "We move slowly through this miserable country. Today we have grass and water." Preuss later wrote, "It is not weakness, but softness of the feet that makes our animals so slow. At Sutter's place (yes, that Sutter, where they camped before heading south) we were, as usual, too impatient to have them all shod" (Preuss, 1958).

Frémont's party was camping in Red Rock Canyon, perhaps at First Creek or Oak Creek.

On May 3 Frémont writes:

> … After a day's journey of 18 miles, in a northeasterly direction, we encamped in the midst of another very large basin, at a camping ground called Las Vegas—a term which the Spaniards use to signify fertile or marshy plains, in contradistinction to llanos, which they apply to dry and sterile plains. Two narrow streams of clear water, four or five feet deep, gush suddenly with a quick current, from two singularly large springs; these, and other waters of the basin, pass out in a gap to the eastward. The taste of the water is good, but rather too warm to be agreeable; the temperature being 71 in the one and 73 in the other. They, however, afford a delightful bathing place (Fremont, 1845).

Leaving Las Vegas and traveling to the northeast Frémont writes:

> In about five hours' ride, we crossed a gap in the surrounding ridge and the appearance of skeletons of horses very soon warned us that we were engaged in another dry jornada [day's journey], which proved the longest we had made in all our journey - between 50 and 60 miles without a drop of water. Travelers through countries affording water and timber can have no conception of our intolerable thirst

while journeying over the hot yellow sands of this elevated country, where the heated air seems to be entirely deprived of moisture....We ate occasionally the bisnada [cactus] and moistened our mouths with the acid of the sour dock (Fremont, 1845).

At the Muddy River, Paiutes suspected Frémont was raiding for slaves and approached the group armed with their weapons:

They were barefooted and nearly naked; their hair gathered up in a knot behind, and with his bow, each man carried a quiver with thirty or forty arrows partially drawn out. Besides these, each held in his hand two or three arrows for instant service. Their arrows are barbed with a very clear translucent stone, a species of opal, nearly as hard as the diamond; and shot from their long bow, are almost as effective as a gunshot (Fremont, 1845).

Frémont made peace, but the Paiutes continued to be an irritation demanding food and gifts. On May 9 along the Virgin River, they murdered one of his men who was searching for a lost mule. The expedition continued up the Virgin into present day Utah where conditions improved and they encountered no additional problems with the Indians.

Mohave Indian guide with similar bow and arrows.

After Frémont's return, Congress printed 20,000 copies of his 1845 report and map and the route through Las Vegas became more traveled. Elizabeth Warren noted in her thesis that the report and map, "became so important that if a group of emigrants did NOT have one, that fact would be mentioned in diaries" (Warren, 1974). Within ten years Mormons would send families from Utah to settle in the Las Vegas Valley.

ENDNOTES

One of the attendees at the 2012 Mojave Rock Art Workshop was an elder from the Mohave Tribe. After one of the presentations he spoke to the group about being politically correct when discussing Indians. He told us that Indians don't understand what the big deal is. Indians call themselves Indians when they talk among themselves, or if need be, by the name of a particular tribe, such as Paiute or Mohave, etc.

The early journals and diaries (some in beautiful handwriting) are interesting because they give life to the story and make the travelers human instead of simply words in a history book. They can also contain racist terms and derogatory comments about non-whites. I chose not to include most of this language, as it adds nothing to the story. I decided instead to include human interest entries such as the one that follows:

Shortly after starting the 1842 exploration, Frémont's party crossed the Kansas River when an accident occurred. Frémont's official report describes what happened:

> The man at the helm was timid in water, and in his alarm capsized the boat. Carts, barrels, boxes and bales, were in a moment floating down the current, but all the men who were on the shore jumped into the water without stopping to think if they could swim and almost everything, even heavy articles such as guns and lead, were recovered. Two of the men who could not swim came nigh being drowned and all the sugar belonging to one of the messes wasted its sweets on the muddy water—but our heaviest loss was a bag of coffee which contained near all our provision. It was one which none but a traveler in a strange and inhospitable country can appreciate, and often afterwards when excessive toil, and long marching had overcome us with fatigue and weariness, we remembered and mourned over our loss in the Kansas (Fremont, 1845).

CHAPTER 2

Travel, Settlement, Explorations, Interventions

By Chuck Williams

In the spring of 1848 Lt. George Douglas Brewerton, stationed in San Francisco, was transferred to a post in Mississippi. He was ordered to report to Los Angeles and accompany Kit Carson who would be delivering military dispatches and mail to St. Louis via the Old Spanish Trail. Several years later, Brewerton, who would become well-known as an artist of Western American landscapes, published a book about this once-in-a-lifetime adventure in which he described overtaking a caravan which stretched for over a mile:

> This caravan consisted of some two or three hundred Mexican traders who go once a year to the California coast with a supply of blankets and other articles of New Mexican manufacture; and having disposed of their goods, invest the proceeds in Californian mules and horses, which they drive back across the desert. These people often realize large profits, as the animals purchased for a mere trifle on the coast, bring high profits in Santa Fe. [This caravan]...did us great injury, as their large caballada [containing nearly a thousand head] ate up or destroyed the grass and consumed the water at the few camping grounds along the route. Their appearance was grotesque in the extreme. Dressed in every variety of costume, from the embroidered jacket of the wealthy Californian, with its silver bell-shaped buttons, to the scanty habiliments of the skin-clad Indian (Brewerton, 1930).

One can only imagine what it would be like to observe such a group traveling through Red Rock Canyon and on to the springs of Las Vegas. As a side note, the dispatches being carried by Carson included the first reports about the discovery of gold at Sutter's Mill.

TRAIL TRAVEL, EARLY SETTLEMENT, MORE EXPLORATIONS AND MILITARY INTERVENTION

So while traders and travelers continued to pass through and even camp in Red Rock Canyon on the way to and from California, there were no settlements in the area. This was about to change. The route would begin to attract California settlers traveling in wagon trains which made progress more difficult. The portion of the trail/route through southern Nevada was considered to be the most difficult of any route to California. Coming from the east, the wagon route up Virgin Hill (located six miles southwest of present day Mesquite) was considered, "the climax of bad places." Addison Pratt described how his party had to chip and break through the ten-foot-high vertical ledge at the top of the hill. "We were compelled to work several hours rolling stone from the top of the hill before we could get up one wagon with eighteen yoke of oxen." After several days hard journey the springs at Las Vegas became the favorite resting place for travelers going in either direction (Lyman, 2004).

What is now Spring Mountain State Park was known as the Bill Williams Camp or Bill Williams Ranch in the 1850s. Based on several accounts, it appears that sometime around 1840 mountain man and explorer Old Bill Williams and a mixed band of renegades "collected" a herd of horses and mules

Charles Nahl

Crossing the Plains

from southern California and drove them across the Mojave to sell at a large profit back east. How the horses were collected, the number collected, and the number that were lost varies on who is telling the story. According to allthingswilliam.com, the group collected about 3,000 abandoned horses and lost half crossing the desert where Old Bill sold his share for a barrel of whiskey. In his 1853 book, George Brewerton relates a story he heard about Old Bill in which the group stole 1,500 head of mules and horses from California ranches. They were pursued by a posse of 200 men and lost half of the herd crossing the desert and the rest were later stolen when they were attacked by Indians. There is enough documentation to conclude that some type of raid or roundup occurred and all of the variations are fun to read (Brewerton, 1930 & William Sherley Williams, n.d.).

In 1855 the Military Commander of the Department of the Pacific requested cartographic information of the lands under his command. Lieutenants Mowry and Chandler were given the task of mapping the route from the Great Salt Lake to Los Angeles. Lt. Chandler's planning map of the route, which closely followed the Old Spanish Trail, shows the mileage between stops and also includes interesting notes along the way. Along the Virgin River in southern Utah and eastern Nevada he noted, "Indians plenty in 1855." Along the Muddy River the note reads, "Indians plenty and impudent," which corresponds with Frémont's experience when traveling through the area. Chandler noted that it was nearly 60 miles between the Muddy and Las Vegas and that, "Water horrible all through this country when any to be found" (Steiner, 1999).

Mormons began to settle in northern Utah in 1847, encouraged in part by Frémont's expedition. In 1855 the church sent a group of 30 men, under the direction of William Bringhurst, to establish an Indian Mission at Las Vegas. The Mormons built an adobe fort alongside Las Vegas Creek, a wall of which still stands at the current location of Las Vegas Boulevard and Washington

Thaddeous Kenderdine

Mormon Fort c. 1858

Avenue. The fort is considered to be the oldest Anglo-American building in Nevada. The missionaries also dug irrigation trenches and planted grain. The Mormons made a treaty with the Indians and taught farming in addition to teaching religion. Additional Mormon families joined the mission to provide assistance; however, the fields could not support 100 members of the mission and the estimated 1,000 Indians that lived in or near the Las Vegas Valley. A drought in 1856 also hurt the traditional supplies of wild food and game and the Indians began stealing grain and melons from the mission's fields. Tempers begin to flare among the missionaries. In May Nathaniel Jones arrived with orders from Brigham Young to take men from the mission to work the lead mine at Mt. Potosi. The mission's recorder reported, "Jones presented his letter of instruction to President Bringhurst and there was a great storm between them calling each other anything but gentlemen." Bringhurst refused to send men or supplies to the mines and when Jones returned to Las Vegas in December he bore a letter from Young notifying Bringhurst that he was disfellowshipped from the church. The lead mine proved to be unprofitable and in the fall of 1858 Indians stole the harvest from the fields. Church authorities officially abandoned the mission. During the Civil War, the fort was renamed Fort Baker, but was never garrisoned (Hopkins & Evans, 1999 & *United States information: Nevada*, 2010).

By 1856 Captain George Johnson, who operated a steamboat transporting goods from the mouth of the Colorado River to Yuma, was looking for ways to expand his operation. He heard rumors that steamboats could navigate as far as the Virgin River. Thinking that he could turn a profit supplying mail and supplies to the new forts and settlements being developed in the Las Vegas area, he approached Secretary of War Jefferson Davis who liked the idea and convinced Congress to approve funding. Johnson bid on the contract but Davis awarded it to a relative, Lt. Joseph Ives. Johnson went home and fumed. Ives had an iron-hulled stem-wheeler named *Explorer* built and shipped to the mouth of the Colorado River. The ship had an unusual design with a howitzer on one end and a cabin on the other. When it arrived at Yuma, the Indians laughed at it and the expedition artist called it "a water-borne wheelbarrow."

Balduin Mollhausen

Steamship Explorer.

It proved to be underpowered with too deep a draft. In fact it ran aground in front of the crowd who had gathered to watch the launching, much to the delight of the Indians. Captain Robinson later claimed that he became able to recognize sandbars ahead by the number of Indians gathered along the banks of the river.

Ives began the upriver journey from Yuma on December 31, 1857. What he didn't know was that Captain Johnson left the same day on the *General Jesup*, a much faster boat with a shallow draft. Johnson wanted to reach the Virgin River first in order to one-up the young Lieutenant. He made it as far as the first rapids about 75 miles from the mouth of the Virgin River, but he was short of supplies and had to turn back. About a week later they met the Explorer which was slowly coming upstream. One has the impression that Captain Johnson received a great deal of pleasure from the meeting.

The *Explorer* did get further upstream than the *General Jesup* but ran aground on a rock at the entrance to the Black Canyon, knocking the boiler off its foundation. Ives determined that "Explorer Rock" was the extent of practical navigation; however, he concluded that steamboats could get as far as the Virgin River when there was high water. His group explored eastward along the south rim of the Grand Canyon before heading back down river. In his official report he labeled the area as "altogether valueless" and neglected to mention anything about the *General Jesup* or Captain Johnson (History of the Colorado, n.d.).

Attached to Ives party was geologist John Strong Newberry who had a very different impression of the canyons. Newberry later convinced John Wesley Powell that a boat could run the river and the survey would be worth the risk (Joseph Christmas Ives, 2013).

River traffic expanded in the 1860s and 1870s, going upstream as far as Eldorado Canyon and Callville; but traffic began to decrease when the railroad reached the Colorado River in 1877. When the Laguna Dam was constructed 14 miles north of Yuma in 1909, the era of paddle-wheeler river transportation became history (History of the Colorado, n.d.).

In 1858 Thaddeus S. Kenderdine, traveling to California from Salt Lake City, described bathing in one of the Las Vegas springs:

> … a spring five yards in diameter and of unfathomable depth, the water of which was at precisely the right temperature for a warm bath. Divesting ourselves of our habiliments we plunged into the refreshing pool, below whose sparkling surface it was impossible to sink; not on account of the density of the water, but of the strong current that boiled up from the bottom (Kenderdine, 1888).

Solomon Carvalho described the spring "...forty-five feet in diameter containing the clearest and purest water I ever tasted; the bottom which consisted of white sand did not seem to be more than two feet from the surface." Unable to sink in the strong upward current he found that, "The water, instead of being two feet deep, was over fifteen, the depth of the longest tent pole we had with us" (Lyman, 2004).

After refreshing themselves, the Kenderdine group moved on to their next camping site:

> Passing over a tract of country almost entirely destitute of vegetation and covered with beds of sand, gravel and stone, we reached, late at night the noted camping place of Williams' Ranch. Old Williams, a hunter celebrated for his daring exploits and recklessness, once ventured here with a drove of horses and mules which he stole from the Mexicans; and after him the camp is called. A considerable stream here gushes out at the foot of a rugged wall of rock, which rises precipitously to the height of one thousand feet above the plain (Kenderdine, 1888).

The Historian Dennis Casebier, an expert on the history of the Mojave Road, published "Carleton's Pah-Ute Campaign" which documents the 1860 campaign against the Paiute Indians. There were three murders in early 1860 that contributed to the campaign, all attributed to Paiutes. The first happened in January when Robert Wilburn was murdered by Indians near the Mojave River in California. The second incident, the murders of Thomas Williams and Jehu Jackman in March, directly led to the campaign.

Some in California thought that the Mormons had instigated the attack on Williams and Jackman. Williams was at odds with Brigham Young and the Mountain Meadows Massacre of 1857 was still recent history. The circumstances of the murders were a bit puzzling because the Indians did not attack the train of fourteen wagons. Several Indians joined the train near Bitter Springs, California and offered to show Williams where water and grass could be found. When Williams and Jackman went ahead with the Indians, they were attacked and killed and the Indians disappeared into the desert.

Most citizens of Southern California blamed the Indians and the Los Angeles Star was demanding that forts be established along the Salt Lake Road (the Old Spanish Trail). The next week a military party heading to Los Angeles discovered that Williams' body had been dug-up, the body stripped of clothing and left exposed. The Star ran an article on March 31, 1860 demanding that, "A severe castigation should be dealt out to these Indians." The Star also suggested, "There is no manner of doubt but that the murder is the result of Mormon counsel and Mormon policy."

Pressure was placed on the Governor who in turn urged General Clarke, Commander of the U.S. Army Pacific Division, to send troops to establish a military post along the Mojave River. On April 5 General Clarke ordered Major James Henry Carleton to march to the Mojave country in order to establish order and punish the Indians. The letter of instruction provided a means to determine who should be punished: "...as it is impossible to ascertain the individuals or the particular band in each case of murder, and is as certain that their acts are connived at by the tribes in the vicinity, the punishment must fall on those dwelling nearest to the place of murder or frequenting the water course in its vicinity."

Public Domain

James Henry Carleton

Carleton had the troops start construction of Camp Cady and dispatched scouting parties to track down Indians. On April 19 a detachment encountered a band of Indians and in the ensuing skirmish one Indian was killed and another taken prisoner but was later killed. Carleton had the two bodies hung on gallows at Bitter Springs where they were left as a warning to the Indians. On May 2 in the area around Kelso Sand Dunes another band of Indians was discovered and immediately attacked by Lt. Carr's detachment. Three Indians were killed and one squaw taken prisoner. That night, acting on instructions from Carleton, the heads of the three Indians were cut off and put in a sack. The heads and prisoner were sent to Camp Cady where Carleton had the heads taken to Bitter Springs and "hung upon the gibbet" along with the two bodies already hanging there.

Carleton kept scouting detachments busy looking for more Indians and in the meantime released the captured squaw, "Who was sent to her people with the word that we were punishing the Pah-Utes for their bad conduct in murdering people who had done them no harm; that we should continue to punish them until they would promise to behave themselves in the future."

In the middle of May he divided his command into two detachments to tempt the Indians into attacking the smaller party. On May 18 at Mountain Springs, Lt. Davis was instructed to conceal his men in the wagons and if the Indians were friendly, to do them no harm: but if they were threatening or insolent, he was to attack them while Major Carleton followed up with the larger mounted detachment of troops. There were no Indians at the springs; the next day the combined detachments proceeded to Las Vegas where Carleton had decided that if the Indians were not hostile, he would give them "a talk" and assure them that if they behaved they would be treated kindly. At Cotton-wood Spring (Blue Diamond) they came upon a Rancheria (a Spanish word for small village) where the fire was still burning but the Indians had escaped. Carleton sent an interpreter out to call to them to come back but to no avail. As the scouts approached the old fort at Las Vegas, two mounted Indians were seen coming from the direction of the Muddy River. These Indians made off to the neighboring mountains "as if greatly frightened."

The troops stayed at Las Vegas that evening and then returned to Camp Cady on the 20th. As they were passing Cottonwood Spring they came upon the same Rancheria "but moved higher in the crags." Everything had again been abandoned in flight. "Three Indians were seen on the peaks and were beck-oned to and called to in their own language to come down-but they hurried off as if terrified."

What is surprising is that Carleton seemed puzzled as to why the Indians were frightened, evidently forgetting about the two bodies and three heads he left hanging at Bitter Springs.

In early June Carleton received the following letter from headquarters:

Sir:

Brigadier General Clarke has received your report of May 14, 1860, covering that of Lieutenant Carr. He desires you to give positive or-ders to prevent mutilation of the bodies of Indians who may fall, and to remove all evidences of such mutilation from public gaze. He can-not approve of such acts, tho' the effect upon the Indians may, or may be thought to be good.

The *Salt Lake City Deseret News* published an article on June 13th denouncing the gruesome display after it was reported by a citizen who just returned from Los Angeles by the way of Bitter Springs. The article also stated that the few Indians who had resided in the Bitter Springs area had now relocated to Las Vegas or the Muddy River.

Carleton continued his scouting patrols, extending into Death Valley and to the Colorado River; but the troops, while finding tracks, failed to make con-tact with any Indians.

Carleton finally decided to return to Fort Tejon after concluding that the In-dians had all left the area, informing headquarters that he planned to leave on July 3. However on July 2nd, "...about 3 o'clock P.M. three Pah-Ute chiefs showed themselves on top of a mountain near this camp. They waved a white flag." Shortly after the three entered the camp, an additional 23 men and one woman joined the group. They had come to make peace. Carleton reported, "The Indians present were from different parts of the desert; here was one Mojave Indian with them, and one Pah-Ute from as far away as the Santa Clara Band." Carleton dictated the peace terms which the Indians agreed to.

In the final report of the expedition, Carleton recommended that if the Indians remain peaceful, they should receive gifts such as blankets, knives, shirts, tobacco and beads. He felt that doing this "would be commencing with them a system of artificial wants which eventually will make them so dependent on us, they will never go to war for fear the supply will stop. The cost would be a bagatelle." And so ended the Pah-Ute Campaign (Casebier, 1972).

Sometime during the 1860s, sandstone buildings were built on the Williams Ranch. The Spring Mountain Ranch State Park staff provided the following:

> At the present time we do not know, with absolute certainty, who actually built the one-room cut sandstone cabin, but Tweed Wilson told Maryellen Sadovich, then local historian, that Ivanpah grain merchants built the sandstone buildings in the 1860s. A core sample taken in 1974 from one of the fig trees by the sandstone buildings indicates that it was between 110 and 115 years old at the time, which indicates they were planted around the same time that the house and blacksmith shop were erected, probably circa 1860 (Nevada State Parks, n.d.).

The Mormons would return to Southern Nevada in 1865 to establish St. Thomas where they hoped to grow cotton along the Muddy River. By 1869 additional settlements were established in St. Joseph, Overton, West Point and Junction City. William Bringhurst would soon rejoin the church and served as bishop of the Springville, Utah Ward as well as a trustee for what would become Brigham Young University. The Potosi mine would be reopened in 1861 when it was discovered that the impurities which caused the lead to be so brittle were zinc and silver ore (Hopkins, & Evans, 1999 & *United States information: Nevada*, 2010).

In 1865 Octavius Gass took over the abandoned Mormon Fort at Las Vegas and turned it into a 640-acre ranch and way station for travelers. He planted orchards and a vineyard as well as vegetables supplying fresh food to settlements and mines in Eldorado Canyon and along the Muddy River, even paying his Indian ranch hands with food. Gass also raised cattle and horses running the ranch until he defaulted on a loan from Archibald Steward in 1879 (Hopkins, & Evans, 1999 & *United States information: Nevada*, 2010).

Lt. George Wheeler conducted military reconnaissance through Southern Nevada in 1869 and 1871. The 1871 expedition included photographer Timothy

Wheeler 1869 Map

H. O'Sullivan. The 1869 expedition followed the eastern boundary of Nevada from Elko to Panaca, then to the Muddy River which they followed to the mouth of the Virgin River. On September 29 he noted the temperature reached 112 degrees and that John Wesley Powell had landed there 15 to 20 days prior to his arrival.

Wheeler estimated an Indian population of 500 in the Muddy River area.

Powell's boats in the Grand Canyon c. 1869

Wheeler sent the wagons and livestock to Las Vegas by the Spanish/Mormon Trail; meanwhile, the rest of the detachment followed the north bank of the Colorado River to Eldorado Canyon where they continued up the existing road to Las Vegas. Wheeler described the trip in his report:

John W. Powell with Tau-Gu Chief of the Paiutes, overlooking the Virgin River c. 1873

The mountain scenery in the locality, to my idea, was the most wild, picturesque and pleasing of any that it has ever been my fortune to meet. The walls of the Black Canyon rise steep, dark and sharp on the south and east and to the north-east those of Boulder Canyon, while the continuation of ranges leading to the north and north-west make our station appear similar to that of a depression of the great basin. The scene encountered upon reaching the river by moonlight, after threading a steep and sandy wash, was one of extreme loneliness and grandeur.

During a reconnaissance mission to the Potosi area, the group camped near what is now the town of Blue Diamond.

On the morning of the 12th October, 1869, I left camp at Las Vegas, taking one ambulance and three men, and Mr. Hamel, Topographer. The road taken was the old Salt Lake road, running in southwesterly direction until reaching a point about five miles from Potosi, when the tail leading to the latter place branches off to the south. The first

Black Canyon c. 1870

Timothy H. O'Sullivan

night's camp was made at the Cottonwoods, a spring at the head of Las Vegas Wash. These springs rise and sink at several places and receive their name from the cottonwoods growing near.

Wheeler's 1869 map shows Bill Williams's Ranch north of Cottonwood Springs, but there is no mention of the ranch in his report (Wheeler, 1870).

Wheeler conducted another reconnaissance in southern Nevada in 1871, where they again camped at Cottonwood Springs which he described as, "a beautiful locality on the eastern slope of the Spring Mountains." There the expedition rested for several days while they waited for supplies to come upriver from Camp Mojave. Wheeler then sent part of the organization via the Colorado River to Arizona and California. Lt. Lockwood was placed in charge of the land parties which proceeded eastward to the Muddy and Virgin River area. Again there was no mention of Bill Williams' Ranch in their reports.

Wheeler Boat Crew c. 1871

Timothy H. O'Sullivan

Wheeler estimated the Indian population of Las Vegas Valley to be 50-60 during the summer months and increasing to 150-200 in the cooler months as the Indians moved between the valley and Cottonwood Springs (Wheeler, 1872).

Cottonwood Spring is now generally associated with the spring in Blue Diamond; an upper spring, about a half mile north, is now known as Wheeler Camp Spring; a third spring, another three quarters of mile north, was known as Bens Spring. Bens Spring later became part of what is now Oliver Ranch. Wheeler's reports identified the camps as either the Cottonwoods or Cottonwood Springs, so it is difficult to now determine exactly where he camped during his two visits.

In the 1860s, travel to and from the Las Vegas area continued to be dangerous because of the harsh environment and possible attacks. Travelers were cautioned to travel in groups and use care. It can be argued that this advice is still valid today.

ENDNOTES

Reading the details of Carleton's Paiute Campaign is disturbing but it was felt they needed to be included in the story. The European and American travelers passing through the Las Vegas area upset the physical and social environment

Timothy H. O'Sullivan

Paiute Indians c. 1872

of the native Indians. The settlers attempted to teach new farming methods and convert the natives to their religion. The natural food sources became scarce and the outsiders seemed to have a never-ending supply of food, clothes and equipment. The Indians began to beg for food and travelers and ranchers had to protect their equipment and livestock from being stolen. The whole Indian lifestyle was undergoing change. And it was not a good omen. In 1855 the Mormons estimated there were approximately 1,000 Indians in the Las Vegas area. Wheeler's 1871 report estimated 500 Indians in the Muddy River area and 200 in and around Las Vegas/Cottonwood Springs (Hopkins, & Evans, 1999 & Wheeler, 1870). Currently there are about 30 members of the Las Vegas Paiute tribe and 320 members of the Moapa (Muddy River area) Paiute Tribe.

Casebier writes about the Pah-Ute peace agreement, "The terms of the agreement required that the Indians leave hostages at Fort Mojave as insurance for the good conduct of the rest of the tribe. By this time their ranks were reduced to the point where they would not have been a threat much longer anyway." (Casebier, 1972).

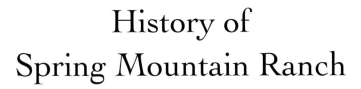

CHAPTER 3

History of Spring Mountain Ranch

By Linda Carlyle McCollum

FIRST SETTLEMENT – BILL WILLIAMS

Campsite Established - 1840

In the 1830s, news of Jose Antonio Armijo successfully developing a trade route from New Mexico to California spread quickly. With large numbers of horses available in California, some trappers and traders, whose business was in decline, resorted to stealing horses. One of those mountain men was Bill Williams who, along with others, stole thousands of horses and mules from the missions and ranches in California around 1839-1840 and drove them across the Mojave heading for the livestock market in Santa Fe. Williams is said to have stopped off in the Red Rock Canyon area to recoup after having crossed the Mojave Desert (Kenderdine, 1888). Williams told the story of the raid when he was living in Salt Lake City, and he may have even returned to the area several times. When the trail developed into the Mormon Road, the emigrants coming from Salt Lake applied Williams' name to the campsite. It was an alternate campsite on the Spanish Trail and is believed to have been used by outlaws involved in the slave trade or attacks on caravans coming through the area (Hafen, 1993).

Visited by Kenderdine (1858), Wheeler (1869), Dellenbaugh (1876)

When Thaddeus S. Kenderdine traveled to California from Salt Lake City, he mentions stopping at the Bill Williams Campsite on December 9, 1858. Leaving the Las Vegas area, they had a thirty-mile trip to the next campsite with food and water:

> …we reached late in the night the noted camping place of Williams' Ranch. 'Old Williams,' a hunter celebrated for his daring exploits and recklessness, once ventured here with a drove of horses and mules which he stole from the Mexicans, and after him the camp is called (Kenderdine, 1888).

When Lt. George M. Wheeler came through the Cottonwood Valley in 1869, his preliminary report included a map which located the Bill Williams Ranch site at present day Spring Mountain Ranch State Park (Wheeler, 1875). In his second expedition through the area in 1871, a large Indian population was occupying Cottonwood Spring so Wheeler camped at a spring to the north known today as Wheeler Camp Spring.

In his report published in 1872, Wheeler reports that "no white man has deemed the place as affording sufficient prospects of success to justify settling there for any time (Wheeler, 1970)." No mention is made of any structures in the area.

In 1876 Frederick S. Dellenbaugh recorded a sketching tour through the area. On a sketch he made of Lost Creek there is a pencil note stating, "Head of a canyon in cliffs near Bill Williams Homestead (Dellenbaugh, 1902)."

SANDSTONE RANCH – WILSONS FLYING 5

WILSON ACQUIRES LAND IN 1875

The property known as the Williams Ranch or Homestead on early maps of the area became the Sandstone Ranch when James Bernard Wilson and George Robert Anderson acquired the 320 acres (160 each) at the base of Sand Mountain in Cottonwood Valley. The acquisition included all the water rights for stock and other purposes. Surveys Book B shows Wilson filing on January 31, 1875, with the records being filed in March at Pioche (the county seat for Lincoln County which was the county of record before Clark County was established in 1909). It was not until 1878 that the Tax Assessment Rolls show both Wilson and Anderson owning 320 acres of land 24 miles west of Las Vegas. In 1879 Anderson paid a possessory claim on 160 acres of land 25 miles west of the Las Vegas Ranch known as the Sand Stone Ranch. The following year in 1880, Wilson claims 160 acres of "land and improvements" on land known as the Sand Stone Ranch in Cottonwood Canyon, 25 miles west of the "Los Vegas Rancho."

James Wilson

James Bernard Wilson was born in New York on September 4, 1828. The 1880 Census and Army Records show his father was from New York, but his mother was from Ohio; when he was two years old, the family moved to Knox County, Ohio. He appears to have been an Ohio farmer before going to California during the Gold Rush and becoming a miner. The 1859 California Census shows him mining at the Rough and Ready east of Nevada City.

On October 7, 1861, the National Archives show Wilson at Camp Union in Sacramento, California enlisting in the California Volunteers as a Sergeant in Company "I" which was one of two companies which were to reestablish Fort Mojave (SMR Files). The Fort had been established in 1858 on the Colorado River to pacify Indians so mining could be conducted in the Eldorado Mining District. During the Civil War, stations were established to protect gold coming out of the Mother Lode country from Confederate threats as well as protecting emigrants going through the area (Warren, 1979). The California Volunteers were used to garrison these forts. Wilson was with a detachment in the area until October 16, 1864 when his term of service expired, and he left for Drum Barricks, California where he was discharged on October 31, 1864 (SMR Files).

In 1865 Pah-Ute County Records show Wilson owning mines in the San Francisco Mining District, Mojave County, Arizona territory with various partners (SMR Files). By 1869 Wilson had visited his old friend Octavius D. Gass in Las Vegas. Gass was also from Ohio and had come west during the gold rush. Gass was involved in mining in El Dorado Canyon from 1862-65 before acquiring the Old Mormon Fort property which became the Las Vegas Ranch. Lincoln County Deeds Book A on page 549 shows Wilson acquiring a portion of the Las Vegas Ranch on September 13, 1869 from an Anne Sewerth.

In 1871 Wilson was buying land in Lincoln County with various partners. Mining claims were located in Bristol District near Pioche, the last named "Poor Man's Lode." Within four years he profited from the sale of his last mining claim "Sweep Stakes" in Pahranagat Lake Mining District (Lincoln County Records).

In 1872 Wilson filed on the Las Vegas Springs (today's Springs Preserve) with John Howell for agriculture and grazing purposes. Survey Book B in 1871 showed both men having 160 acres of the property which was surveyed by Wilson, Howell and a George Anderson. The Assessment Rolls for Lincoln County in 1875 show the value of the 320 acres being $50 and having 150 bushels of barley, 17 cattle and two mules and the taxes being $25.02.

On February 9, 1874, Deeds Book M, page 358 shows Wilson selling out his "undivided interest" in the Spring Rancho to Howell for $100 which included the Flying 5 Brand and the cattle from Howell. Since supplying the mines was no longer a profitable livelihood, Wilson decided to begin an extensive cattle operation business (Sadovich, 1972).

When Frederick Dellenbaugh came through the area on a sketching tour in 1876, he mentions meeting Howell and Anderson in Cottonwood Valley on March 19, going after stock out on the road to Pahrump by a ranch he refers to as the Bill Williams Homestead (Dellenbaugh, 1902). Obviously Wilson's former partner Howell continued to be aligned with Wilson in some capacity at his new ranch. Four years later, the 1880 Census shows Howell in El Dorado Canyon as a teamster.

George Anderson, Annie and Son "Tweed"

Spring Mountain Ranch Archives

The "red-headed" George Robert "Bob" Anderson was born in England of a Scottish father and an English mother. It is said that he came to America when he jumped ship at San Pedro, California on January 16, 1864 to "test his luck in the gold fields" (Sadovich, 1972). He wound up at Mohave City in the 1870 census which said he was a 23-year-old laborer from England. After becoming bored with the mines, George became a successful freight wagon driver from San Bernardino to Fort Mojave and El Dorado Canyon, as well as Las Vegas, and became a part of Las Vegas' early history. Wilson and Anderson may have connected when Wilson was mining in the area.

George Robert Anderson

Anderson had a Paiute wife named Kayer, known as Annie, from the Panamint Mountains on the western edge of Death Valley. She had given birth to a son named Jim by a transient miner named Jim Betts or Beck on October 14, 1874 (Rogers, 2000). George and Annie had a son named George Twison "Tweed" Anderson on October 28, 1876.

Numerous stories have circulated over the years about Tweed's birth. Some say that Anderson's wife died giving birth to Tweed on one of their freight trips. Tweed claimed he was born under a mesquite bush somewhere between Las Vegas and Boulder City and his mother died when he was three and his father died five years later. On April 13, 1959, the *Las Vegas Sun* claimed Tweed had been born in a primitive shack in 1876 at the Old Ranch on South Fifth St.

Anderson seems to have continued business operations outside of the ranch he shared with Wilson. Some claim that Anderson and his wife drove supply wagons to remote mining camps. There is some evidence that after his wife died Anderson left the ranch and may have been running a saloon in El Dorado.

The 1880 census shows Wilson aged 42 (when he would have been 52) with a thirty-year-old Indian woman named Annie and three half-white children named Jonathan (age 6), Mary (age 3) and James (born in June). None of this matches the known information on Wilson or Anderson.

Possibly the Indian woman worked at the Sandstone Ranch and lived there with her offspring. The same 1880 census also shows a James Wilson living at Pahrump Springs and a Robert Anderson, a 32-year-old butcher born in England of Scottish descent, at El Dorado Canyon.

ANDERSON LEAVES THE RANCH

In the fall of 1880 and spring of 1881, accounts with Poppet and Clark in Ivanpah show George Anderson buying 1800 cigars, 44 gallons of whiskey along with beer, wine, cider and cards as well as making payments on the merchandise. The 1881 Assessment Rolls show Anderson owning a lot in Eldorado Canyon with a man named Marsh and improvements being made (SMR Files). The *Weekly Record* of October 13, 1883 mentions Anderson owning the Bobby Burns Saloon in El Dorado Canyon which was the chief pleasure resort owing to Anderson's pleasant and genial disposition. The article goes on, under "El Dorado Canyon Items," to mention Anderson being open-handed and free-hearted and helping all those who land at El Dorado broke. This, along with receipts and account sheets in the early 1880s, shows Anderson trading in Ivanpah, California with Poppet and Clark for whiskey, beer and other merchandise and confirms him running a saloon. In 1885 he seems to be in Daggett, California purchasing wood for a 20 x 32 foot building with eight windows and ten doors. In January of 1886 George Anderson is mentioned as starting up a new business, and after this date there is no mention of Anderson in the area.

Family correspondence reveals Wilson spending Christmas in 1881 visiting his relatives back in Ohio and Iowa. When he returned to Las Vegas, he brought Robert Wilson's son, James H. Wilson, back with him for a visit. Wilson's brother, T.J. Wilson, wrote Anderson in March of 1882 stating he was glad to hear from him and to learn that Jim had returned home all right as he had not heard from him since he left St. Joseph, Missouri (UNLV Special Collections, Wilson File). He goes on to ask Anderson "to keep up correspondence in order to stay in touch with Jim." Letters indicate Anderson was in touch with T.J. Wilson until 1886. Family letters also indicate that William and Lizzie Wilson later came out west to settle, and in October of 1890 were living in Daggett, California.

With Wilson back east in the winter of 1881 and Anderson in Eldorado Canyon, one wonders who was taking care of the Sandstone Ranch and the cattle operation?

In the fall of 1885, Helen Stewart mentions both Wilson and Anderson visiting at her ranch. Wilson and the two boys celebrated Christmas at her ranch in 1885 and the next day at the Kiel Ranch. In January of 1886, Anderson is mentioned starting up a new business and that it was not a saloon.

WILSON ADOPTS JIM JR. AND TWEED AND DEEDS THE RANCH TO THEM

In 1887 Wilson hired a Scotsman, James MacGarigle, who had been a teacher at the Moapa Indian reservation in the 1870s, to teach the two boys to read and write as well as do math. This indicates that Anderson was no longer around. Octavius Gass's wife is also mentioned as helping the young boys. In 1890 the sixteen-year-old Jim Jr. worked for a while at the Stewart Ranch. At some point Wilson seems to have adopted two boys who were henceforth known as James Bernard Wilson Jr. and George Tweed Anderson Wilson.

Jim Wilson with adopted sons Tweed and Jim Jr. Wilson
Boy in bushes to the left is Willard George c. 1900

In 1888 Wilson's ranch served briefly as the Sandstone Precinct for voters; prior to this, voters had to cast their ballots in El Dorado. In 1890 the Las Vegas Ranch became the voting precinct for the area.

When Wilson filed for an increase on his military pension in 1893, he listed a James N. Pickett, whose residence was Cottonwood Springs, as a witness to his character. He needed two character references to testify that his disability was not the result of "vicious habits." Pickett was a fifty-nine-year-old man who stated that he had known Wilson for ten years (Military Service Records). The other character witness was the James MacGarigle who Wilson had hired to teach the two Indian boys.

In August of 1902, Lincoln County Real Estate Deeds show Wilson deeding the ranch to James B. Wilson Jr. and George T.A. Wilson and retaining personal control until his death.

In 1904 Tweed Wilson was appointed as a Deputy Constable by the Mojave County Sheriff of Arizona, apparently for the purposes of arresting the party that had stolen his horse (UNLV Special Collections, Wilson file).

The railroad came to Las Vegas in 1905 and changed the cattle operation in the area on a large scale. Cattle were trailed to market and feed lots and then shipped to other locations. That same year Tweed was hired by the Union Pacific Railroad as a surveyor. He was paid with a deed to Lot 3, Block 24 of the original Vegas townsite. When he failed to pay taxes for the property, the county acquired the property by default.

WILSON DIES IN 1906

Jim Wilson passed away on May 3, 1906 and was buried at the ranch on May 6. The surgeon's Certificate for Pension in 1899 had shown Jim Wilson to be partially deaf in the left ear, along with a partial loss of sight, rheumatism, heart murmurs, varicose veins and Brights disease of the kidneys. He was also a big man, six-foot two-and-a-half-inches tall.

The two half-Indian boys, Jim Jr. and Tweed Wilson, inherited the Sandstone Ranch in 1906 and seem to have continued to reside on the ranch periodically during their lifetimes even though the ranch was owned by others. Maryellen Sadovich claims they were probably the wealthiest young men in the area, but their limited education and lack of commercial experience combined with non-payment of taxes would result in the boys losing a great deal (Sadovich, personal correspondence).

Nearly a year after inheriting the ranch, the two Wilson boys leased the Cottonwood Ranch (today's Blue Diamond) on April 15, 1907 for one year for

James Bernard Wilson Jr. and George Tweed Anderson Wilson

$120. When they did not give up the Cottonwood Ranch until June lst, they were a month and a half past due, increasing the bill to $135. One wonders why the Wilsons leased the Cottonwood Ranch since they owned the Sandstone Ranch just a few miles away.

TWEED'S SON BUSTER

Tweed's wife Annie, who was the daughter of Indian Ben of Mormon Green Springs (today's Oliver Ranch) bore Tweed a son Buster (Russell) at the Stewart Ranch in Las Vegas on August 8, 1908. Olive Lake, in her interview in 1977, mentions that there were some suspicions that Buster wasn't Tweed's boy as it was thought he looked more like his uncle Jim who had always been so good to him over the years.

RANCH SOLD TO KAISER IN 1909 AND RETURNED IN 1910

A little over a year later on October 2, 1909, the *Las Vegas Age* reports that the "Wilson Brothers Ranch" was sold to Charles Kaiser, head of Kaiser Livestock Company in Elko. The sale included the ranch, water rights and the large stock range with about 400 head of cattle. Kaiser's intention was to transfer a large portion of his sheep business to this area. About 10,000 sheep were shipped from the north, unloaded at the Arden station and driven to the Wilson Ranch on December 25, 1909. In January Kaiser and his partner B.G. McBride moved their families to the ranch. By April the sheep shearing produced over 75,000 pounds of wool that were sacked and made ready for shipment. The company was planning numerous improvements at the Wilson ranch and the building of a substantial stone farm house was underway. Clark County saw this as the beginning of a new and very important source of wealth for the county. But by June of 1910, Kaiser used 64 rail cars to move the band of sheep north to Red Rock, Montana. From there the sheep were driven to new range in Idaho since the feed and water supply was too scant in the Spring Mountains to keep the animals in good condition.

WILSON BROTHERS RECLAIM RANCH/TWEED'S SECOND SON BOONE

During the time the Kaiser Corporation owned the ranch, Jim and Tweed continued their own cattle operation and in 1909 filed for the water at Upper Cottonwood Springs. It is unclear where they were living at this time. They were able to recover the ranch when the Kaiser Corporation decided to give up on the sheep operation, and in 1910 they bought out the water rights from the Kaiser Corporation (Kaiser Land and Livestock Company) securing rights to the springs at the northern end of the canyon and around the other side (Warren, 1974). In the middle of all this, Tweed's second son Boone was born on June 3, 1910.

In their oral interviews in 1975 and 1977, Olive and Ada Lake, who came to Las Vegas as children around 1903 or 1904, mention going to the Cottonwood Ranch, the Wilson Ranch and what is today the Oliver Ranch in their early teens during the summer and riding their horses. Sometime before Jack Naylor acquired what is today's Bonnie Springs, there was a young woman named Mabel living there who "used to come over to the Wilson Ranch and go riding with Jim (Lake-Eglington, 1975)." This would have been Jim Wilson Jr. as the *Las Vegas Age* reports the Lakes vacationing in the area during the second decade of the twentieth century.

On October 23, 1915, the *Las Vegas Age* had an ad mentioning that J.W. Woodard, the agent for Dodge and Ford cars in Las Vegas, had sold three cars that week and one was a Dodge purchased by stockmen Jim and Tweed Wilson. Two months later, the *Las Vegas Age* reports the Wilson brothers filing on Lone Pine Spring, Railroad Spring and Willow Spring for permission to appropriate water for stock and domestic purposes.

A year later on December 9, the *Las Vegas Age* reported that Tweed was driving to Arden from the ranch with Roy Beebe when his hat blew off his head. As he turned to see where it went, he accidentally turned the steering wheel and the car plunged off the road and began rolling over. Beebe suffered some bruises and a general shaking up; but Tweed's face was badly lacerated, his nose smashed and several ribs were broken and severely bruised. He was cared for in Arden, and it was several weeks before he recovered (*Las Vegas Age*, 1916).

In 1917 Jim and Tweed Wilson invested in ore wagons in order to cash in on the freighting boom in the Goodsprings District during World War I. This was a little late, because when the war ended in 1918, mining halted and the Wil-

Jean Fayle

sons were unable to pay off the debt for the wagons and horse team. Jean Fayle of Goodsprings (Yount and Fayle Store) took the ranch as security on a major loan for repayment of debts (Warren, 1985).

While the Wilsons were running the freight operation in 1917, Tweed's son Buster was living with his guardian Mrs. R.E. Lake and going to school at the Las Vegas City School with Helen A. Sander as his teacher. Olive Lake Eglington, Mrs. Lake's daughter, changed Buster's name to Russell when he started school since she felt it was a more proper name. (She had a cousin named Russell whom they called Buster.) Wilson never really appreciated the name change, but it followed him to his grave (Lake, 1977).

In 1918 Annie left the ranch with her son Boone and divorced Tweed. The following year Buster was in the second grade at the Sherman Institute, an Indian school in Riverside, California and did not return to the ranch until the 1930s. Boone and Buster had a poor relationship and did not stay in touch with each other.

The *Las Vegas Age* reported in January of 1919 that the Wilsons were having trouble over their cattle. In April of 1919, James and Tweed repeatedly ran an article in the *Las Vegas Age* with a drawing of a cow with both ears split and the Flying 5 brand on its left hip. By the end of the year, the picture had been published nine times with an offer of a reward leading to the arrest and conviction of any person stealing stock in Nevada. In May of 1920, John Esser, a butcher who had been arrested on rustling charges and convicted of embezzlement months earlier by shipping a carload of livestock claimed by the Wilson brothers as their property, was denied parole (Board Denies Parole Clark County Man, 1920).

FAYLE AND YOUNT ACQUIRE RANCH IN 1920S

The Clark County Mortgage Records show the Wilsons mortgaged the ranch on March 4, 1919 to the Fayles for "various and sundry bills and debts" at their store in Goodsprings. The following year, the *Goodsprings Gazette* reported people enjoying the Fourth of July Picnic at the Wilson Ranch. They were transported by Fayle early in the morning in a big truck along with fourteen cars, each loaded to the top. They lunched under the big trees at "the picturesque ranch in the shadow of the great 'Castle Rock' in the Spring Mountain Range," bathed in the pool and played various sports. "Some picknickers came home by way of Vegas where they took in the movies. The last crowd reached home about midnight. Several parties drove to the ranch Sunday evening and camped overnight" (All Good Springs Awakened Early, 1920).

On February 7, 1925, the *Las Vegas Age* reported Sam Yount purchasing the "Old Wilson Ranch" which was being used as the headquarters for the Wilsons' cattle business. The ranch is mentioned as "one of the most delightful spots of the desert country and would make an ideal home place or resort" (Sam Yount Purchases Old Wilson Ranch, 1925). Since Yount was Fayle's partner at the Goodsprings Store, the acquisition of the ranch may have been a business agreement between Fayle and her partner over the money the Wilsons owed them. Fayle did not foreclose on the Wilsons but did sell off the cattle to Yount who failed to renew the Flying 5 brand on the cattle in 1929.

Jim Jr. & Tweed Are Deeded 5 Acres to Live on Their Entire Lives

On February 9, 1929, Mrs. Fayle sold the ranch to Willard George with a codicil in the deed giving Jim and Tweed Wilson five acres on the ranch that included the old houses and cemetery. Even though the ranch would have different owners over the years, Jim and Tweed Wilson were entitled to live at the ranch their entire lives.

Jim Jr. lived on the ranch for fourteen more years. He passed away in the Las Vegas Hospital on November 23, 1943 and was interred at the Wilson Ranch the next day. Indians in the area came up to the ranch, dug the hole and lowered Jim's casket on their lariats while chanting around the grave.

Tweed suffered a tragic accident in February 1949. He had taken off across the mountains to his own cabin 18 miles over the ridge on the Pahrump side of the range. He ran into a blizzard on the crest and was forced to spend the night waiting for the snowstorm to subside. He stayed three weeks alone in the cabin awaiting aid. A neighboring rancher came and summoned help from the Bar Nothing Ranch (today's Spring Mountain Ranch State Park). Tweed was brought to the hospital with gangrene in both feet. He had not realized that his feet were frozen which necessitated the amputation of one foot completely and part of the other. It was three months before he was released from the hospital as he had to be fitted with an artificial leg and learn to use it (Warren, 1979). When Olive Lake-Eglington saw Tweed for the last time, Tweed was still unable to get around since he had lost part of his foot. It had been a long time since he had had a haircut or a shave and he had a long white beard and hair.

Ten years later, Tweed died on April 12, 1959 of cardiac arrest and carcinoma of the colon at Southern Nevada Memorial Hospital. Vera Krupp, who owned the ranch at the time, gave Tweed a beautiful funeral (*Las Vegas Sun*, 1959).

After graduating from the Sherman Institute, Buster spent a short time painting sets for Hollywood movies before returning to join his father, Tweed, at the ranch in the 1930s. The ranch was then owned by Willard George.

The June 13, 1935 issue of the *Las Vegas Evening Review Journal* reported the sheriff being summoned to the ranch by Willard George's foreman, Ed Relitz, who reported that Buster Wilson was lying in his bunk with his throat cut. When officers arrived at the ranch they found the "corpse" lying beneath a tree with blood oozing from a gash in the head. While the sheriff investigated the scene, he began noticing signs of breathing coming from the "corpse." Buster suddenly woke up, clambered to his feet and explained he had fallen against the door

Buster Wilson c. 1960s

UNLV Special Collections

of his car. Relitz had been told by Tweed to call the sheriff as Buster was dead. The investigation revealed that Jim, Tweed and Buster had been drinking and that Tweed struck his son during an argument. The cut and the flow of blood gave the impression that Buster's throat was cut.

In the 1930s and early 1940s, even though the codicil established in 1929 still gave Tweed the right to live on the ranch, he and Buster periodically spent weeks or months on the western slope of the Spring Mountain range at today's Lost Cabin site. Jim Wilson Sr. is believed by some to have built the original adobe structure, as well as the one in today's Blue Diamond. He used it to live in while he tended to cattle herds in the area when he was running the Sandstone Ranch. Tweed and Buster are believed to have built the second cabin. The upper adobe cabin, made from mud poured in corrugated sheet-metal forms, still remains. The lower adobe cabin, which was converted to a concrete structure, became known as Lost Cabin when it was mistakenly razed by a Forest Service fire crew during a clean up in 1998 (Rogers, 2000).

Beginning in 1943, Buster served in World War II in North Africa with the American Indian Company under George Patton. He was decorated several times for combat heroism. He received the American Defense Medal, European-African Middle Eastern Service Medal, Purple Heart and medals for expert marksmanship and good conduct.

Buster worked for various owners of the ranch. He helped Chet Lauck build the Main Ranch House in 1948, worked as a ranch hand for Vera Krupp, and was employed by Hughes as a spring tender to keep the stream beds free of debris as part of the cattle operation. He also painted local landscapes and animal portraits as well as making wooden carvings of animal heads. Many of his works were created as gifts for his friends.

Buster continued to live in the area. In 1967 Ann Layton, who owned the Blue Diamond store with her husband, said that Buster use to hang out in the village and was drunk all the time but was always a gentleman. He drank Seagrams 7, 16 oz. Bud and malt liquor. He had a flatbed truck which went about two miles per hour. He use to pick up Indians and come to Blue Diamond where he had credit at the store (Layton, 1982).

At the time of his death in January of 1972, Buster was living in a cabin at the foot of Mt. Potosi and looking after range cattle for Howard Hughes. He was killed in a nighttime highway accident on Highway 538 near the Pahrump Highway when his truck overturned and crushed him. He was buried on the ranch in the family cemetery.

Boone Wilson

Buster's brother Boone had married Juanita (Clyde) Lee on the Moapa Reservation. They had four children, three girls and a boy, before they divorced. In April of 1962, Boone was 63 and living alone in a small trailer in the Indian Village. He fought many years to gain legal possession of the five acres and two houses on the Sandstone Ranch (Boone Wilson Homestead Fight, 1972). In March of 1973, the *Review Journal* reported that Boone filed a deposition challenging the sale of the ranch (Indian Fights Sale of Krupp Ranch, 1973). He claimed that he and his family had rights to five acres of ground on the ranch since his grandfather, James Wilson, founded the ranch in 1865. His attorney, Kermit Waters, said any sale of the ranch would be made subject to the suit. Boone's claim was based on the codicil which all owners of the ranch inherited since 1929 when Fayle sold the ranch to Willard George. However, this codicil only included Jim Jr. and Tweed.

Boone claimed Howard Hughes refused to listen to him but heard that Fletcher Jones was a concerned person and a local man, so he might listen. Jones denied knowledge of the Wilson claim to the property and said that, "since the ranch does not belong to him, it isn't his problem right now" (Lewis, 1973).

Boone died February 28, 1975 and was buried on the ranch in the family cemetery. The ranch was closed a half day for the ceremony. Several veterans officiated at the funeral, indicating that Boone had also served in the military. Rumor had it that another coffin with a "handle like patent 1895" was already lying in the ground under Boone's plot. (This may be where Anderson's wife Annie was buried.) Boone was survived by his children Gloria Wilson Shearer, Elaine Wilson, Marie "Lulu" Wilson and Marvin Wilson.

Early Ranch Improvements

The Sandstone Ranch had a one-room stone cabin that was allegedly built by grain traders from Ivanpah, California in early 1867. The traders were looking for land to raise hay and grain to sell to the miners in Ivanpah that was in an isolated area some sixty miles away. However, Lt. Lyle's survey of the area in 1871 makes no mention of any buildings in Cottonwood Valley and states there was "no rancher in valley" at the time. Ivanpah was founded in 1869 and was a short-lived silver mining town on the lower slopes of the Clark Mountains in California. It became a trading center in the 1870s before closing down in the mid-1880s, so the timing does not make a lot of sense. Sadovich claims that Wilson and Anderson moved into the stone cabin in 1867 and built the log cabin in the spring of 1868. This also does not match the documented evidence (Sadovich, 1972).

The sandstone cabin had two windows without panes, a door and fireplace. The sandstone came from blocks that had tumbled from the cliffs behind the ranch. The timbers in the structure were ax-trimmed logs and the construction was low-roof, shed style. The original roof line can be seen on the south wall of the cabin above the south door. A fig tree by the sandstone cabin, dating from the 1860s, was either planted or accidentally started.

The blacksmith shop on the property began as a retaining wall against the slope with an open shed roof. It is unknown whether this was on the property when Wilson acquired it or he built it himself because it was needed for his cattle operation. The forge was built into one end. Smoke escaped through the open walls since there was no chimney. The bellows were added later and

Wilson Cabin c. 2015

Blacksmith Shop c. 1900

their size, nearly six feet long, required breaking through the stone curtains and creating a small jog in the building. The window on the east wall fell out in 1976 when the wall collapsed during a rainstorm.

Blacksmith Shop c. 2015

RANCH IMPROVEMENTS BY WILSON

Wilson built a log house a few yards from the stone cabin. Before 1895, two modifications were made to the log house. The roof was raised and a room added to the north end of the building. Since the fireplace wall was enclosed in the middle of the house, the room addition was only accessible via the porch. At some time a board and batten bunkhouse was also constructed near the site.

The ranch grew to include grazing lands within a fifty mile radius. Wilson also planted grain and a vegetable garden to provide fresh produce, along with meat and other products, to mines in the vicinity and for travelers coming through the area. Old timers mention that in his youth Tweed used to ride out bareback on a pony to the edges of the valley to greet wagon trains and lead them to water.

By 1894 Wilson is believed to have built an earthen dam across the creek to the south of the ranch in order to irrigate some dozen acres, but it was wiped out by floods. The water was later diverted by means of a ditch in front of the blacksmith shop to a natural reservoir (site of the old reservoir). In 1895 he planted apple trees that are located in front of today's Park Superintendent's house. The grapes on the ranch are probably grown from slips from the O.D. Gass Ranch, which was formerly the Old Mormon Fort. Since the original plants at the Fort no longer exist, the grapes on the ranch are the oldest domesticated plants in the area.

The green shed that is attached to the old cabin at the Sandstone Ranch had copper tubing that dates from 1908 indicating the house was being used as a still. During the period of prohibition, many stills were located wherever water could be found in the desert and in the mountains. It became such an industry that the cattle in the area frequently became ill from drinking the seepage from the stills (SMR Files).

SANDSTONE RANCH – WILLARD GEORGE K BAR 2

GREAT GRANDSON OF CONRAD KIEL

Willard George was a prominent furrier (known as the "furrier to the stars") and real estate investor in Los Angeles who had lived in Las Vegas as a boy. Willard was born in Lincoln, Nebraska in 1889 and his family moved to Las Vegas when he was three or four years old. His father was Hampton Ellis George. His mother Sadie was Frank Kiel's daughter, making Willard a great-grandson of Conrad Kiel of Las Vegas. The George family lived on the Kiel Ranch in North Las Vegas from 1892 until 1902, and Willard George frequently visited the Sandstone Ranch as a boy. He felt he owed his highly successful livelihood as a furrier to his Indian instructors who taught him to trap and treat furs while he was a boy. A picture of Jim Wilson standing in front of the cabin at the Sandstone Ranch with Jim and Tweed Wilson has Willard sitting in the bushes to the left of Wilson in the picture.

Willard was sentimentally attached to the Sandstone Ranch and was interested in owning the ranch for the purpose of naturalizing chinchillas in order to improve their quality. On February 9, 1929, he bought the Sandstone Ranch from Jim and Tweed Wilson by paying off the mortgage owed to Fayle and agreeing to the covenant that gave Jim and Tweed the right to reside on the ranch during their natural lives. The mortgage was approximately $13,000. He also gave the Wilsons a share of the cattle and later paid them $100 a month in place of their cattle interest when they were too old to assist on the ranch. The cattle operation continued to carry the ranch and the brand was the K Bar 2 which was registered in the name of Wilson Brothers (Anderson, 1974). When Willard went to file on various water rights, he discovered that Jim Sr. was using water for which he had no permit (Anderson, 1974).

Developed Blue Mist Strain of Chinchilla at Ranch

Willard developed the Blue Mist strain of chinchilla at the Sandstone Ranch. In the late 1930s or 1940s, a stone shed was built to house the chinchillas being raised on the ranch. Since the climate in the canyon was similar to the chinchilla's natural habitat in Peru, Willard thought by releasing them in the canyon he would be able to naturalize them and improve their coats. Unfortunately, their numbers were decreased by coyotes and bobcats. A few chinchillas were still roaming the ranch when Chet Lauck leased it in 1944.

Even though his experimental attempts with breeding chinchillas at the Sandstone Ranch failed, he was still a successful furrier. In 1947 he owned The Antelier Shop which was an exclusive salon on Wilshire Blvd in Los Angeles with the slogan, "we search the earth for furs of worth." He developed the first nationally-used grading system for chinchillas that was formally adopted by the National Chinchilla Breeders Board. He was known as "The Chinchilla Industry's Greatest Friend" and was one of the foremost judges in the industry, giving lectures at seminars and shows. "Keystone to Quality" became the bible for early ranchers. By 1953 he was the oldest judge in the industry.

Absentee Landlord

Willard George was the first absentee landowner and the ranch operation was

Old Reservoir with Willard George House in background c. 1930s

Spring Mountain Ranch Archives

Willard George House c. 1930s

left to the Wilsons. However, he was at the ranch in January of 1941 and saw Carol Lombard's plane passing over in the twilight with what appeared to be the tail bobbing up and down and acting in a peculiar manner.

Willard George built a home next to the old reservoir. The house would later be torn down by Vera Krupp and a guest house built on the site. Other improvements Willard made to Sandstone Ranch are still present today.

In 1929 he built the Foreman's House, which is a one-bedroom house with a milk spring cooling system in the basement. It was known as the "farmer's house" referring to the tenant farmer on the ranch. Willard also had a workshop which was located on the site of today's modern shop. He also planted an orchard in the pasture area near the main ranch house (built later on by Chet Lauck); a few trees still remain. The Old Reservoir, which the Wilsons had started, was expanded. The reservoir was low in elevation and irrigated fewer acres than the present one.

BAR NOTHING RANCH – CHET LAUCK BARS NOTHING

In 1944 Chet Lauck leased the Sandstone Ranch from Willard George with the option to buy in four years. The ranch was renamed the Bar Nothing Ranch and the cattle brand was Bars Nothing. Like Willard George, he was another absentee landlord.

Lauck, who was Lum of the "Lum 'n' Abner" radio show, was born in Allene, Arkansas on February 9, 1902. He grew up in Mena, Arkansas with his school friend Norris Goff, who would become Abner of "Lum 'n' Abner." In 1912 the two school friends would do a blackface act for their friends. Both boys went to the University of Arkansas in the early 1920s but returned to their home town of Mena and married their childhood sweethearts.

They performed blackface comedy until they changed their skit to a hillbilly act for an audition in 1931 on Radio Station KTHS in Hot Springs, Arkansas to benefit flood victims. The pair was such a hit that they got their own radio show which was on the air five nights a week until 1954. They were picked up nationally by the NBC Radio Network. Lauck played a number of recurring characters in the "Lum 'n' Abner" series including Cedric Weehunt, Grandpappy Spears and Snake Hogan (Lum n Abner, 1982).

Lauck and Goff made seven motion pictures in Hollywood between 1940 and 1956 playing the 65-year-old characters of their radio show. Their films were a success because they did their own censoring. The most noted films are "Dreaming Out Loud" (1940), "The Bashful Bachelor" (1942) and "Two Weeks to Live" (1943).

When Lauck leased the Sandstone Ranch in 1944, his partner was W.J. Walshe. Unfortunately, Walshe never came up with his part of the financing; yet the Bars Nothing brand was registered in both their names from 1944-49.

Chet Lauck with his family c. 1950

Spring Mountain Ranch Archives

Lauck Buys the Ranch

When Lauck picked up the option to buy the ranch in 1948, there was a codicil stating that it was subject to the life estate of George T.A. Wilson. Tweed was to have a furnished home that he had the right to use, occupy and enjoy during the term of his lifetime as well as the sum of one hundred dollars per month (SMR Files). Lauck bought the ranch with 350 head of cattle on the range to which he added 20 registered cows. The ranch continued as a cattle operation. It was at this time he began building the ranch house that today serves as the visitor center.

In a letter to the park personnel Lauck wrote:

> It would have been a highly successful ranching operation but the cattle rustlers kept pretty busy thinning them out for me. They didn't drive them off in herds like in the western movies but since it was not fenced they would drive out in a pickup truck, shoot a steer and take off. Sometimes they would dress them out on the spot. In one year by actual count, they had stolen over 400 head (SMR Files).

In 1954 Lauck and Goff retired from radio due to Goff's ill health. Unfortunately, they retired before they ever got into television. The following year Lauck sold the ranch to Vera Krupp.

Twenty years later Lauck was executive assistant to the Chairman of the Board of Continental Oil Company of Arkansas where he was living with his wife Harriet and their three children Shirley, Nancy and Chester, Jr. Goff died in 1978 and that same year Lauck and Harriet visited Spring Mountain Ranch State Park. Lauck died in his home in Hot Springs, Arkansas on February 21, 1980 (Lauck, Internet).

Ranch Improvements by Chet Lauck

Lauck made many improvements on the ranch. As early as 1945, he built the new reservoir which covered nearly three acres and was 15 to 20 feet deep. It was used for irrigation as well as recreation. Lauck stocked the reservoir with blue gill and large mouth bass and had an island for the ducks. The lake was named Lake Harriet after his wife.

The pipe is the original pipe that Lauck put in (Lauck, 1978). The lake had a gas pump that Vera would later remodel.

After buying the ranch in 1948, Chet started building the main ranch house. His wife Harriet was an interior decorator and did all the decor in the main Ranch House. It was a New England style farmhouse with a cedar shake roof,

Lake Harriet c. 2015

cut sandstone and redwood board-and-batten siding. The original house built by the ranch foremen Paul Warner and Buster Wilson was based on a drawing by Lauck. The house had an open kitchen, dining nook, living room, sun porch, two bedrooms and a bath upstairs, along with two bedrooms and two baths downstairs. The house was designed to be only one room wide and offered a view of the mountains from both sides of the house.

The large beams in the house are redwood which was purchased at Basic Magnesium Inc. in Henderson at a surplus sale at the end of World War II. The bricks in the fireplace and gun cases were from Olivera Street in Los Angeles. Paul Warner went to Los Angeles in a cattle truck and got two loads of used brick from Olivera Street (Warren, 1979). The sandstone was recycled from a small building at Sandstone Quarry on the Red Rock Canyon Scenic Loop.

The kitchen had copper-fronted propane ovens; the floor, which may have originally been brick, was replaced with oak planking; the paneling and woodwork were knotty pine. The only thing separating the kitchen from the living room was the stone wall that had a cabinet in it.

Paul Warner started construction but got hurt. He did all the wiring, plumbing and a lot of carpenter work, even hanging wallpaper. Curley Pumbley became the foreman and finished the house, and a man named Holley was hired to finish the carpentry. He lived in the two-story house and brought his wife out for about five months. Buster did all the brick and rock work and built the fireplace out of used brick (Lauck, 1978).

The furniture was pine made into antique replicas by Rennick of Beverly Hills. There were two four-poster beds in the upstairs bedrooms with curved canopies. Some antiques were also used. The upholstered furnishings and window valances were chintz. Mrs. Lauck collected Meissen china which was displayed on a stone wing with a pine breakfront. When the ranch was sold to Vera Krupp, she insisted it be left furnished. While visiting the ranch later, the Laucks saw that she had replaced everything with French furniture from Bel Air (Lauck, 1978).

The floor was made with random boards that buckled in spots. The lumber was two-inch tongue-and-groove that the government had used for water tanks in Henderson where it was stored (Warner, 1975).

In 1953 the back of the house had a swing. The patio was screened in halfway up and there was no pool. The Laucks wanted a pool down below in the pasture so that the view would not be cut off.

In 1950 an east wing was added. The garage was connected to the main house by a breezeway, which was enclosed to house Lauck's racing trophies. It was later converted into a sitting room, pantry, kitchen, bath and laundry, with a bedroom and bath above the garage. Lauck had racing horses at his L&A Stables, the initials standing for Lauck and Ameche Stables (Warner, 1975).

In 1952 a water-powered generating system was installed at the reservoir to run lights in the blacksmith shop and the cabin. It was called "Boulder Dam Jr." Also in 1952, a birdhouse was built in the patio area. White fences with red caps, which were the colors of Lauck's racing stables, were built. The modern shop was started and a stone watering trough replaced the old wooden trough at the Old Cabin. Lauck's children's names and ages are etched in the cement of the trough.

When the Lauck's arrived, there were still about a dozen chinchillas that looked like rats roaming the property. The Laucks fenced in the cemetery for Tweed. The fence was put up to keep cattle from grazing on the graves, and it pleased Tweed very much to have this done (Lauck, 1978).

A Boy's Camp was built. The story goes that Chet's son wanted to go away to camp; rather than send him away, Lauck built a camp on the ranch. The Boy's Camp operated for two years. Boys aged eight to thirteen paid $25 a week and were issued a horse and lariat. They would work the ranch in the morning and play in the afternoon. Approximately fifteen to sixteen boys attended the camp. The Boy Scouts also helped with the camp construction and used the facility. Girl Scouts also used it and Paul Warner's wife was their leader.

SPRING MOUNTAIN RANCH – VERA KRUPP DIAMOND V

Vera Krupp Acquires the Ranch in 1955

Vera Krupp, the wife of German munitions industrialist Alfried Krupp, acquired the ranch in May of 1955 from Chet Lauck with the water rights to 27 springs and renamed it the Spring Mountain Ranch. Alfried Krupp is alleged to have purchased the 518-acre ranch in 1955 for approximately $270,000 as a hobby for Vera. It was Vera's principal residence until 1967.

When asked why she bought the ranch and worked so hard to make it a success, she said "I bought a dream—a dream of complete freedom for myself, a dream of seeing a horse run free, a dream of hearing the stirring of leaves in the breeze, and being made breathless by a beautiful sunset and awed and enriched by nature" (Connell, 1982).

Vera wanted a working ranch. Her intent was to raise a hybrid strain of white-faced Brahmas and Herefords. She purchased prize stock for this purpose and leased over 300,000 acres of Taylor Grazing Land. She learned to ride so she could participate in cattle roundups.

Vera loved animals of all kinds and had a houseful of cats, dogs and even a pet toad. Wild burros frequented the ranch at night, as all animals were welcome except predators that could endanger her livestock. She raised pedigreed Black Great Danes and kept large flocks of chickens and milk cows.

Vera's Youth

Vera Krupp von Bohlen und Halbach was born Martha Vera Wilhelmine Hossenfeldt in Dusseldorf, Rhein, Germany on July 17, 1909. Her father Franz, who was in insurance, passed away when she was quite young. She came into a sizeable fortune when her mother Anna Louise married Heinrich Flottman, a wealthy German industrialist and inventor who held world patents and owned a heavy industrial machinery plant.

Vera was tutored at home until she was thirteen when she began attending private schools in Germany. After graduation she went to the Sorbonne in Paris and the University of Frankfurt where she studied art history, medieval art, architecture and literature.

Vera's Multi-Marriages

In 1929 Vera married Baron von Langenn, who was quite a bit older; it is from this marriage that she derived her title of Baroness. They spent a great deal of time at the mountain resort of Davos, Switzerland to facilitate the Baron's recuperation after he contracted tuberculosis. While in Davos, Vera became interested in films after becoming acquainted with some of the German movie stars and filmmakers. From 1933 to 1938 she acted in movies in Berlin playing Olga in "Verklungene Melodie" in 1937, Mary Waverly in "Kautschuk" in 1937-38, "Mitternachtswlzer" in 1937 and Hix in "Millionen Suchen Einen Erben" in 1937-38 (SMR Files).

When she started coming to the attention of some in the Nazi regime, she saw the "handwriting on the wall" and decided to immigrate to the United States. She came with German producer and director Franz Wisbar either late in 1937 or early 1938, and divorced Baron von Langenn in 1938. Since her finances were tied up in Germany, she had to take odd jobs to get by. Vera did small parts in films, worked at Bonwit Teller and did the concessions for Elizabeth Arden in various department stores.

She traveled to Cuba in order to reenter the U.S. and obtain American citizenship. She obtained her first papers in April of 1940. It was at this time that she married Franz Wisbar in Phoenix, Arizona and they lived in Hollywood and New York while Wisbar directed several films. She became a naturalized U.S. citizen on May 23, 1947. It was at this time she legally changed her given name to Vera.

After World War II, Vera's mother, who had become a widow when her husband died unexpectedly of a heart attack in October of 1947, planned to immigrate to the United States. Vera obtained an immigration visa for her mother and was making final arrangements when her mother passed away unexpectedly. Vera divorced Franz Wisbar in 1948 in Las Vegas and married Sigfrid Knauer, a physician in California. She divorced Knauer in Las Vegas in 1952.

On May 19, 1952 she married Alfried Krupp von Bohlen und Halbach in Berchtesgarten in Germany. Vera and Alfried Krupp had been teenage sweethearts and while events in Europe caused them to go their separate ways, they kept in touch. They reconnected when Vera returned to Germany during the postwar years to take care of family affairs. After their marriage, she had to commute back and forth to Germany as she did not want to lose her American citizenship. The couple traveled to England, the Bahamas and Mexico, but Alfried could not come to the United States because of his war crimes.

In October of 1956, nearly a year and a half after Alfried purchased the ranch for her, Vera filed for divorce asking for $5 million and a yearly alimony of $250,000, claiming he had willfully and without cause withdrawn from the marriage bed, refused her a home life and demanded she give up her American citizenship (Connell, 1982). The German aristocracy was shocked. Alfried was stunned and embarrassed and sought a quick settlement to the divorce. Vera withdrew her original demands and they were divorced on January 9, 1957. Vera is quoted as saying, "I can support myself and prefer the simple life of a Nevada ranch to an existence in Mr. Krupp's 380 room castle in Essen." As part of the divorce settlement, Alfried, allegedly since the divorce agreement is sealed, paid $200,000.

After the divorce, Vera was frequently seen at Strip casinos and even became an owner of the New Frontier by investing approximately $200,000 in the hotel before it went bankrupt. The New Frontier was leased to Krupp, Louis Manchon and Sidney Bliss in 1956. Krupp did not see eye-to-eye with her partners and returned the property to the owners on St. Patrick's Day 1957. The casino closed down and they operated the hotel as a motel until December 1957. In 1959 the casino reopened. She also had a home in the Bel Air section of Los Angeles which she had purchased in the early 1950s.

Spring Mountain Ranch Archives

Vera Krupp wearing diamond ring
Unknown date

On April 9, 1959 the thirty-four carat diamond ring that Vera wore regularly was stolen by three armed men who broke into the ranch house after staking out the ranch for over a week. The diamond was recovered at the Cadillac Motel in Elizabeth, New Jersey on May 23, 1959 but was held in evidence before being returned to Vera. In 1968, the diamond, which had been cleaned and reset, was purchased at auction by Richard Burton for his wife, Elizabeth Taylor.

Vera suffered from diabetes for several years, complicated by goiter and in 1964 went to live in her Bel Air home. She offered the ranch to Clark County for $750,000 but the county could not raise the money. She divested herself of the ranch property in June 1967 by selling it to Howard Hughes. Four months later she was stricken unexpectedly, lapsed into a coma and died on October 16, 1967 at the age of 58 at Mt. Sinai Hospital in Los Angeles. Her former husband Alfried Krupp had died three months prior to her death on July 30, 1967 (Connell, 1982).

Spring Mountain Ranch Archives

Spring Mountain Ranch Archives

(top) Krupp House after pool construction and prior to enclosing porch

(bottom) Pool with enclosed porch c. 1960s

Ranch Improvements by Vera Krupp

After buying Spring Mountain Ranch in 1955, Krupp modified the main ranch house, added a swimming pool and built a guest house, a three-bedroom residence and the modern bunkhouse.

Louis Manchon, who was vice president of Catalina Construction Company, which Krupp owned, built the 75,000-gallon swimming pool and a flagstone patio. Krupp deeded the ranch to Spring Mountain Ranch Corporation with Manchon named secretary/treasurer (Spring Mountain Ranch Corporation, 1981). The main entrance to the house went past the pool and patio. Krupp modified the main house interior by putting bluestain on the wood, painting the fireplace white, installing a bar in the dining nook and adding a new kitchen in the trophy room.

Around 1961 she modified the main house bedroom by installing a wardrobe and a hidden passage to a concealed bedroom and bath which she used as a hobby room. The screened porch/game room from the Lauck period was converted into a covered patio used for dining and a bath/changing room for swimmers. A guest house was built on the site of the Willard George home and was later used by Krupp's secretary, Peggy Westburg. An implement shed, stable and kennel for her Great Danes was built. The dogs were often encountered laying on the chaise lounges around the pool. After her generators failed in 1964 and she was without electricity for a few months, the Nevada Power Company installed power to the ranch.

SPRING MOUNTAIN RANCH – HOWARD HUGHES

Howard Hughes, investor, aviator, aerospace engineer, filmmaker, philanthropist, business magnate and one of the wealthiest men in the world, arrived in Las Vegas in 1966 on Thanksgiving Day by train with his entourage of personal aides who became known as the "Mormon Mafia." Hughes began investing in Nevada real estate and allegedly wanted to change Las Vegas' image into something more glamorous. He moved into the 9th floor penthouse at the Desert Inn which he purchased early the next year. Hughes then went on to purchase The Castaways, New Frontier, Landmark, Sands and Silver Slipper hotels and casinos.

Hughes Purchased the Ranch in 1967, But Never Stayed There

In 1967 Hughes also purchased the Spring Mountain Ranch from Vera Krupp for a reputed $600,000 (Whitaker, 1972). The ranch was supposedly for his third wife, actress Jean Peters, whom he had met in the 1940s and pursued until they were married in January of 1957.

*Howard Hughes and
Jean Peters c. 1940s*

There is no positive evidence that Hughes or his wife ever used or lived at the ranch. In 1971, only a few years after Hughes purchased the ranch, Jean Peters filed for divorce claiming they had not lived together for years and their only contact had been by phone.

The head of Hughes' business interests, Robert Maheu, along with his son and nephew, are known to have stayed at the ranch periodically. The changes at the ranch were probably made by Maheu and not Hughes. When Maheu was dismissed in 1969, the ranch went into caretaker status with many articles on the ranch disappearing during this time.

Sold in 1972

The ranch was sold in 1972, the same year Hughes left Las Vegas to live in Nicaragua and the Bahamas. Hughes passed away on April 5, 1976 during a flight from Mexico to Houston, Texas and is buried in a family plot in Houston.

Ranch Improvements by Howard Hughes

Changes in the ranch under Hughes' ownership included replacing the buckling wood floors with a concrete slab and a blue wool shag rug. A "Kool Deck" was put in around the pool. Heavy artificial graining was done to the woodwork and the fireplace was repainted. A black cocktail bar was installed which was later used as the desk in the Visitor Center. Wall finishes and wallpaper were installed. A helicopter clearing was made between the stable and the kennel.

The pool was drained when Maheu left and was never refilled. Attempted repairs to the old reservoir were made and failed, and the reservoir became totally unusable.

SPRING MOUNTAIN RANCH –
FLETCHER JONES AND WILLIAM MURPHY

Real Estate Speculation in 1972

Fletcher Jones and William Murphy acquired the 528-acre ranch in 1972 for $1.5 million for real estate speculation (Confirm Hughes Ranch Sold for $1.5 Million, 1972). Jones and Murphy had plans for an equestrian-oriented community with 387 one-acre lots, 175 half-acre tracts, 117 townhouse units, a three-acre lake, a nine-hole golf course, an equestrian center and 10.7 miles of bridle trails (Jones, 1973). The Nevada Open Spaces Council and the Red Rock Advisory Committee opposed the plan. Jones and Murphy made three zoning requests for a proposed townhouse/condominium community of 5,000 residents. They sought a zone change from rural open land to rural estates residential which would allow two units per acre (Scenic Land Plan Tabled for Further Study, 1973).

Zoning Change Rejected/ Sold to the State in 1974

The Clark County Regional Planning Council snubbed a proposal to turn the ranch into a state park (Confirm Hughes Ranch Sold for $1.5 Million, 1972). In May, the Clark County Planning Commission voted against rezoning the Red Rock Canyon area from rural open to rural estates residential (Red Rock Rezoning Plan No Go, 1973). At the same time, the plans were underway to acquire the Red Rock land under a Phase I plan which would take $300,000 from state funds that would be matched by federal funds to hire rangers, erect a building and make road improvements. By June the Nevada State Parks System was trying to negotiate an agreeable price for the purchase. Jones and Murphy showed no interest in negotiating with the park system and dropped their bid to rezone the property (Jones, 1973). Jones and Murphy withdrew their application and eventually sold the property to the State of Nevada, Division of State Parks.

SPRING MOUNTAIN RANCH STATE PARK – DIVISION OF STATE PARKS, DISTRICT VI

District VI includes the Valley of Fire State Park, Floyd Lamb State Park at Tule Springs, Red Rock Canyon Recreation Lands and Spring Mountain Ranch. In 1974 the Nevada Division of State Parks purchased the 528-acre Spring Mountain Ranch for $3.25 million. The financing was one-half state funds and one-half Federal Bureau of Outdoor Recreation, Land and Water Conservation Funds. They also purchased the eighty-acre Pine Creek ranch from Art Lullis.

With the purchase, the Division of State Parks acquired the rights to 52 springs in the valley and surrounding mountains. There are six springs on the ranch itself. They are: Sandstone 1, Sandstone 2, Fig Spring, Green Spot Spring, Heart Spring and Conglomerate 1.

The ranch is operated by State Parks. The park staff also administered the recreational use of Sandstone Quarry, Whiterock Spring, Red Springs and Brownstone Canyon (all north of the Loop Road) before the Red Rock Canyon National Conservation Area was established.

The "Sand Stone Ranch" was listed in the United States National Register of Historic Places on April 3, 1976.

There are 28 acres of pasture on the ranch which includes the two-and-a-half-acre play field. Water to the pastures is gravity-fed from the reservoir. The pastures are irrigated six days a week from spring until fall. Use of the pastures by cattle is on a lease/bid basis from mid-March through mid-October on a rest/rotation basis. The ranch has historically been a cattle operation and having the cattle present retains the nature of the ranch's history which aids in the area's interpretation.

The Visitor Center is open in April, May, September and October from 10-5. In June, July, and August it is open from 11-7 and from November to March from 10-4.

TOURS

The location of the ranch at the 3,800 foot elevation located so close to Las Vegas makes it an easy retreat for local residents to get out of the heat during the summer for a small entrance fee.

There are self-guided tours of the ranch house with park docents available to answer questions. Guided tours of the park are available along with picnic areas and a group-use area that accommodates up to 200 people. Because of its elevation, it also offers a diverse opportunity for plant study of four plant communities: desert scrub, black brush, pinion juniper and riparian.

PLAYS AND OTHER EVENTS

From May through September, the Super Summer Theatre is in operation. This local non-profit program offers outdoor performances where people can picnic and experience live theatre.

During Pioneer Days in September, music, spinning and weaving demonstrations, gold panning, black-powder rifle shooting, candle dipping and Dutch oven cooking takes place. During the Nevada Day Celebration in October, Civil War battles are reenacted. There is also a Living History Program in the spring and the fall that began in 1992. Actors depict the lives of early settlers of the area presented in the first person or as a narrated description of events in the settlers' lives.

NOTE

More information about the people in this chapter can be found in the End-notes which follow.

ENDNOTES

SANDSTONE RANCH - WILSON AND ANDERSON

The Assessment Rolls of Lincoln County in 1876 show a Charles Wilson possessing a claim to 160 acres of land southwest of Las Vegas and a George Anderson possessing a claim to 160 acres 200 miles south of Pioche at Cottonwood Island. In 1877 the Tax Assessment Rolls show Wilson being taxed on land situated 24 miles west of Las Vegas, known as the "Old Williams Ranche."

Local historian Maryellen Sadovich's article on the Sandstone Ranch has Wilson and Anderson moving their stock and personal possessions to the ranch in 1867 and living in the deserted stone cabin that winter. They then built a log cabin a few yards from the stone cabin and planted grains and garden vegetables in the spring of 1868. Anderson's Indian wife and many of her friends and relatives also lived and worked on the ranch. Wilson provided fresh produce, meat and other materials to the travelers who passed the ranch on their way to and from California. The source of much of Sadovich's information on the ranch was Tweed Wilson, who was Anderson's son; the information does not correspond with today's documented information (Sadovich, M. 1968, October; James Bernard Wilson, *The West*, V.9, #9. Las Vegas, NV: pp. 38-39, 64-66).

James Wilson's Mining Interests

Wilson's name is found on numerous mining properties in the Sacramento Mining District in the late 1850s and in Mohave County, Arizona in 1865-1866. Records show Wilson and his partners buying, working and selling various mining interests.

Octavius D. Gass

O.D. Gass was born in 1827 in Richland County, Ohio of Scotch-Irish descent and came to San Francisco in the employ of a man named Gilman who shipped two room pre-fab houses to California. Gass became interested in mining and headed for the goldfields in El Dorado. Not having much luck in mining, Gass went to San Bernardino, California before heading to St. Thomas on the Muddy River with two other miners, Nathaniel Lewis and Lewis Cole. On the way they stopped at the abandoned Mormon Fort. After restoring and improving the property, it became a way station for travelers on the Old Spanish Trail. The three of them supplied food to the settlements. By 1872 Gass bought the 640 acre ranch outright from his partners. He produced grain, vegetables and fruits and raised horses and cattle for El Dorado.

Gass invested in Calville on the Colorado River, hoping that steamboats heading for Utah would be the chief means of transportation. However, the railroad came first. Gass excelled in politics and served as the postmaster for Calville from 1867-1869 and as Lincoln County justice of the peace.

In 1872 he married Mary Virginia Simpson of St. Thomas and they had three children. He was heavily in debt and mortgaged the Las Vegas Ranch to Knapp in 1876. After borrowing money from Archibald Stewart of Pioche in 1879, Gass was out of the ranching business after Stewart foreclosed on him in 1891.

Gass moved to California and tried to raise grapes. By 1900 he was living with his son in Redlands, California. Gass passed away on December 10, 1924 and was buried there (Evans, K. (1999, February 7) Part I: The Early Years. At the Right Place at the Right Time, Almost. *Las Vegas Review Journal*. Las Vegas, NV.)

Spring Rancho

Records show the Spring Rancho changing hands over the years with Mary V. Gass purchasing it on February 15, 1876 [Book O p. 147-48] and O.D. Gass acquiring the springs that formed the Las Vegas Creek the following day [Book O p. 144-7]. O.D. Gass purchased the ranch on January 22, 1878 from a J.B. Baird (Sadovich, M., 1972, April 9). James Wilson Settled Sandstone in 1867 (*Review Journal Nevada*. pp 4-5.)

John Howell

The 1870 Pah Ute Co. Census shows Howell to be a thirty-year-old Ohio farmer living with Indian Sally and two eighteen-year-old Indian girls. The 1880 Census shows Howell being a thirty-eight-year-old male mulatto from North Carolina who worked as a teamster, was widowed and could not read or write.

George Anderson

George Anderson served as a cook in Company B, 6th Regiment California Infantry. He enlisted March 7, 1865 at San Francisco California and deserted at San Francisco when he was 24 years old (Krauskopf, R. (1974, June 14). Letter from Chief, Old Military Branch, Military Archives Division. General Services Administration, National Archives & Records Service, Washington D.C. SMR Files.)

Boone's daughter, Gloria Wilson Shearer, claims that Kayer died in 1878 and Anderson left the Sandstone Ranch and his two sons behind. Shearer said he was shot to death in California a year later (1879). However, Helen Stewart mentions Jim Wilson and George Anderson visiting her at the Las Vegas Ranch in the mid 1880s and Jim Wilson's family mentions being in touch with Anderson until 1886 (Rogers, K. (2000, October 30) Lost Cabin. *Review Journal*, Las Vegas, NV.)

Spud Lake mentions Anderson being killed down in Jean by a drunk about 1903 or 1904 (Lake, S., 1978, February 25, Oral Interview, Nevada Division of State Parks File, p. 18.)

Jack Coyle

Foreman of the Boss Mine, Jack Coyle, is mentioned in the *Las Vegas Age* on March 4, 1917 as purchasing an 80-acre ranch near the Wilson ranch and building a comfortable house on the ranch and making other improvements (Boss Mine in Goodsprings Mining District, State Rt. 53 and Sandy Valley Road).

Fayle and Yount Acquire the Ranch in 1920s

Spring Mountain Ranch files claim Boone was older than Buster. In an interview, Paul Warner mentioned that he didn't know Boone. Tweed hated Boone and loved Buster. Tweed asked Warner to get Boone out of here or he was going to kill him. So Warner ran Boone off and never saw him again.

Jim Jr. and Tweed Deeded Five Acres to Live On For Their Entire Lives

On January 27, 1932 the *Las Vegas Age* reported a Notice of Contest concerning the Black Jack Mining Claim, a non-mineral site which adjoined Red Rock Canyon. It was an abandoned mine owned by numerous people, some deceased. The Wilson Brothers were included in the list of owners and were given twenty days to file after the fifth and final notice in order to have the right to be heard concerning the allegations (Black Jack Mining Claim, 1932).

Hampton George

Hampton George had interest in the Indian Springs (Cactus Springs) Ranch with George Latimer in the early 1900s. When his father became ill, the family moved up north to Idaho and his mother went to Long Beach. George went to school at the Old Fort but never finished school (NDSP Anderson 11-9-74). They may have lived at Indian Springs before coming to Las Vegas.

With his second wife Florence Schrodt, he had two sons named Hampton and Lowell. His son Lowell Thomas George (April 13, 1945 to June 29, 1979) went on to become an American singer and songwriter. He was the main guitarist and songwriter for the rock band Little Feat in the 1970s. He also produced the Grateful Dead's 1978 album "Shakedown Street." His solo album "Thanks I'll Eat It Here" was also produced that year just before his death in 1979. George passed away in 1956 and his wife married C.E. "Andy" Anderson.

Vera Krupp's Brahma bulls

Barbara Conover, the Postmistress in Blue Diamond, mentions that her children were unable to catch the school bus one morning because Krupp's Brahma bulls were on their porch in the village and they couldn't get out of the house. Conover's house was located at the corner of Cottonwood and Cerrito. Barbara always wondered if the teacher believed the story.

The Krupp Diamond Robbery

The Krupp Diamond, one of the world's largest diamonds, was stolen from Vera Krupp at the ranch on April 9, 1959. The nearly 34-carat diamond was set in a platinum band with two baguettes that were nearly a carat each. Vera wore the diamond almost all the time, even when horseback riding, and a former housekeeper claimed she kept it in a coffee cup on the sink when she wasn't wearing it.

While Vera was out of state, three men became partners in the plot to rob Krupp after a mutual friend informed them that there was a fortune in jewelry, cash and German gold at the Krupp Ranch. Curly Bowman, Jimmy Reves and Bill Davie took turns staking out the ranch for over a week. Vera returned to the ranch on April 8; and the next day the three armed men burst into the ranch house at night. They tied-up Vera and her foreman Harold Brotherson and stole the diamond ring off her finger, $700 in cash from her purse, a Minox camera and a .38 revolver; the thieves accidentally left a bag with other jewels behind. On the way to McCarran Airport to return the car they had stolen from the parking lot, the trio threw the gun out the window of the car. Two days later a nine-year-old boy, riding his bicycle to school, found the gun lying along the side of the road.

After splitting the seven hundred dollars between them, the three men agreed to separate and meet in Miami to dispose of the diamond. Bowman, the one who could easily be identified, was to lay low for a few days while Reves and Davie headed for Ogden, Utah to meet their wives and head for Miami. With all the publicity in the press, Bowman discovered that they had left $200,000 in jewels behind and was furious. He contacted the informant Eddie Hay in Texas, and they agreed to meet at the Singapore Hotel in Miami Beach.

Because of all the national press the robbery had generated, the $300,000 ring was going to be hard to sell. The thieves located a potential buyer in Chicago, and they agreed to meet at the La Sands Western Hills Hotel. The Chicago deal fell apart and Reves and his wife went to St. Louis to find a buyer. While in St. Louis, Reves managed to sell the two baguettes for $150, and he and his wife went to Birmingham, Alabama to lay low for awhile. In May Reves made a connection for another potential buyer, and he and his wife went to New Jersey.

The ring was recovered on May 23, 1959 at the Cadillac Motel in Elizabeth, New Jersey when the FBI arrested Reves and his wife. The diamond had been removed from its setting and was hidden in the lining of Reves' coat. The diamond was held as evidence and not immediately returned to Vera Krupp. Reves agreed to sign a confession if his wife could go free. This was done and all the others who were involved were located, arrested and brought to Las Vegas to stand trial on November 1, 1959.

After her death, the Krupp Diamond, which had been cleaned and reset, was sold at an auction on May 24, 1968 to an agent of Richard Burton for $305,000. Burton gave the ring to his wife, Elizabeth Taylor. After Elizabeth Taylor's death in 2011, her jewelry was auctioned by Christies in New York. On December 13 the ring containing the Krupp diamond was sold for $8.8 million.

When Tweed Wilson died at Southern Nevada Memorial Hospital on April

12, 1959, two days after the diamond robbery, it was Vera Krupp who made the arrangements for his funeral (Connell, B. (1982, May 9). Yesterday's Headlines: The Great Krupp Diamond Caper. *Las Vegas Sun* Magazine. Las Vegas, NV: pp 10-13 Connell, B. (1982, December 12). Yesterday's Headlines: Conclusion: The Great Krupp Diamond Caper. *Las Vegas Sun* Magazine. Las Vegas, NV: pp 10-11, 18.Find No Clues to Vera Krupp Diamond Theft. (1959, April 13). *Las Vegas Sun*. Las Vegas, NV: p.1.)

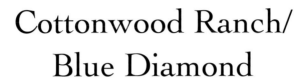

CHAPTER 4

Cottonwood Ranch/ Blue Diamond

By Linda Carlyle McCollum

COTTONWOOD SPRINGS AND THE OLD SPANISH TRAIL

What is now named Blue Diamond was once a stopping place on the Old Spanish Trail known as Cottonwood Springs. It was located near the base of the Spring Mountain Range in the Cottonwood Valley, today's Red Rock Canyon.

The area is believed to have been first visited by non-Native Americans in 1829 when Antonio Armijo, a Santa Fe merchant, brought his first pack train from Abiqui, New Mexico to Los Angeles to trade woven goods for horses and mules (two blankets per animal). Armijo used parts of Jedediah Smith's routes of 1826 and 1827 and Raphael Rivera's route of 1828 to be sure that a route to California was possible for a large trading expedition.

The new route resulted in a lucrative market for horses in Santa Fe. Caravans of up to one hundred men would leave Santa Fe in the fall, arrive in Los Angeles two-and-a-half months later and return to Santa Fe in the spring with several thousand horses and mules ready for trade to pioneers from Missouri.

Armijo's journal, due to its brevity, brings some disagreement among historians as to the exact route taken through the Las Vegas area on the initial trip. The journal lists stopping at Salado Arroyo on January 9, 1830, which is believed to be the Whitney Mesa area, and proceeding to a dry lake on the 10th, "the little spring of the tortoise" on the 11th, followed by a pass without water on the 12th and a salty spring on the 13th. The "little spring of the tortoise" is believed by some to have been the spring at today's Blue Diamond, while others believe it to be the spring at Goodsprings because of the dry lake in the area of Jean. The pass without water is more characteristic of the Goodsprings area than Mountain Springs Pass.

Regardless of which route was initially taken through the Las Vegas area, the springs in the vicinity of Blue Diamond known as Cottonwood Springs (or Pearl Spring, Ojo de Cayetana) was one of the stopping places as the Old Spanish Trail developed over the years. Unfortunately any spring in a canyon with cottonwood trees was referred to as "Cottonwood Springs" in the pioneers' diaries, which confuses the exact location of where different expeditions actually stopped in the vicinity.

In the autumn of 1847, a small party with ox teams was sent from Salt Lake to Los Angeles over the Escalante and Spanish Trails to secure seeds and grain for the spring sowing. Mormons occasionally used the southern route and established small colonies at various points along the route to support those traveling on it. One of the reasons the Old Mormon Fort was built in Las Vegas (Las Vegas Boulevard and Washington Avenue) was to have a stopping place on the route. Some parts of the Spanish Trail route developed into a wagon road known as the Mormon Road or Trail which was used mostly in the winter. Wagons traveled from fifteen to twenty miles a day. Some reports mention leaving the Las Vegas area at six in the morning and not arriving at the Cottonwood Springs until eleven at night.

On October 12, 1869, Lt. D.W. Lockwood, three men and a topographer from Lt. George Wheeler's United States Arms reconnaissance team took the Mormon Road from Las Vegas to Potosi and camped at the Cottonwoods, a spring at the head of the Las Vegas Wash. They camped there again on October 14 on their return. In September 1871 Cottonwood Springs was the rendezvous camp for Lt. George Wheeler's expedition.

Most of the Spanish Trail markers have been destroyed with urban development. The route basically went from the area of the Mormon Fort (Las Vegas Boulevard and Washington Avenue) or the Springs Preserve (Valley View Boulevard and Highway 95), crossed the Las Vegas Valley (in the vicinity of Decatur Boulevard and Alta Drive, Jones Boulevard and Charleston Boulevard, Rainbow Boulevard and Oakey Boulevard, Buffalo Drive and Sahara Avenue, Durango Drive and Edna Avenue, Spring Mountain Road and Fort Apache Road) before exiting the valley on the east side of the Blue Diamond

Hill. The caravans would exit at the narrows (just past the current wallboard plant) and come to Cottonwood Springs (today's village of Blue Diamond). From Cottonwood Springs it would take another full day to travel to Mountain Springs before descending into Pahrump Valley and on to Stump Springs, Emigrant Pass, Resting Springs and Tecopa. Frequently travelers would come to a spring but there would not be enough forage for their animals. They would then have to travel to another area in the vicinity to find food.

The Spanish Trail/Mormon Road was one of the longest used wagon roads in the American West. The road was replaced in 1905 with the San Pedro, Los Angeles and Salt Lake Railroad.

Chapters 1 and 2 offer more details and additional information about the discoveries of Antonio Armijo, John Fremont and Lt. George Wheeler, along with the early settlements near Cottonwood Springs. This chapter will tell the story of Cottonwood Ranch and the establishment of the Village of Blue Diamond.

COTTONWOOD RANCH

The first evidence of non-Indians residing and ranching at Cottonwood Springs was the adobe house that stood in the private park in the Village of Blue Diamond from the 1880s until the late 1970s. In his 1970 article "Blue Diamond's Mystery House," Ray Chesson attributed the building of the house to miners from Ivanpah in the 1860s. The same story exists for the original structure at Spring Mountain Ranch. However, when Lt. George Wheeler described and mapped the area in 1871, there is no mention of a house in the area. It was Wheeler who is credited for naming the area Cottonwood Springs even though the name appeared on earlier maps of the area.

In the 1970s Claude Warren of the University of Nevada Las Vegas (UNLV) Anthropology Department did an archaeological examination of the adobe at Cottonwood Springs and found a 1902 newspaper stuffed in a crack in the wall. Its position suggested it had been used to fill in the gaps caused by the shrinkage of the adobe bricks. This would indicate that the building had been built ten to twenty years prior to the date on the newspaper, sometime after 1882.

The internal dimensions of the original room structure were twenty-one feet by seven feet. It had a foundation of limestone rocks reaching up approximately three feet, from which the two adjacent columns of adobe bricks commenced.

Overview of the limestone and adobe walls, Unknown date

Adobe house c. 1970s

Due to the thickness of the limestone rocks and the double thickness of adobe bricks, the external dimensions were about twenty-five feet by ten feet. A fireplace was built in one corner of the room and hand-hewn beams, roughly chopped-out and shaped with an axe, supported the roof. The house later had two wooden rooms added with a cellar excavated under the addition.

In 1893 when James Wilson Sr. at the Sandstone Ranch filed for his military pension, he needed two character references to testify that his disability was not the result of "vicious habits." One of his witnesses was a fifty-nine year old man named James N. Pickett whose residence was Cottonwood Springs. In his affidavit, Pickett stated that he had known Wilson for ten years. This is the first documented evidence of anyone other than the native Indians living at Cottonwood Springs. It is possible that Pickett may have worked for Wilson or that Wilson may have built the adobe house.

The Division of State Lands in Carson City dates the first patent at Cotton-wood Springs on October 7, 1901 for eighty acres and water rights with the original claimant being Charles Stewart. All Stewart needed to show was that the land had been improved and did not have to indicate who actually improved the land. This required that the property had a house. Right after receiving the patent, Stewart sold the Cottonwood Ranch to W.H. Bancroft (Warren, 1979). Bancroft sold the ranch and the water rights to the San Pedro, Los Angeles and Salt Lake Railroad in 1903 (Lincoln County Deeds, 1903). The railroad company leased out the eighty-acre ranch property to a number of tenants during the next three decades, who in turn subleased the property to others. The tenants were required to take care of the water line to Arden for the railroad as well as the house and property.

In their oral interviews, Olive and Ada Lake, who came to Las Vegas as children in 1903-1904, mention (without giving a specific date) spending two or three summers out at today's Oliver Ranch and riding their horses over to the Cottonwood Ranch and the Wilson Ranch and spending the day there. When they first came up to the Cottonwood Ranch, they remembered an Elmer Wooden either owned or leased it: "There was a woman and her son on the ranch and she was sitting out in the yard smoking a pipe and the pigs were running around."

Ada remembered the ranch being in the narrows and Olive remembered it at the Cottonwood Springs (Lake, 1975 and 1977). They also mention a Jim Robson having the ranch for one year. Mary Hurtado, who lived in Arden as a child, remembers going to the Cottonwood Ranch to buy half a pig from a French woman who raised pigs there (Hurtado, 2003).

On March 3, 1906 the *Las Vegas Age* mentions J.R. Hunter leasing the "old Cottonwood Ranch on the California road between Vegas and Good Springs" and spending the spring and summer there. A little over a year later on April 15, 1907, Hunter subleased the ranch for $120 for one year to Jim and Tweed Wilson, who had just inherited the Sandstone Ranch in May of 1906. The Wilsons' lease expired in April of 1908; but since they did not leave the ranch until June, they owed Hunter $26.45 (RR Letters, 1908).

In 1909 C.P. Ball, who was in the freight business in Las Vegas, leased the property and began experimentally farming the Cottonwood Ranch. On August 14, 1909 the *Las Vegas Age* had an article entitled "Cottonwood Ranch, An Example of the Wonderful Fertility of Vegas Soils." Almost everything that Ball planted had been successful, except the potato crop. He reportedly grew onions, sweet potatoes, tomatoes, cabbage, cantaloupes, cucumbers, cane, corn, peas, beans, peaches, apples, grapes and figs. Anyone desiring more information on varieties and the proper time for planting was encouraged to write Mr. Ball.

Even before Ball acquired the property, the "Local Notes" section of the *Las Vegas Age* mentions many well-known Las Vegans going out to the Cottonwood Ranch between 1906 and 1914 for the weekend or camping with their families at the springs.

Vincent Matteucci of Caliente came with his family to Las Vegas in 1905 to get involved with railroad work and was associated with mining, a roadhouse and the tourist trade.

In the spring, summer and fall of 1907, ads in the *Las Vegas Age* mention Matteucci and Boyce selling "Fresh Fruits and Vegetables" at the Las Vegas Rancho in Las Vegas. An article on June 15 mentions the two of them managing the Las Vegas/Stewart Ranch. Back in 1902, all but a few acres of the Stewart Ranch property, including the springs and water rights, had been sold to the San Pedro, Los Angeles and Salt Lake Railroad to supply water for the steam-powered locomotives and beef for the railroad workers. By 1905 fifteen hundred people lived in the tent town and the old ranch was a recreational area, giving birth to the city of Las Vegas. Lots were sold off at a public auction on May 15, 1905.

There is some speculation that Matteucci and his family may have made arrangements to work the Cottonwood Ranch for C.P. Ball when he leased it. In June of 1910 the *Las Vegas Age* mentions the Matteucci family returning to Vegas from Arden, where they had been for some time. While there is evidence that he was selling produce in the Las Vegas area, there is no documented evidence he was personally farming at the Cottonwood Ranch until the spring of 1914 when he acquired a five year lease on the property that Ball had been farming. The lease from the Railroad Company went from March 1, 1914 to March 1, 1919 (RR Letters, 1914).

In 1912, two years prior to obtaining the lease on the Cottonwood Ranch, Matteucci had acquired the Katie Quartz and Millsite at Beck Spring in the narrows of Section 8 from Charles Beck (or Lambert of Las Vegas according to Liz Warren) which is in the vicinity of Cottonwood Springs. Even though Matteucci acquired the lease on the Cottonwood Ranch in the spring of 1914, Mrs. Ball and her family were still vacationing at the ranch as they are reported in the *Las Vegas Age* returning from the Cottonwood Ranch in August of 1914 where they had been for several weeks.

Ethel Bowler Matteucci remembered her in-laws bringing wagonloads of vegetables into Las Vegas and peddling them. The cottonwood trees between 3rd and 4th Streets, where the railroad houses were located, were from seedlings from the Cottonwood Ranch (LV Age, 1910). Matteucci is believed to have added the two wooden rooms with a cellar to the adobe house. In 1917 Matteucci filed a homestead claim in Sec. 8 (NDSP Files).

Matteucci also owned property on First St. in Las Vegas. On April 28, 1917 the *Las Vegas Age* reported a fire from a gasoline stove completely destroying the property. The loss was estimated at two thousand dollars with insurance to the amount of six hundred dollars.

Beginning March 31, 1919 to March 1, 1920, C.P. Ball again leased the ranch from the Railroad Company for one year for $10.

When Mrs. Vincent Matteucci died in Las Vegas on February 5, 1920 of influenza pneumonia, the family took her remains to Gilroy, California for burial. The family stayed in California for awhile and then scattered. In 1920 Vincent Matteucci is listed in the *Las Vegas Age* on the delinquent tax list for 1919 owing $28.11.

The same year Matteucci again leased the Cottonwood Ranch for one year from April 1, 1920 to March 31, 1921 and on May 18th reported a cyclone had destroyed the building. After his lease had expired in March of 1921, Matteucci rented a house in the Goodsprings area and the Goodsprings Gazette on May 14, 1921 reported his arrest along with two other men for bootlegging. Matteucci was guilty of selling jackass brandy as well as having and keeping intoxicating liquor at his Raineer Saloon in Block 16 of Las Vegas which was a "drinking joint and dance hall" and one of the first saloons in the area.

In 1921 when Matteucci got into trouble for bootlegging in Las Vegas, the ranch had been leased for three years at $100 a year, with semiannual payments, to a locomotive engineer named Lou Martin. Before this time the railroad was only receiving $10 a year for the ranch with the objective of having someone living there and taking care of the water line intake. The tenant had use of portions of the spring that were not required by the railroad company for its use. There really was not enough water to do anything but a little gardening and caring for a few fruit trees. It appears that Martin moved to the ranch to take care of the property.

By 1922 Martin had subleased 1.53 fenced acres of the ranch to Great Western Gypsum of Los Angeles for $100, the price he was paying for the whole ranch. The Great Western Gypsum Company had a sublease from July 1, 1922 to December 31 and set up a tent community for its employees on a "piece within the enclosure under the shade trees." Tents were placed on the property along with sufficient water for camp purposes. Later Martin demanded $250 a year on land that was high and dry and could not be cultivated. The company offered $5/month rent which would be the equivalent of $40 an acre a year. Martin refused and served notice for them to vacate. Great Western Gypsum went directly to the railroad company who owned the land and complained. (Great Western Gypsum may have been mining the bluff immediately southeast of the ranch as there is evidence of some mining having occurred on that hill.) In 1924 Martin gave up possession of the ranch when his lease expired.

A new pipeline from the ranch to Arden had been installed by March of 1924, but it ran from the springs through the house yard and the orchards taking all the water to Arden. It was going to require a great amount of work to put the ranch in rentable shape. For a while the Railroad Company was unable to secure a renter and with all the water going to Arden, the Railroad Company did "not care anything for the little ranch."

In November of 1924, the Blue Diamond Materials Company of Los Angeles bought the Buol Gypsum Deposit on the hill northeast of the Cottonwood Springs area to which Peter Buol and Vincent Matteucci owned the mining rights (LV Age, 1924).

Four years later in 1928, Charles Rodman received a five year lease on the Cottonwood Springs property from the Railroad Company and agreed to have a man go up there to raise chickens and rabbits. In May of 1929 Rodman agreed to let the Blue Diamond Materials Company have someone occupy the "shack" at Cottonwood Springs from day-to-day for protection of the property and the water system. An employee was allowed to live there during the summer months.

In 1930 the School District requested permission to build a small frame schoolhouse at the Cottonwood Ranch with a sublease from Rodman; he agreed to it on September 19, 1930. By March of 1931 the company, renamed the Blue Diamond Corporation, had been leasing Cottonwood Ranch from Rodman and kept it in very good shape at their own expense. As a result, they acquired the lease of the property on May 29, 1933 for five years at $120 a year; it was renewed in June 1938 for another five years.

When Blue Diamond Corporation began leasing the ranch property in the 1930s, the adobe house was used by employees. The Company planted several new trees and grass around the pool and made other improvements. On November 18, 1941 the Blue Diamond Corporation obtained a 25 year lease at $120/year with an option to buy in order to build housing facilities for their employees.

The adobe building was in continual use until the 1960s when it was used as a boy's clubhouse (Ritenour, 1975). When it was abandoned, neglect and vandalism resulted in its deterioration. After UNLV's excavation of the site, it was fenced off to avoid future vandalism but the deterioration continued and the adobe bricks disappeared. While there is no evidence that either UNLV or Claude Warren ever obtained permission to come onto private property and excavate it, the artifacts from the site are said to be in storage at UNLV for further research. All that remains of the adobe house at the site today is a corner of the foundation where the fireplace once stood.

BLUE DIAMOND COMPANY TOWN AND ITS STRUCTURES

HOUSING

The Blue Diamond Corporation leased the Cottonwood Ranch from the railroad with an option to buy and in 1941 began building a company town to provide housing for married supervisory and key employees. With the board plant in Los Angeles being moved to the mine site, there was a significant increase in the number of employees. Approximately twenty houses were built in the original phase and there were still ten units for families living at the mine site.

In 1946, twelve more houses were built along with a new pumping station and an additional storage tank. About the same time, a trailer park was also constructed to accommodate fifteen more families. In 1955, another twenty-five houses were added to the east side of the village. An aerial view picture shows the village laid out in the shape of the state of Nevada.

When the Flintkote Corporation acquired the mine in the 1960s from the Blue Diamond Corporation, they wanted to divest themselves of the responsibility

Blue Diamond laid out in the shape of Nevada, Unknown date

of maintaining a company town and the village was sold to the Castella Corporation, which in turn sold all the houses and facilities to individuals.

VILLAGE MARKET

Today's Village Market was built in 1942 by the Blue Diamond Corporation and was a privately owned and operated grocery store maintained for the convenience of the village residents. It carried fresh meats, cheese, vegetables, dairy products, drug items, beverages and other basics in moderate amounts and became a gathering place for the community. Credit for employees was

available in the form of "script," to be used only at the market and deducted from the employee's next paycheck. Originally, script was in paper form with denominations of 5 cents, 10 cents, 25 cents, 50 cents and $1, totaling $20 per book.

Used script was disposed of by burning. Later a copper-colored metal coin with "Blue Diamond Script" embedded in it was used. One could trade off script for real money at the market. Most major shopping was done in Las

Inside the Blue Diamond Market c. 1960s

Closer view of the town streets and water tanks, Unknown date

Vegas. Since employees were paid every two weeks, smaller shopping was done at the market, like bread and milk or anything needed at the time. When the village was sold in the mid-1960s, the store was sold to private ownership.

POST OFFICE

Before the Village of Blue Diamond was established, mail delivery was fifteen miles east in Arden, Nevada. Mailbags were thrown off the train at Arden and the timekeeper, Pat Mahoney, or the mine manager, Mr. King, went to Arden to pick up the mail. Mahoney sorted the mail in his office, kept mail that belonged to him or the company and put everything else in an open box nailed to the wall in the recreation hall. Everyone went to the rec hall to pick-up their mail. When the mail service at Arden ended, mail for Blue Diamond was picked-up at the Las Vegas Post Office.

The Blue Diamond Post Office, which was located in a small room in the back of the company store, was established on July 1, 1942 and was recorded as Blue Diamondville. The name was officially changed to Blue Diamond on December 1, 1942. Stella Phelps was the original postmistress and served for many years.

George Bogdanovich, who lived at the mine, remembers that Assistant Plant Manager Ken Zahn or Office Manager "Shorty" Schaefer would pick up the mail from the Las Vegas Post Office on their way to work in the morning. Company mail was separated and resident mail delivered to the Village Post

Blue Diamond Post Office c. 2015

Office by 10:00 a.m. It was then sorted and placed in individual P.O. boxes or held for request. Sometime in the late 1950s, mail was picked-up at the Las Vegas Post Office by the school bus driver who bussed high school students to and from Rancho High School in Las Vegas. It arrived at 3:00 p.m., so there was always a crowd waiting for their mail at the company store.

Dexter Thomas is believed to have pushed to get the current post office. The Post Office was built on private land by Charlette Cope in 1968, was leased to the government and still is today.

PHONES

Prior to the building of the board plant in 1942, the only phone was a direct line to the mine manager's office. With the building of the plant and accompanying facilities, a public telephone booth was located adjacent to the medical building at the plant. Residents could make outgoing calls twenty-four hours a day. Incoming calls or messages were handled through the office switchboard. Only in cases of emergency were employees permitted to receive personal phone calls at the plant. Emergency messages were delivered to employees as quickly as possible. In the mid-1950s, phones were installed in the residences of key management personnel.

MEDICAL

The Company provided a registered nurse who lived in the Village. Her main duties were caring for workers hurt in industrial accidents at the plant, but she was also available to the Village residents. The Company maintained an ambulance at the plant for emergency use. Dr. B.L. Houghton had an office in the back of the company store two days a week.

SCHOOL

Due to the sparse population in the area in the early 1900s, Nevada law permitted the establishment of a school district for a minimum of five children. Once opened, a school could continue as long as there was a minimum of three children. The Blue Diamond School began in 1929 and although its location varied, it is one of the oldest continually operating elementary schools in Clark County.

When the miners moved their families up to the mine camp in tent houses at the top of the bluff, the six children living in the camp at the time went to school in a little shack at Indian Ben's Place, today's Oliver Ranch. Rebecca Park taught there.

> You wouldn't believe that she could have a school in this little shack, but she did. She taught the Blue Diamond children. You know the Blue Diamond Mine was around the mountain then. They did all their work up over the mountain and they brought their children down here to the school (Ritenour, Blue Diamond Adobe).

On September 12, 1930 the Blue Diamond School District asked Charles Rodman, who had the lease from the railroad, for a sublease on some property at Cottonwood Ranch to build a small frame schoolhouse under the cottonwood trees. On September 29 Rodman agreed to a sublease for the School District. The railroad required that the school be built so it could be moved once the lease expired. Ingress and egress and a public road was also negotiated. A fully executed agreement was made in February of 1931 for five years at $1 a year, with the five years paid in advance (Lake, Tape). The school was later moved up the hill and placed at the base of Indian Hill.

Angie Bogdanovich Delong's school experiences, which she shared with the Blue Diamond History Committee, spoke of the blue, one-room school on top of the hill of the Blue Diamond Mine that she attended for the first six grades. Grades 1-4 were on the east side of the room and grades 5-8 on the west side with a fuel-burning stove on the north side of the room. It was a two to three mile walk from their tent house to the school. When she began school in the first grade on September 14, 1936 there were 13 students and the teacher was Flora Holden.

The first class in the New Village School in the village of Blue Diamond was held in 1942 and became a focal point for the community. It was one long room with a divider curtain that separated the two areas, with the first four grades in one room and the next four in the other. When needed, the divider was opened and all the students came together. An additional room was added in 1947 and another in the 1980s. There were two teachers for grades 1-8. The children who lived up on the hill were transported to the school in the village. The children went to high school in Las Vegas either rode on a company bus, moved into Las Vegas and lived with friends or relatives, or made other arrangements.

From 1942 to 1957, the school bus would leave Blue Diamond at approximately 7:30 a.m. to arrive at Las Vegas High School before the start of school at 9:00 a.m. Stops were made at Arden and at the Highway 91 intersection to pick-up additional children. School was out at 3:00 p.m. and the bus would leave at 3:30 p.m., arriving in Blue Diamond prior to 5:00 p.m.

After 1957, the high school students were bussed to Rancho High School and the school hours were changed. This required the Blue Diamond bus to leave at 5:30 a.m. in order to arrive at Rancho High School by 7:00 a.m.

LIBRARY

Since there was no library in the village, sixth grade teacher Mr. Riding wanted to have a library at the Blue Diamond School. He came out every weekend and with about three students helped get the library started. The Blue Diamond Library opened in 1970 and was located in a small trailer which was purchased with a Federal Library Grant. The trailer was parked near the school in the private park.

Today's library was established in 1989 when a local resident constructed the present day 1,000 square-foot library which opened in 1992. It now houses over 7,000 volumes and serves the 260 residents of Blue Diamond.

COMMUNITY BUILDING

A community building in the park was built in the mid-1950s to a great extent by the volunteer labor of the Village residents. It had kitchen facilities and rest rooms and was available for use by the various social organizations, churches and other groups. Permission to use the building was obtained from the Employees' Facilities Manager. Today it is referred to as the Quonset Hut.

Swimming Pool

The swimming pool was originally a small pond that was fed by spring water. In the late 1920s, under the direction of Mine Manager I.E. King, the pond was converted to a concrete-lined pool still fed by continually running spring water.

Over the years it was expanded, diving boards added, grass planted around the edges, fencing installed and changing rooms built. It was the central place for recreation in the summertime. Lifeguard attendance was not provided until the mid-1950s. Today the pool has been redone and is maintained by the Blue Diamond Charitable Association.

Blue Diamond History archives

I.E. King (then Mine Superintendent) with wife and daughter at the pool c. 1930

Church

Although there were no churches in the Village, the Community Building in the private park was available for use by different denominations holding services on different weeks. The Baptist Church conducted regular church services and Sunday School classes. The Catholic Church held weekly Mass and Catechism instructions. The present-day church by the Post Office opened in November of 1980.

The Volunteer Fire Department's first fire truck-Unknown date

VOLUNTEER FIRE DEPARTMENT

There was no fire department in the village. Residents were given tanks to hang in their houses that had a fire extinguisher. There was an old jeep with a pumper on it that had to be hooked to a fire hydrant, some of which were in backyards. The fire hydrants had 2 ½ inch standpipes that needed an adapter. A fire truck coming from Las Vegas would have to adapt to the fire hydrants in order to be able to pump water. After the Layton house burned down in 1969, a meeting was called to start a volunteer fire department. There was no equipment but the town got an old 1948 Jimmie (GMC) from county commissioner Saylor Ryan. It was painted and fixed-up with an old 150 gallon water pumper.

There was a set of old garages that had to be dug out with a loader so the vehicle could be backed in to avoid the water freezing in the winter. At this time most fires were out on the highway and were either car wrecks, accidents or brush fires.

The volunteer fire department firehouse was located down at the bottom of the village. One of the first emergencies was when Barbara Conover's vacation trailer, parked in her backyard, caught fire when some mice chewed matches. John Murphy was the chief then and the firefighters were all volunteers.

Money was needed to keep the trucks in order, buy gas and equipment. Funds were raised with the annual Fireman's Ball which was held on the Saturday closest to the 4th of July and was the biggest event of the year. Everything was donated and hundreds of people attended.

RED ROCK ADVISORY BOARD GOVERNANCE/VILLAGE

The Red Rock Advisory Board was begun by Don Slesinger, a member of the state assembly, to establish a "grassroots" level of community governance. It began in several small communities with an actual election of board members. The Red Rock Advisory Board represents not only Blue Diamond but Calico Basin and residents in the rural area of Highway 160. The advisory boards are one of the best levels of governance in the county allowing communities to be heard. But unfortunately being heard and listened to by the commissioners does not always happen. It can be hard to get the attention of the commissioners and they don't always understand the communities' reasoning.

IT TAKES A VILLAGE

The Flintkote Company, which had bought the mining and plant operations from the Blue Diamond Corporation, sold their interest in the village in August of 1964 to the Castella Corporation of Columbus, Ohio who specialized in buying company towns and reselling the real estate to individual owners (Jim Stultz, Historical Society). By May 11, 1966 all the homes in Blue Diamond had been sold. Blue Diamond was now a village without company protection.

The original residents were mostly people associated with the mine; but over the years as houses were sold or property purchased, various newcomers without any association with the mine or the residents began buying property in Blue Diamond.

In his book "Vanishing Village," Evan Blythin, who became a resident in the late 1970s and served on Red Rock Advisory Board for twenty-two years and as chairman for ten, speaks of how the community came together to solve problems over the years.

Blythin points out that when it was a company town, the mine company maintained the community center, the store, the private park and swimming pool as well as the residents' lawns. When the town was sold, the maintenance ceased and things began to degenerate and fall apart. Originally every deed had a provision which required the owners to pay dues to maintain the park, pool and community center. An association was formed to oversee this, like a homeowner's association does today. Later, as houses were sold, the provisions in the original deeds were omitted and the money for maintenance was no longer available. The new residents were not paying even on a volunteer basis and the community became divided on what should be done.

Gradually as new people began buying property and being more task-oriented, they began to get the community center, pool and park in working order. Some of the older community members spent their own money to get things started and little by little more people joined in to help. "And little by little the community center became the heart of the community by virtue of everybody interacting. And little by little there was a renaissance" (Blythin, 2010).

Today the Blue Diamond Charitable Association maintains the private park in the village and raises funds from memberships, special events such as the Spring Fling, Fall Festival, Gourmet Dinners and Easter Brunch, and rental of the recreation hall to outside groups for special occasions.

What brought people to Blue Diamond was the rural nature and natural environment located only about twenty-five miles from Las Vegas. Living in such a community required people to work together to get things accomplished. Little by little differences were overcome. "It takes a village."

As a former resident Donna Phelps said, "When I think of things in life that I really enjoyed, I think about Blue Diamond."

More information about the people and events in this chapter can be found in the Endnotes which follow.

ENDNOTES

SPANISH TRAIL THROUGH THE LAS VEGAS AREA

Historians disagree on the exact route taken through the Las Vegas area on Armijo's expedition in 1829-30. Many assume the expedition crossed the Las Vegas valley, heading west towards the Spring Mountain Range, camping at Cottonwood Springs (today's Blue Diamond), before crossing the mountains at today's Mountain's Pass and on into Pahrump Valley.

Armijo's journal does not support this route on the initial trip. His journal mentions camping at "Yerba Manso Arroyo" for several days. Since Yerba Manso is an herb that grows in the Las Vegas Wash, it is assumed that this is the location Armijo is referring to. The scouts were out looking for Rivera at the time. "Citizen Rivera," who had been looking for the location where he had crossed the river in 1828 on his way to New Mexico, returned to the base camp at the Las Vegas Wash on January 7. He had discovered a path dotted with springs all the way to the Mojave River.

The scouts returned and the expedition continued on, camping at a "Salado Arroyo." This salty arroyo is believed to have been the location where Rivera had crossed the river the year before. It is in the vicinity of Duck Creek, in the area of what is today's Whitney Mesa. The following day they camped at a dry lake which is probably Jean, Nevada before proceeding on to "the little spring of the turtle" which would be Goodsprings. The next day the group proceeded through a "pass without water" which is Wilson Pass, and then on to a "Little Salty Spring" which is probably Tecopa Springs or Salt Spring.

For twenty years Mexican and American traders used variants of the route that Armijo had pioneered, depending on the amount of available forage for the animals and water in the springs. Caravans are reported using the trail annually until the winter of 1847-48. Over the years other expeditions clearly crossed the Las Vegas Valley, camped at Cottonwood Springs or other springs in the Red Rock Canyon area, before crossing the mountains at Mountain Springs. The name of Old Spanish Trail was not given to the trail until John C. Fremont came through the area in 1844.

Antonio Armijo (1804-1850) was the son of Jose Francisco Armijo, one of the first New Mexican traders on the Santa Fe Trail in 1821. In 1829 Antonio received the necessary trade documents and passports to authorize him to take an expedition to California to trade New Mexican hand-woven blankets and serapes for horses and mules. This was the first round trip from Santa Fe to Los Angeles. Upon his return, Armijo's diary was published resulting in commercial possibilities of the route. The Governor of New Mexico named Armijo the "Commander of the Discovery of the Route to California."

After his return to New Mexico, Amijo convinced his parents to immediately move to California and they were residing in the San Francisco Bay Area in 1830. On April 30, 1831 he married Dolores Engracia Duarte y Peralta, whom he met on his first trip to California. Between 1832 and 1844 they had seven children. In 1840 Antonio acquired 13,000 acres in Solano and Napa Counties known as Rancho Tolenas. When he passed away in 1850, he was listed as a farmer north of Suisun Bay in Solano County. A high school in Fairfield, California is named after him.

Rafael Rivera was a Mexican teenager who served as a scout on Armijo's expedition in 1829-30 and was probably the first non-Native American in the Las Vegas valley. He separated from the other scouts who were riding down the

Virgin River in late December. He chose to head along the Colorado River where it merged into Black Canyon and the Las Vegas Wash. He is said to have camped at the top of a mesa overlooking the Las Vegas valley where he saw the springs and meadow and is credited with naming the area "the meadows." He went on to find the Mojave River crossing he had made the year before and rejoined the expedition on January 7, reporting an abundance of springs along the route ahead. Rivera's route became a vital link on the Old Spanish Trail. It was Fremont who mapped the trail in 1844. After Salt Lake was linked to the trail in 1847, it became known as the Mormon Road.

EARLY COTTONWOOD RANCH RESIDENTS

Frank Williams came to the area in 1892 and in his autobiography refers to Jim Wilson as the "old rancher who lived at the Cottonwood Ranch." Since Wilson had lived at the Sandstone Ranch (today's Spring Mountain Ranch) since the mid 1870s, this may be why any spring with cottonwood trees was referred to as Cottonwood Spring/Ranch.

Charles Stewart was born in Pennsylvania in 1844, spent his childhood in southeastern Ohio, lived in Kansas in 1870 and then went on to Colorado. In 1880 he was in Overton, Nevada and spent much of his time working in the mines. In 1894 he was living at the "Root Well Cabin" at the mouth of a north and south wash that emptied into the main wash directly south of the Boomerang Mine. In 1896 he was working for Mr. Campbell on contract for five dollars a ton. After acquiring the Cottonwood Ranch and selling it to Bancroft, he bought a half-interest in the Towner Ranch at Indian Springs which he soon sold. He returned to Ohio where he married (Frank Williams autobiography).

J.R. Hunter and his family appear to be residing at the Cottonwood Ranch during the time Jim and Tweed Wilson were subleasing it for one year from April 15, 1907 to 1908. The *Las Vegas Age* on June 8, 1907 mentions the Hunters coming in from the Cottonwood Ranch to visit friends. The Hunters are later mentioned moving into town from the Sierra Madre mine in November of 1907. While the Wilsons were leasing the ranch, J.R. Hunter had moved to Carson City in February of 1908 and was appointed Adjutant of the Nevada State Police in July.

LAS VEGANS VACATIONING AT THE COTTONWOOD RANCH

From listings in *Las Vegas Age* editions in the early 1900s, it seems that Cottonwood Ranch was a popular getaway for Las Vegas residents. This is a sampling taken from the paper's pages.

On October 20, 1906 Mrs. Peter Buol is mentioned going to the Cottonwood ranch to visit her friend, Mrs. J. R. Hunter. Even before acquiring the lease on the property, C.P. Ball's family is mentioned camping at Cottonwood Ranch in August of 1908 and being joined by Mrs. R.E. Lake to "continue vacation pleasures." The same month Mrs. Castle and her son are also mentioned "sojourning at Cottonwood Ranch" and the following month Mrs. Ball and her children are reported coming in to Las Vegas from the Cottonwood Ranch and Mrs. R.E. Lake and children returning from a "delightful outing at the Cottonwood Ranch."

In June of 1910 Mrs. Ball and the children are reported taking up their residence for the summer at the Cottonwood Ranch and on July 23 are mentioned returning to the ranch with Mrs. Stanton. At the end of July Mrs. Lake and the children are mentioned returning to Las Vegas from the ranch and in October Mrs. Frank Wengert is reported enjoying an outing to the ranch.

In August of 1911 Miss Nellie McWilliams is reported visiting the ranch and a Mrs. George Hooper being seriously ill after having been bitten by some poisonous insect at the ranch. A George Hooper is mentioned as bringing in some delicious fruit from the ranch and it being the only ones raised in this section.

In August of 1912 Mrs. Ball is again mentioned going to the ranch with the children for the remainder of the summer. The following month Mrs. J.D. Richards and her son Arthur, and Mrs. Lake and little Emily as well as Mrs. Ball and her family are returning from their outings at the Cottonwood Ranch. In August of 1913 Mrs. Ed Von Tobel and children are reported returning from the Cottonwood Ranch where they had been for several weeks "enjoying the delights of the mountains."

RESIDENTS OF THE ADOBE HOUSE

Chico Duarte, his wife Annie and their six children lived in the adobe house. By March of 1940 a family named Masons was living in the adobe building and taking care of the property. Eldon Cunningham's wife worked in Blue Diamond and lived in the house while her husband was in the army. Roy and Minnie Miller had the house in the 1950s. Kitty Cahill remembers Minnie ironing in the adobe part of the house because it was cooler and one of the rooms served as a kitchen.

Angie Bogdanovich's school records tell the story of some of the teachers in the school's early years. In 1938 Angie was in third grade and her teacher was George W. Wood; he was also her teacher for fourth grade. In fifth and sixth grades, Mr. R. Joseph was Angie's teacher. For seventh grade she had M. Erickson; by eighth grade Angie was the only eighth grade student and Mrs. Florence Melburn was her teacher. After eight years in a one-room schoolhouse, Angie found "it was strange" when she went to high school. All the students began the day by meeting in homeroom and then went to different rooms for every class.

CHAPTER 5

Pine Creek Canyon

By Norm Kresge

THE WILSON/HUNT ERA

What would motivate someone to give up the home they know and move with their wife to a place in the desert—not just in the desert but a place removed from a city by a fair distance for its time? Was the West settled by people in search of a better life or did some make the move for other reasons?

Horace Wilson had been a bricklayer in Indiana, but he had dreams of growing strawberries and cultivating fruit trees. He and his wife left Indiana and drove west, coming to Las Vegas in 1922 (Vincent, 1967). The population of the city in 1920, five years before Fremont Street was paved, was 2,304. The Clark County population for the same year was 4,859 (*Las Vegas Sun* Timeline). The Wilsons didn't stay in Las Vegas. Rather, they headed for what we now call Red Rock Canyon and started a homestead six miles from the end of the road.

The original settlers in the Pine Creek area had been Scott and Ada Bearden. They soon left this idyllic area for the city where they were closer to the things most people depend on—schools, doctors, stores and entertainment. The Wilsons took over the Bearden's homestead.

Horace Wilson—no relation to the Wilson brothers living nearby at Sandstone Ranch—first had to put in a road so he could drive to the farm. He built the six-mile road by hand with a pick and shovel, and sandy stretches had to be covered with yucca and Joshua leaves. Horace used a drag to level the roadbed. Every time they went to town, Mrs. Wilson would drive and Mr. Wilson would stand on the drag to level out the roadbed. First they owned a Flivver, a Model T Ford and later a Dodge. The Wilsons left the drag at the end of the road when they went anywhere and then used it again on their way back home.

The Wilson house was a two-story home with 12-inch-thick adobe walls. Pine needles were used as a binder with the adobe to seal the walls. There were no fields of hay, so straw was not an option for Wilson. Horace built a large fireplace to keep the house warm in colder months because the sun disappeared behind the mountains as early as two in the afternoon.

Wilson planted a variety of crops at the new homestead. There were the strawberries that he wanted and many fruit trees. He also planted a large area of alfalfa (that gave him up to seven cuttings per year), a watermelon patch and green beans which were sold at market. They raised goats and chickens and there were rabbits raised to sell at local markets as well.

While Mr. Wilson was busy with his crops, Mrs. Wilson did much to beautify the homestead. She planted roses and the end of their driveway near the house was lined with zinnias. She recounted that the circular drive was often filled with friends who came out for a weekend picnic that included having some of the watermelon grown on site. It was a good place for the friends to be for the weekend with the cooler temperatures of the higher elevation. The creek was also a draw for the friends because you could always splash in the cool water. On one day, Tweed Wilson and his son Buster came to visit and had their photo taken on the porch.

The Nevadan June 30, 1974

Tweed Wilson and his son Buster c. 1930

Vincent states, "To distinguish between the two families, Las Vegans of that day referred to them as the Indian Wilsons and the White Wilsons."

In 1929, the Wilsons sold their homestead to Leigh and Jessie Hunt. Mrs. Wilson said, "He was a millionaire and wanted a mountain lodge and retreat for himself and friends." Hunt had been the owner and publisher of The Seattle Post-Intelligencer that he sold in 1893. He was involved in mining and land development in Las Vegas, and the Huntridge neighborhood of Las Vegas was developed on land that was his farm (Vincent, 1967).

The Wilsons stayed on as caretakers for Hunt, and Mr. Wilson built a large room with a verandah for Leigh and Jessie. The stone was native, which Mrs. Wilson said turned white after exposure to the elements. The Wilsons set up a weather station and sent reports to the weather bureau. They watched the weather very closely because of their crops. Mrs. Wilson related that after one downpour, she counted 26 waterfalls in Pine Creek.

Hunt died in 1933; and shortly after that, the Wilsons moved to Las Vegas. Mr. Wilson resumed his bricklaying trade, but it wasn't to be for long. In 1938, the Wilsons moved to Oregon where he farmed again. After six years, they returned to Las Vegas but stayed in the city.

In 1929, Hunt had hired Walter S. Hunsacker, a recent Pomona College graduate, as his private secretary. Hunsacker said that the estate looked for a buyer for several years with no luck. Eventually, the estate sold an option for 80 acres in Pine Creek to a Las Vegas attorney named John Spann. Spann then sold it to Garland Barnaby, who lived in Boulder City and worked for the Los Angeles Water and Power Authority. Barnaby sold the land to Art Lullis.

Mrs. Wilson described how the homestead went downhill after they left. Some kids let a log roll out of the fireplace and it burned the house down.

The Wilson Foundation as it appears today c. 2013

The fruit trees were cut and people parked their cars where the trees had been. The tank that had been put up to hold water for the wild grapes had been shot at and now was full of holes. The grapevines had died. In the 1950s, Ruby Richardson, who lived at Oliver Ranch for two years, said that she moved to "Hunt's Ranch" for a month or two before moving to Blue Diamond. Ruby Richardson's brother, Glenn, remembered moving to the Hunt Ranch for just one winter. He remembered, "… a nice big spring with lots of water. It was a nice home and had a big garden" (Rankin, 2012).

MOVIEMAKING IN PINE CREEK

In 1968, much of the film entitled "The Stalking Moon" was filmed in Pine Creek. The remaining scenes were filmed at the back of the park at Tule Springs and some extra scenes were filmed at Valley of Fire State Park. The film starred such notable actors as Gregory Peck, Eva Marie Saint and Robert Forster. Photos provided by Jules Mayhew show that the cabin built for the set is located on the meadows near the Wilson home site. (Mayhew does not know who the photographer was.) Other photos show desert with a train station built for the movie. One can pick out various areas of Pine Creek, including a rider coming down what is now the Arnight Trail as it comes down the ridge to Pine Creek. Other photos provided by Mr. Mayhew show a pine tree being set in place for the film and there are various angles of the Pine Creek Canyon area. The Clark County Library District has multiple copies of "The Stalking Moon" available for loan in DVD format.

Public Domain

"The Stalking Moon" set with Mescalito Peak in the background c. 1968

LATER PINE CREEK HISTORY

In the late 1960s, Art Lullis became the owner of the homestead in Pine Creek. Records at Spring Mountain Ranch show that the State of Nevada purchased the 80-acre Pine Creek Ranch from him. From 1969 to the spring of 1971, University of Nevada, Las Vegas Art History Professor Dick Wist was invited to visit Pine Creek by a friend who was familiar with the area. Wist "fell in love" with Pine Creek and began spending his leisure time exploring the area. Wist relates:

Another view of "The Stalking Moon" set with the Pine Creek cliffs c. 1968

> By a quirk of circumstance I met a person who had the rights to the property. Pine Creek was at that time, to the best of my knowledge, 'patent land' owned by a person I knew as Art Lullis. At that time, there was a couple living in a semi-permanent camp just above the cabin that was part of "The Stalking Moon" movie set. I asked Art if I could move a house trailer up there and he said 'fine.'

Wist goes on to say that there was a locked gate below the movie set and a road of passable quality came all the way up to the base of the promontory. He says he began to call the promontory "Mescalito" after the name of the elixir in Carlos Castaneda's "The Teachings of Don Juan: the Yaqui Way of Knowledge."

During the two years he lived there in a double-wide trailer, he didn't need any government permits as he had the permission of Lullis to be there. He stated in his e-mail that "…it wasn't a 'meadow' then but more of a flat spot, adjacent to the creek itself." Further he says, "Based on Google Earth images, it looks quite different now and we almost couldn't recognize the spot with the meadow there now."

When asked about what life was like living in Pine Creek from 1969-1971, Wist said that the only water they had was the creek. During their first year, they only had butane and kerosene lamps. In their second year just before Thanksgiving, he purchased and installed a 5-kilowatt generator. The generator was used for the first time making Thanksgiving dinner. Wist, his wife and their three children came to the conclusion that "…the convenience of electricity was not worth the cacophony and clatter of the noise caused by the generator. It was never used again."

Finally, he said that to the best of his recollection, the entire set of "The Stalking Moon" was still on site when he lived in Pine Creek. There were no trails in that area and they did not see horseback riders or other people doing outdoor exploring. He did not know any of the people who lived at the Oliver Ranch at the time and he had no knowledge of the Wilsons being in Pine Creek (D. Wist, e-mail message to the author, 2013, January 16). In the spring of 1974, the Nevada State Parks acquired Pine Creek.

Today, Pine Creek is one of the most popular hiking and climbing areas in Red Rock Canyon. The foundation from the burned Wilson house is all that is left to remind us that people lived in Pine Creek at one time. The meadow stretches from the foundation toward the base of Mescalito Peak. There are two small creeks that flow from canyons on both sides of Mescalito. The joining of these two make up Pine Creek. Both creeks run underground for a distance, but there's usually water in them year-round. A two-and-a-half mile loop hike goes from the parking area off the Scenic Drive to the floor of the canyon. From there it goes to the base of Mescalito and back to the area of the Wilson home foundation. In 2005, there was a fire in Pine Creek that burned several hundred acres. The damage done by the fire can still be seen, but the desert is coming back and the yuccas and chollas are growing slowly.

CHAPTER 6

Morgan Ranches

By Chuck Williams

In the late 1800s and into the early 1900s, the land that is now Bonnie Springs Ranch and Oliver Ranch was used as grazing ground for the Wilson Ranch (now Spring Mountain Ranch State Park). J. T. McWilliams' 1914 Clark County map shows "Bens Spring" at what would become Oliver Ranch. Ben was a Paiute, sometimes called "Indian Ben," whose daughter would marry one of the Wilson boys. The 1914 map labels what is now considered the core area of Red Rock Canyon as "Fruitland Valley," with the road to the Wilson Ranch passing through Cottonwood Ranch (Blue Diamond) and continuing on to Frye's Camp. Arthur Frye was part owner of the Panchita mine located in the mountains above La Madre spring ("Shipping Ore," 1911).

Brothers William and Reese Morgan homesteaded stock ranches on this un-claimed federal land in the late 1920s. The two ranches were not adjacent to each other, being separated by a forty acre parcel of open land. As both men maintained homes in Las Vegas, it doesn't appear that either brother ever lived on the Red Rock property full time.

Of the two, Reese, the younger, seemed the most settled and eventually be-came a police officer. William was a real cowboy who moved from place to place and wore several hats during his life. He strikes me as a man who wasn't opposed to putting one or two toes over the legal line on occasion. In fact he once walked clear across the line but was never arrested.

Their journey from a boyhood home in Utah through ownership of a ranch in Red Rock Canyon is interesting, to say the least, and is intertwined with the pioneer history of the Las Vegas Valley.

BILL MORGAN

By all accounts William "Bronco Bill" Morgan was an excellent horseman. His second wife Edith was also an accomplished rider and quite forgiving as well. Shortly after 9:00 on a Wednesday evening in October 1912, the Morgans were at their home in what is now North Las Vegas. Bill was sitting in the room where Edith had already gone to bed. He was attempting to fit a screw into his shotgun when it went off. "I didn't know it was loaded," Bill explained. The charge passed through Edith's forearm, shattering one of the bones and then struck her in the face, breaking her jaw and tearing away a portion of the bone and several teeth. Bill mounted a horse and came "with all speed" to Las Vegas, which lay four miles southeast from their home. After securing aid from a doctor and the sheriff, he mounted a fresh horse and returned home "as rapidly as possible." Though terribly injured, Mrs. Morgan would survive the trauma of a gunshot wound, recover, and evidently forgive Bill for the accident ("Unloaded Gun Claims Victim," 1912).

UNLV Special Collections

Bill Morgan riding at his Las Vegas Ranch c. 1907

Thirty years later the Morgans would ride in the 1942 Heldorado Parade where Mrs. Morgan would ride her 32-year-old horse, Pete, and wear a fringed buckskin suit with skirt, jacket and leggings made from five deer skins. She designed and made the outfit herself in 1916 and had worn it for 20 years when she and her husband were operating stock ranches in the area. Mrs. Morgan was proud of her horse that she acquired in 1914 and had ridden ever since ("Pioneer Las Vegans Ride in Parade Here," 1942).

Bill was born in Ogden, Utah in 1869 and first came to southern Nevada in the 1890s. Bill married his first wife Sophia prior to 1890. The Morgans either moved several times during their marriage as Bill became involved in various occupations, or Sophia sometimes stayed home with the children in Utah while Bill traveled. Almost all the 1890 census records were destroyed in a fire so we don't have a record of where Bill and Sophia lived at that time.

Bill won the Champion Cowboy award at the 1893 Chicago World's Fair for breaking horses to harness where he unseated the former champion, Tex Gleason. Afterwards, Buffalo Bill Cody hired Bill as a horse wrangler for his Wild West show. He was said to have doubled for Cody in some performances. Newspaper articles described him as a "Pony Express Rider" in 1895 delivering mail between the Moapa Valley and Vanderbilt, California, a station on the Santa Fe Railroad that required several changes of horses. The real Pony Express ended in November 1861. Between 1895 and 1905 Bill sometimes worked at the Stewart Ranch and served as foreman at a time when the ranch had 4,000 head of cattle. During the Tonopah boom c1900-1901 he drove 16-horse freighters delivering supplies from Las Vegas, a 400 mile round trip.

In 1901, he formed *Bronco Bill's Wild West Show* which employed 50 Paiutes and toured the Midwest and eastern United States. It was there he received his nickname of "Bronco Bill" ("W.C. 'Bill' Morgan, Vegas Pioneer, Dies After Illness in California," 1948).

During the 1900 census Bill and Sophia were living in Salt Lake City, Utah with his occupation listed as "Horse Dealer." The Morgans had five children at that time, three born in Utah, one born in Idaho in 1892 and one born in California in 1895. Two more children were born before Bill and Sophia divorced, sometime prior to 1905 when Bill married his second wife, Edith.

Beatty Museum

Freighter delivering supplies to Tonopah from Las Vegas c. 1907

The 1910 census shows Bill married to Edith (lct's assume legally) and living in Los Angeles, California with his occupation "Stock Dealer." That same census shows Bill's first wife Sophia living in Salt Lake City, Utah with her and Bill's seven children. She is listed as the "Head of Household" and married for 22 years. Surely she and Bill were divorced by this time. Perhaps Sophia was embarrassed or her pride didn't want her to admit she was divorced. In the 1920 census she changed her status to "Widow," perhaps as a way to explain having no husband; but finally on the 1930 census, she listed her status as "Divorced." Sophia passed away on February 16, 1934. The limited information available suggests little, if any, contact between Bill and his children after the divorce.

As noted in the shotgun accident, the Morgans had moved back to Nevada by 1912 and were living in what is now North Las Vegas. A newspaper notice in 1914 announced that, "Mrs. Grace Bentley had given birth to a ten pound girl. Mrs. Bentley is a daughter of Mrs. W.C. Morgan of this city and her husband is employed in Los Angeles." As Bill and Sophia did not have a daughter named Grace, it would stand to reason that Mrs. Bentley is a daughter from Edith's first marriage ("Born: Bentley," 1914).

In December 1914 Bill submitted an application to appropriate water from Mud Spring located between McFarland and Macks Canyons in the Spring Mountains. The water was to be piped to troughs for watering stock. I assume this was used as a summer grazing area for the Morgan's cattle on public land. Access to the area is from the Cold Creek Road. The application received final approval in December 1918. The survey map that was included with the application shows there was a "Log House" located by the water troughs ("Notice of Application," 1915). Bill maintained these water rights until February 1936.

Bill and Edith also purchased a seven acre parcel of land in December 1915 located east of I-15 between Owens Avenue and Tonopah Avenue. They sold this property in March 1920 (Clark County Recorder Book 4, Pages 366-367 and Book 7, Pages 47-48).

Reese Morgan

Reese Morgan had a reputation as a rough and tumble outdoors man who was quite capable of taking care of himself. On Christmas Eve 1930 Police Officer Reese was making his rounds of the local bars and, at that time, illegal gaming establishments. Reese entered one of the establishments and found himself in the middle of a fight when one man "banged smack dab" into Reese. At this point Reese took exception and floored the man with one left-hand punch, dislocating his middle finger in the process. When the other man demanded to know who he was, Reese backed him into a wall and explained he repre-

sented "Old Man Law." This seemed to stabilize the situation and both men became docile. When Reese found that the fight started because of an eight cent dispute during a penny-ante card game and that both men were willing to patch things up, he permitted them to return to the game without making an arrest, it being the Christmas Season and all ("Card Games Cause Fracases on Xmas," 1930).

We don't have much information about Reese prior to his move to Nevada in 1916 since we have to rely on census records and his obituary published in the newspapers. Reese was born in Toelle, Utah in 1876, the younger brother of William. The 1900 census shows Reese as a single man living in a boarding house in Salt Lake City and listing his occupation as "Horse Dealer." Reese is not listed in the 1910 census which would not be unusual if he was moving from place to place. He married Rosella Fuller in 1913 and shortly thereafter they moved to Idaho Falls, Idaho where he was engaged in ranching and stock raising ("Reese T. Morgan Pioneer Vegas, Dies Saturday Eve," 1941).

THE BROTHERS IN PARTNERSHIP

In 1915 Bill and Edith homesteaded 160 acres in the southern Las Vegas valley in what is now the city of Henderson centered at Coyote Run and Hemsdale (Clark County Recorder Book 4, Page 319). His younger brother Reese and his wife moved to Las Vegas in 1916 to join them as partners. In 1918 they again partnered on 160 acres of land north of the city in the area that is now Grand Teton Drive and North Buffalo. Reese had homesteaded 80 acres and Bill and Edith purchased 80 adjacent acres. The two families submitted an application to appropriate water from Lower Tule Spring in May, 1918. The application indicates that the water was to be moved by ditches and used for a truck garden, orchard, alfalfa and corn fields. In 1925 L.L. Gilcrease amended the water application to irrigate his orchard and gardens. The revised application is still active (Clark County Recorder Book 6, Page 46 & Book 10. Pages 294-295 & "The Public Waters of the State of Nevada," 1918).

Reese would later sell his half of the cattle to Bill and move into Las Vegas where he owned several pieces of income property near the Gilbert Brothers store in Westside ("Reese T. Morgan Pioneer Vegas, Dies Saturday Eve," 1941).

In November of 1919 Edith applied for a homestead on 40 acres of land which is now the southeast corner of Grand Montecito Way and Centennial Parkway. Reese Morgan was one of the witnesses. There have been several owners over the years but it doesn't appear that the land was ever developed as it remains a 40 acre empty parcel ("Department of the Interior U. S. Land Office," 1922).

Bill and Edith as well as Reese and his wife Rosella continued to buy and sell property in the city of Las Vegas until the late 1930s. While both families maintained a home in Las Vegas, it is likely that most of the property was for investment and rental income.

The 1920 census records show that both Bill and Reese were living in the "Old Town Addition" of Las Vegas. Reese listed his occupation as "Hay Farmer" and Bill listed his occupation as "Stockman."

THE RED ROCK YEARS

In December 1926 Bill purchased 80 acres of land from Charley Keats, a Paiute Indian, which would later become the core area of Oliver Ranch including the water rights for "Ben's spring" (Clark County Recorder Book 12, Page 80).

25475

THIS INDENTURE, made this 31st day of December, A.D. 1926, BETWEEN Charley Keats, a Pahute Indian, of Clark County, State of Nevada, the party of the first part, and William Morgan of the City of Las Vegas, County of Clark, State of Nevada, the party of the second part,

WItnesseth:

That the said party of the first part, for and in consideration of the sum of Ten Dollars ($10.00), lawful money of the United States of America, to him in hand paid by the said party of the second part, the receipt whereof is hereby acknowledged, does by these presents remise, release and forever quitclaim unto the said party of the second part, his heirs and assigns all the right, title, interest, claim, and demand, both at law and in equity, as well in possession as in expectancy, of the said party of the first part of, in, and to all that certain property situated in the County of Clark, State of Nevada, and more particularly described and bounded as follows, to-wit:

The East one-half (½) of the Southwest quarter of Section one (1), Township Twenty-two (22) South, Range Fifty eight (58) East, M. D. B. & M., containing eighty (80) acres, more or less, Together with that certain spring situate thereon known as and called Ben's Spring.

TOGETHER with all and singular the tenements, hereditaments and appurtenances thereunto belonging, or in anywise appertaining, and the reversion and reversions, remainder and remainders, rents, issues and profits thereof.

TO HAVE AND TO HOLD, all and singular the said premises, together with the appurtenances, unto the said party of the second part, heirs heirs and assigns forever.

IN WITNESS WHEREOF, the said party of the first part has hereunto set his hand and seal the day and year in this instrument first above written.

Witness:
      His
   Joe X Smith
      Mark
  A. S. Henderson

                                His
                       Charley X Keats (Seal)
                              Mark

State of Nevada, {
            :ss
County of Clark.}

On this 31st day of December, A.D. 1926, before me, the undersigned, a Notary Public in and for the County of Clark, State of Nevada, personally appeared Charley Keats, a Pahute Indian, to me known to be the individual described in and who executed the foregoing instrument; and he acknowledged to me that he executed the same freely and voluntarily and for the uses and purposes therin mentioned.

In witness whereof, I have hereunto set my hand and affixed my official seal at my office in said County of Clark the day and year in this certificate last above written.

                              Edgar F. Dupray
                        Notary Public in and for the County
                        of Clark, State of Nevada.

(Notarial Seal)
                        my commission expires November 20th, 1928.

Filed and Recorded at Request of Mr. W. C. Morgan Jan. 12, 1927 at 45 Min. past 10 A.M.
In book 12 of Deeds Page 80 Clark County, Nevada, Records.

LW
                     . S. R. Whitehead, Recorder.

Keats – Morgan Deed c. 1927

Carson City 015606   4—1028—R

The United States of America,

To all to whom these presents shall come, Greeting:

WHEREAS, a Certificate of the Register of the Land Office at **Carson City, Nevada,**

has been deposited in the General Land Office, whereby it appears that full payment has been made by the claimant **William C. Morgan**

according to the provisions of the Act of Congress approved March 3, 1877, entitled "An Act to provide for the sale of desert lands in certain States and Territories," as amended by the Act of March 3, 1891, **for the southeast quarter of the southwest quarter and the southwest quarter of the southeast quarter of Section two in Township twenty-two south of Range fifty-eight east of the Mount Diablo Meridian, Nevada, containing eighty acre ,**

according to the Official Plat of the Survey of the said Land on file in the GENERAL LAND OFFICE.

, NOW KNOW YE, That the UNITED STATES OF AMERICA, in consideration of the premises, and in conformity with the several Acts of Congress in such case made and provided, HAS GIVEN AND GRANTED, and by these presents DOES GIVE AND GRANT, unto the said claimant and to the heirs of the said claimant the Tract above described; TO HAVE AND TO HOLD the same, together with all the rights, privileges, immunities, and appurtenances, of whatsoever nature, thereunto belonging, unto the said claimant and to the heirs and assigns of the said claimant forever; subject to any vested and accrued water rights for mining, agricultural, manufacturing, or other purposes, and rights to ditches and reservoirs used in connection with such water rights, as may be recognized and acknowledged by the local customs, laws, and decisions of courts; and there is reserved from the lands hereby granted, a right of way thereon for ditches or canals constructed by the authority of the United States.

IN TESTIMONY WHEREOF, I, **Franklin D. Roosevelt,**

President of the United States of America, have caused these letters to be made Patent, and the Seal of the General Land Office to be hereunto affixed.

(SEAL)   GIVEN under my hand, at the City of Washington, the   **TWELFTH**

day of   **MAY**   , in the year of our Lord one thousand

nine hundred and   **THIRTY-NINE**   , and of the Independence of the

United States the one hundred and   **SIXTY-THIRD**

By the President: *Franklin D. Roosevelt*

By   *Jeanne Kennedy*   , Secretary,

R.J. Clinton

RECORD OF PATENTS: Patent Number **1102673**   Acting   Recorder of the General Land Office.

W. Morgan Patent Record

The following December, Bill submitted a Desert Land Entry to homestead 80 acres of land to the west of this ranch which would later become part of Bonnie Springs Ranch. At some point about this time Bill became aware that Charley Keats didn't own the 80 acre ranch that he sold to Bill in 1926, most likely to the amusement of the local Paiutes. The land was still part of the public domain and in May 1929 Reese submitted a Desert Land Entry to homestead 160 acres that included the 80 acres Keats had sold to Bill three years earlier ("Notice for Publication Department of the Interior," 1937 & "Notice for Publication Department of the Interior," 1932).

The Desert Land Entry Act of 1877 was an amendment to the Homesteading Act signed by Abraham Lincoln in 1862, and it allowed arid western land to be included in the Homestead Act. The petitioner paid a fee of $1.25 per acre and had to provide proof that the required land improvements had been completed. However, the proof process mainly consisted of providing witnesses who testified that the work had been completed and was not carefully monitored. Once Final Proof had been filed and accepted by the State Land Office, a Homestead Patent, signed by the President of the United States, granted ownership to the petitioner.

The brothers were witnesses for each other's filing and it is a little puzzling that the brothers left a forty acre parcel of land between the two ranches. These forty acres were never homesteaded and remained public land until

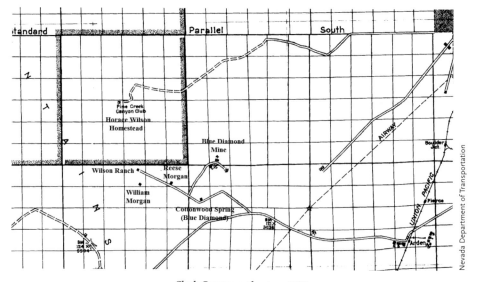

Clark County road map c. 1937

acquired by the Oliver family in 1947. This may have been because the road to the Wilson Ranch crossed this land and there are still remains of the Wilson gate on the property.

In the 1920s and 1930s access to the Morgan Ranches was by what is now Blue Diamond Road / State Route 160. After passing through the former town of Arden, you would turn north on a dirt road that ran through what is now the town of Blue Diamond. The road then ran west of Reese Morgan's Ranch, east of Bill Morgan's Ranch, and continued on to the Wilson Ranch.

Bill and Edith's 1930 census record indicated that they lived in Las Vegas and listed his occupation as "Stockman at a Cattle Ranch."

Reese and Rose's 1930 census listed their home as Steward Street in Las Vegas and Reese listed his occupation as "Policeman." In fact Reese served as a public official in several departments between 1924 and 1937 including Fire Department Officer, Truant Officer, Street Superintendent and Police Officer ("Reese T. Morgan Pioneer Vegas, Dies Saturday Eve," 1941).

Because of Reese's job and management of his rental property, it could be assumed that Bill and Edith were responsible for operating both ranches, perhaps in partnership with Reese. However, in August 1930 the newspaper reported that, "Reese Morgan planned this morning to make a trip this afternoon to his ranch near Arden, where heavy rains have affected the highways during the past few days." So Reese must have maintained some involvement with the ranch ("To Ranch," 1930).

MORGAN RANCHES

During prohibition Bill seems to have supplemented his income by doing a bit of moonshining. In June 1928 Federal agents found two stills at the Morgan ranch, one 50 gallon and another 450 gallon. One was in a shed on the premises and the other in a dugout 2,000 yards from the house. Neither still was working. The agents found four more working stills a quarter of a mile from the ranch. Bill was away at the time, moving a house, and was not arrested. It is unknown if his brother Reese, who was on the Las Vegas police department, had anything to do with the fact that Bill was away at the time or was never arrested. There were several raids that year and some of those arrested included the mayor, the police commissioner and a former police chief ("One of Six Caught in Federal Dry Raid out on Bail," 1928).

The distances stated in the article, if accurate, would seem to indicate that the shed was located on property Bill thought he purchased from Keats, now the Morgan Ranch. The dugout 2,000 yards west would place it at Bill's homestead which is now Bonnie Springs. When the Olivers purchased the ranch from Reese there was only a single structure that may have been built by "Indian Ben." The building's single window (now a part of the main Oliver

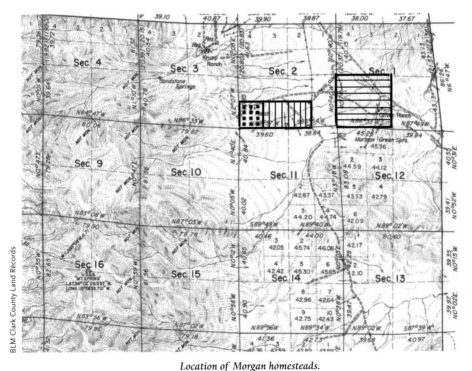

Location of Morgan homesteads.

||| William Morgan
||| 1927 Homestead

━━ Reese Morgan
━━ 1929 Homestead

∎∎∎ William Morgan
∎∎∎ 1939 Purchase

ranch house) is protected by iron bars which has led some to speculate that moonshine had been stored there.

Bill and Edith's Las Vegas homes suffered two fires; the first in December 1925 was caught early and caused $100 damage to the roof. In June 1928 the home was completely destroyed, but fortunately no one was home. Since Bill was away from the ranch "moving a house" during the 1928 moonshining raid, that house may have been the new Las Vegas residence for the Morgans. Another indication that the Morgans primarily lived in town is a 1931 newspaper article which tells of Bill initiating a free employment bureau for ex-servicemen. The Morgans, living at the corner of Main and Ogden streets, provided their telephone number for anyone looking for a veteran to do odd jobs, restaurant work or similar duties, on a temporary or permanent basis ("Sunday Morning Fire Damages Morgan Home," 1925 & "Westside House Razed by Flame," 1928 & "Free Bureau for Jobless," 1931).

Officer Reese suffered a painful bullet wound in January 1934 when his pistol accidentally discharged while he was getting into the back seat of one of the police cars. He was carrying the pistol in a shoulder holster and no one was able to explain just how it discharged. The bullet entered his leg just below the belt and emerged in the upper thigh. The wound was not considered serious and after obtaining treatment at the hospital he was reported resting easily at home ("Reese Morgan is Accidentally Shot," 1934).

UNLV Special Collections.

Bill Morgan delivering mail to airplane by horseback c. 1936

In 1935 Reese and Rose were remarried after being divorced in 1932. When Rose, who had been an invalid for several years, was informed she had only a short time to live, she expressed a last wish that she and her husband remarry. A marriage license was quickly obtained and the couple remarried. Rose passed away on March 26, 1936 with Reese at her side ("Death Bed Vows Unite Divorced 2," 1935 & "Death Calls Vegas Matron Last Night," 1936).

When airmail service to Las Vegas was initiated in 1926, Bill Morgan was asked to deliver a bag of mail to an airplane via horseback to demonstrate how times had changed since Bill carried mail in 1895. In 1936 Bill was asked to recreate the delivery in order to celebrate the tenth anniversary of airmail service ("Re-Enact Scene of 10 Years Ago," 1936).

In January 1937 Bill applied to the State of Nevada for permission to appropriate public water from Point Spring which was located on open range land southwest of his ranch to water livestock. Willard George, who now owned the Wilson Ranch, promptly protested the application. In May a Mr. Hugh Shamberger, Assistant State Engineer, came to Las Vegas to mediate the water fight and the application was approved in February 1938. The application stated that he planned to water 50-200 head of cattle, 3 work horses and 20 head of range horses. The water survey was completed by J.T. McWilliams (see Chapter 11) who also drew the map that was filed with the application ("Notice of Application for Permission to Appropriate the Public Waters of Nevada," 1937 & "Water Hearing," 1937).

Another source indicating that Reese Morgan was an absentee owner comes from an oral interview by Mary Hurtado who describes living at the Morgan Ranch.

> I married my husband in 1934, we moved to Morgan Ranch, which is just a little stone house, just a little stone building with its own spring [The description matches the house located on Reese Morgan's Ranch.] ....We used to pay eight dollars a month rent there. I can remember that's when the Indians used to come, you know, Buster and Tweed and Jim [Wilson.] They used to come over by horseback looking for their cows. And they would ask me have you seen this cow, have you seen that cow? I knew Mr. Morgan, his wife and they had a little daughter by the name of Rose like my girl. She was a redheaded little girl, yeah (Hurtado, 2006).

Asked when they moved from the Morgan Ranch, Mary responded, "We moved in 1938, later in 1938 after my daughter was born." Mary's husband worked at the Blue Diamond mine. He would also help construct some of the

Bill Morgan obituary photo - Unknown photo date

stone buildings added by the Oliver family. The "little stone house" that the Hurtado's lived in would become the kitchen in the main house.

The statement about Mr. Morgan and his wife having a little daughter named Rose does not fit either Reese or Bill. Reese and Rose did not have any children, and Bill and Edith were in their late 60s. Perhaps the little girl was a grandchild of Bill's. The 1940 census lists a Rose Morgan, age six, the daughter of Virginia Zacucke, a divorced head of household living in Las Vegas. I have been unable to find a direct relationship to the Morgans.

On April 11, 1938 Reese was granted a homestead patent on the 160 acre ranch which he sold to Chauncey and Edith Oliver fifteen days later. Reese's health began to fail and that may have been the reason for the sale.

On February 28, 1939 Bill and Edith purchased the adjacent 40 acres west of their ranch from Frank Wait. The land later became the site for the restaurant and old west town of Bonnie Springs Ranch. Shortly after, on March 7, 1939 they sold their now 120 acre ranch to T.S. Thebo. I'm not sure how valid the sale was because Bill did not receive the homestead patent until May 12, 1939. Evidently the sale went through okay as the Thebos remained friends with the Morgans (Clark County Recorder Book 25, Pages 283, 284 and 435).

An article in April 1939 describes a seventieth birthday party for Bill held at "The old Morgan ranch in Red Rock." The article mentioned that Bill was in excellent shape for his age, rounding up cattle during the day (one hopes they were the Morgan's cattle) and riding for over thirty miles before returning home for the party. The party was hosted by Mr. and Mrs. Tom Thebo who purchased the ranch from the Morgans just a month prior ("Bill Morgan Feted on 70th Birthday," 1939).

In the 1940 census Bill and Edith lived at 10 W 4th Street in Las Vegas. Reese, who was in poor health, was living with his sister Beth at 506 W 5th Street. Reese would pass away at his home on December 20, 1941. Bill and Edith remained in Las Vegas until 1946 when they moved to California to be close to their children as Bill's health failed. Bill passed away on August 2, 1948 and Edith on November 27, 1950.

ENDNOTES

The Morgan Ranches would fade from the community memory as generations passed away and the population exploded with a flood of new arrivals. New owners would add buildings, fences, indoor plumbing, electricity and swimming pools. One ranch would become a vacation retreat and tax shelter; the other would end up with a tourist attraction, zoo, equestrian center and residential plots. Cowboys could no longer herd cattle over unfenced grazing land. While both properties retained the title "Ranch" neither would function in the true definition of the word.

When William Morgan died in 1948, the *Las Vegas Review-Journal* paid tribute to a man they called a Western hero. He was someone who saw the area grow from the days prior to the railroad into the teeming community it is now:

> One by one the old timers are leaving us, and it won't be long until the romance of the Old West will be lost in the limbo. Mr. Morgan, while he could not be considered one of the civic leaders of the area, nonetheless probably had as much to do with laying the foundations of this section as anyone. Mr. Morgan came to the Las Vegas area in 1895, before there was any community at all….There weren't more than 100 persons in the whole territory…. He was a restless soul, like most of those early pioneers, and never stayed still long enough to think about helping in the building of a city. The great outdoors was

his home, the sun and moon his blanket and the songs of the wild birds his lullaby. With that he needed nothing else. He was free to roam wherever he desired and able to do anything he felt himself big enough to accomplish... History has been written about the men like William C. Morgan, but that history deals in cold facts and loses the glamour which surrounded the lives they led. The color rests only in the minds of the Bill Morgans of the west and it is being lost because no one takes the time during their lifetime to get the colorful stories which they had to tell. It was men like Bill Morgan who wrote that history and each and every one of them could spin a yarn that would make your hair stand on end. Of course there were some fairly lurid details which were added to their stories as they were told and re-told. However, that was the way the folk lore of the west was built... The Old West is rapidly dying out and it is the hope of the real westerners that someone, somewhere will recapture the exploits of such men as Bill Morgan and document them in song and story for posterity ("Old Timers," 1948).

CHAPTER 7

Oliver Ranch History

By Chuck Williams

It is now a ranch in name only—structures with missing walls and roofs in disrepair. The horses are gone and so is the corral. There are no sounds of children's laughter, running feet or the slamming of a screen door. Broken-down fences no longer keep the wild burros away, which is not necessarily a bad thing. People don't live there anymore. It has become a storage area and dumping ground for items no longer needed.

Chauncey Oliver purchased the 160-acre ranch from Reese Morgan in 1938 (see Chapter 6), and his family used it as a retreat for fifty-five years. After they sold it to the Bureau of Land Management in 1993, it became part of Red Rock Canyon National Conservation Area.

However, the memories remain and we are fortunate to have them recorded by people who lived on the ranch. Their stories don't always agree, but that is okay. Aren't our own memories sometimes clouded by time?

CHAUNCEY OLIVER

Chauncey Bristol "CB" Oliver was an engineer and inventor who had acquired several patents for water filters and cooling. He founded a water purification company in Chicago called Everpure. Chauncey also owned a mine in Vernal, Utah where he gained an appreciation of the west. He decided he wanted to own a place where he could bring his wife and two children and perhaps raise some cattle. According to his son Robert Oliver and April Edner (Robert's long-time secretary), CB decided on the Morgan ranch after checking topographic maps of the area with a Mr. Bracken. The main buildings were constructed between 1938 and 1942. Caretakers lived in a big tent until their house was completed. The main house was built by adding on to a structure already on the property, the original structure becoming the kitchen (Oliver, R., 1993 & Edner, 1996).

CB may have had another reason to own a residence in Nevada. A letter written by Walter Bracken, a Nevada land agent, to the San Pedro, Los Angeles and Salt Lake Railroad requested information on behalf of Mr. Oliver about water rights of the Morgan spring. In the letter, Mr. Bracken indicated CB was looking to secure a small ranch, "Where he would be free from the nuisance taxes imposed by other states" (Bracken, 1938).

The Olivers did obtain water rights to Ben Spring in December 1938; but the application is dated January 1927, which is the date Reese Morgan initiated the application. According to the map that accompanied the application, it would appear that Reese Morgan did not complete the application until February 1937. The water rights are now owned by the Bureau of Land Management (Nevada Division of Water Resources Application 7987).

Inscription on stone wall c. 2015

Whatever the reasons, the Oliver family clearly loved the ranch and enjoyed visiting whenever they could. And you surely can't fault Chauncey on his choice of location. In addition to family, the Olivers opened up the ranch for business associates and friends, with some visiting the ranch on an annual basis.

April Edner was told the stone used for the buildings was quarried from the east side of Blue Diamond Hill. However, there is an inscription cut into one of the boulders on the outside wall of the guest/bunk house that reads:

> FROM AV RANCH N.M.
>
> AUG. 1881 APACHE
>
> ATTACK - WHEN

AV is the cattle brand for the American Valley Ranch in New Mexico which was owned by Mrs. Oliver's maternal grandfather, John P. Casey. It also appears that there may have been additional words on this stone or other stones after the last word of "When." This could indicate that at least this one stone came from the New Mexico Ranch.

The stone commemorates an important event in the life of Mrs. Oliver's mother, Anna Casey Patton, who at the age of seventeen almost single-handedly fought off an attack by approximately twenty Apache Indians on the New Mexico ranch. Her father and oldest brother were away from the ranch and Anna was the only one who knew how to shoot a rifle. Her mother and a wounded ranch hand helped load the rifles with ammunition and care for the younger siblings inside the adobe ranch house. Four ranch hands who were away from the ranch buildings were killed in the attack. According to Mrs. Oliver, the Apaches had raided a wagon train before attacking the ranch and had been celebrating with stolen whiskey. This may have degraded their riding and marksmanship abilities but does not lessen Miss Casey's spunk and efforts to protect her family (Oliver, E., 1967).

The book *Miss Anna*

At this point we are not exactly sure when the stone was placed in the wall. Ken Frejlach, whose parents were caretakers at the ranch in the mid-1940s, recalls hearing Mrs. Casey tell stories about the attack and saying the stone came from the New Mexico ranch (Frejlach, 2015). Alfred Hurtado's parents rented the one-room stone cabin from Reese Morgan for eight dollars a month during 1934-1938 (Hurtado, M., 2006). Later on his father Alfonso helped construct the Oli-

*Miss Anna Patten,
age nineteen c. 1885*

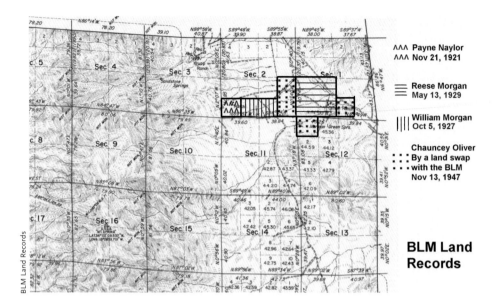

∧∧∧ **Payne Naylor**
∧∧∧ **Nov 21, 1921**

≡ **Reese Morgan**
≡ **May 13, 1929**

||| **William Morgan**
||| **Oct 5, 1927**

Chauncey Oliver
By a land swap
with the BLM
Nov 13, 1947

BLM Land Records

Plat map showing Morgan and Oliver Ranches

ver Ranch buildings. He remembers his mother talking about the stonework, "She said my dad couldn't understand why they hauled stones from other locations when they had all this sandstone in Red Rock." Alfred was born in 1935 but remembers little about the ranch except helping to feed the chickens (Hurtado, A, 2013).

In the 1940 census, the Oliver family listed the Nevada ranch as their residence and Mrs. Anna Casey Patton was listed as the head of household for the Oliver's Oak Park house. However, she was reported to have stayed at the ranch in the early 1940s, especially during the winter months. Staying at the ranch would have rekindled memories of her teenage years so the stone could have very well have come from the New Mexico ranch.

In 1947 through a land swap with the Bureau of Land Management for property he owned in the Spring Mountains, CB added 160 acres to the ranch, bringing the total acreage to 320 (Clark County Recorder Book 46, Page 205).

There are portions of old trails and roads that cross

Kathy Clinesmith

Wilson Gate 1995—The gate has since fallen down.

the ranch property. These include one of the variations of the Old Spanish Trail/Mormon Trail. The original entrance to Oliver Ranch, as well as the Wilson Ranch (now Spring Mountain Ranch State Park) and Bonnie Springs, was located off an old road approximately 300 yards west of the ranch buildings. There are remains of the original "Wilson Ranch" gate alongside the now abandoned road on the Oliver Ranch property.

The 1937 Clark County road map confirms this route, showing the only road to these three ranches coming from what is now the Blue Diamond Road, passing behind the Oliver Ranch buildings, and terminating at the Wilson Ranch. April Edner recalls that the Olivers had problems with people [from Bonnie Springs] drinking and then coming through the fence in the back. That is why Mr. Oliver wanted the entrance to the other two ranches changed to their present location when Highway 159 was constructed (Edner, 1996).

When the ranch was owned by the Olivers, the spring flow was much stronger than it is today. The caretaker families all remembered the water flowing down the wash to the east of the ranch buildings and how the wash became impassable after a rain. In the 1940s and 1950s the ranch had its own alfalfa fields which produced more than one cutting of hay to feed the livestock.

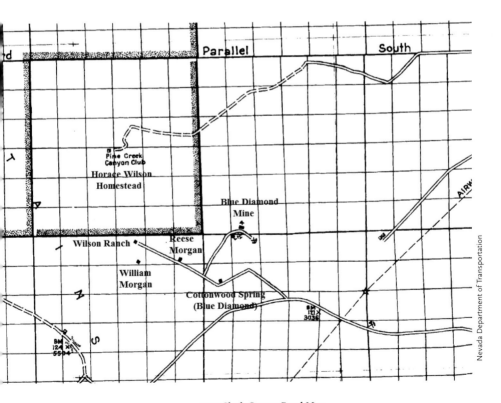

1937 Clark County Road Map

VICKI RICHARDSON

Vicki, whose mother and stepfather Arnulfo Duarte were caretakers circa 1941-1944, recalls living at the ranch as a young teenager. Prior to moving to the ranch, the Duartes had lived in the original adobe house at what would become the town of Blue Diamond. Vicki recalls, "All we knew about the Olivers is that they lived in Oak Park, Illinois. The Ranch was acquired, I think, to accommodate the grandmother. She would come out in the summertime or sometimes in the winter when it was so cold in Chicago." The rest of the family would occasionally come and their visits could last anywhere from a couple of weeks, to a couple of months. "Like I say, we really didn't get a chance to meet anybody except the grandmother. And my mother's duty was to make sure she had enough to eat and supplied her cooking to her and she was supposed to be just made comfortable."

Arnulfo worked at the Blue Diamond Mine, and during the school year he would take Vicki and her younger siblings to the mine on his way to work so they could attend the one-room grade school located on top of the hill. Vicki recalls that there were very few children who attended the school, her class of four students being the biggest.

Vicki's mother had most of the responsibility for taking care of the animals, pool and keeping up both houses. "Since we didn't have a telephone, sometimes people would show up at Oliver Ranch and they knew the house would be in order. My mother would take us into the big house so we had our own duties to do and there was an organ in the house and she would tell us if we did our chores and if we had time, she would crank up the organ and play us a tune because she could play almost any instrument sort of by ear."

Vicki said her mother was also responsible for keeping the Oliver's two limousines maintained as the family seldom drove out from Illinois. "They were Rolls Royce [sic]. One was brown and one was black. That black one, I can remember that it had vases in the back so that people could put flowers in there. It was really a fancy vehicle." Vicki enjoyed going with her mother to get the cars serviced. "You should have seen people's expression. There my mother is with the three or four of us in a Rolls Royce going down to Cashman's dealership." She also remembered the ranch vehicle. "They had a little Ford that had a canvas top they used as a jeep, what people would call a jeep nowadays but this was just a Ford, a little roadster I guess."

Vicki recalled, "Occasionally when it rained we would not be able to get across that creek that ran in front of Oliver Ranch and we would be stranded on one side. We couldn't get to town, or coming from town we couldn't get back home. And that is only all the recollections I can even remember except that we loved being at Oliver Ranch" (Richardson, V. 2013).

KEN FREJLACH

Ken's mother Audrey was stricken with severe rheumatoid arthritis about 1943, and it was suggested that she relocate to a warmer and drier climate. His father Allen decided to look for work in the west by placing a newspaper ad. Eventually, contact was established with Mr. Oliver:

> I remember Mr. Oliver coming out to our house [in Oak Park, Illinois], a very professional looking man. And he brought slides to show us this ranch. Gosh, the slides showed horses, a big dog, ducks and, of course, a pool. My folks made an arrangement with Mr. Oliver to have a modest income if they would be caretakers on the ranch known as the Oliver Ranch a few miles outside of Blue Diamond, Nevada.

The Frejlachs traveled west in 1945 by train, arriving in Las Vegas late at night and were met by Mrs. Oliver who had hired a taxi to take them to the ranch. Ken remembers the lights of Fremont Street, "Good grief, I had never seen anything like that in my life, not even in the circus." After leaving the bright lights of Las Vegas, "It was so dark you couldn't see anything at all outside."

When they arrived at the ranch, a massive dog escorted the family to the caretaker's house. "This was Smokey, a German Shepard mix and fierce looking, but [he] turned out to be a very protective and gentle dog." When Ken went outside the next morning, he was stunned by the view. "I was so impressed when I ran out, here were these huge mountains in all different colors. The ranch had three horses, a pool, ducks and...holy cow, just everything [was] there!"

The Olivers had two old Fords: a coupe with a rumble seat and an old pickup that they kept at the ranch for their family to use. There was an orchard which provided fresh peaches and a spring that fed into a little stream that ran by the tack house. Ken remembers:

> That was another thing that was a joy for a kid...it was loaded with frogs and we would have a ball there. We had a pool, but you know how kids are, we made a little tub-like swimming pool in the stream. I remember taking off in the morning with my dad, and we would go riding in the hills.

Ken's mother was barely able to walk when they arrived, and her hands were so deformed that she could hardly pick up anything. The family contacted a Las Vegas doctor who wanted her to spend time outside. "He told her to go outside in the sun at least 45 minutes a day, soak up that sun and I'll have you walking fairly soon. Sure enough, within six months or so she was able to start getting around taking only aspirin for pain."

The Olivers were very concerned about Audrey's health and took her to see a specialist in Los Angeles. Ken remembered how impressed she was with their car and seeing a freeway for the first time. "They were most generous people in this regard as well as friendly, down-to-earth folks."

The ranch had a one-cylinder gasoline powered washing machine near the back of the house. Ken's dad started it like a motorcycle. "It had a pump that made all this noise and if you were within an acre or so of the house, you could hear it. My mother hung the clothes up when she could and my dad would finish up."

The big house where the Olivers stayed when they came down was a beautiful home, but Ken doesn't remember being inside often. It was generally Mrs. Oliver or the boys who would visit.

Mrs. Oliver's mother also visited the ranch a couple of times. Ken remembers:

Ken Frejlach c. 1945

(top left) Allen Frejlach with ducks Joe, Molly and family (top middle) Ed Price and Ken Frejlach by the ranch back gate (top right) Looking at the guest room tack house from the front yard of the main house (bottom left) Frejlach family ready for church standing by the caretaker's house (bottom right) Pool and changing room

She was a lovely lady, quite sophisticated. She would tell us about what went on with her as a little girl and how she had to fight off the Indians. We would sit there by the Coleman lantern and listen to her stories. She was fascinating.

There were remnants from her time as a girl by the tack house, a couple of old wagon wheels and parts of an old pistol and rifle. When I asked if the stone engraved with the details of the Apache attack came from the New Mexico ranch, Ken replied, "Well, that was what I was told as a young kid. And it wasn't like she was old and feeble. She was an older woman but well-kept and very knowledgeable and, at my age, she was like a grandmother."

Ken attended the Blue Diamond School and would normally catch a ride with the caretakers of the Bar Nothing Ranch (now Spring Mountain Ranch State Park) who had two children in school. They drove an old army ambulance and the three kids would rattle around in the open area behind the seats. But his most memorable times were when his dad would ride into town on his horse to pick him up after school, "We would ride double back home. That was fantastic."

Ken's dad learned to plow with horses and to grow cantaloupe and other

Ken Frejlach c. 1945

(top left) Chicken coop with Ken, father Allen, uncle, his sister Karen and Smokey (middle left) Ken, Karen and his uncle with ranch pickup truck (bottom left) Ken and Karen with a neighbor who was visiting (right) Allen Frejlach plowing garden with saddle horses

vegetables. He had a hard time getting the saddle horses to plow but cowboys from the Bar Nothing Ranch helped him get the horses in line. Ken remembers his dad ordering chickens through the Sears and Roebuck Catalog and building a chicken coop behind the caretaker's house in order to protect the chickens from predators.

Ken also recalled the ranch behind Oliver Ranch which would become Bonnie Springs:

> After we were there about a year, they opened up this little like tavern, with a juke box, next to our spread. I don't know, it was probably set up in some guy's barn. I just remember it was all lit up and people would go there. They would probably have drinks and dance and so forth… The man that owned it wasn't married at the time but he had a son about my age, a tall lanky kid. The dad was a rough kind of guy and whenever the son didn't listen to him, he would kick him in the butt to get him going.

One summer when Bob Oliver was home from Annapolis, he arranged to take Ken and his dad to Mt. Potosi and see the airplane crash site where Carole Lombard was killed in 1942:

> That, as a young boy, was quite an experience; just getting up there and seeing that airplane along with a beautiful vista. We could even see a big portion of Lake Mead. Part of the fuselage was still there as they had not been able to clean much of it up at all. There was a lot of little remnants that we were able to pick up. The story was that her diamond wedding ring was never found.

When I first spoke to Ken over the phone, he described the crash site as "foreboding" as there were still bits of bone and personal items scattered about. The wreckage would glisten in the afternoon sun and could be seen in Las Vegas.

Ken reflected on his stay at the ranch:

> Our total time on the ranch was probably a period of two years or so and then we moved to Blue Diamond. During this time my mom was getting better and my dad was starting to work full-time. I still marvel at my folks. They left Oak Park, Illinois, where they had a phone, electricity, running water, a heater, and all of that… and then to come out to the ranch where they have Coleman light, no running water, no telephone and it took about a week and a half for a letter to go from Blue Diamond to Chicago (Frejlach, 2015).

ED PRICE

I think most boys from my generation played at being a cowboy when they were growing up. I know I did even though we lived in Indiana and I didn't have a horse. Who could resist daydreams of riding a horse among the western scenery seen in cowboy movies? Ed Price, whose father was caretaker of Oliver Ranch circa 1946–1951, could act out that dream for real. He and his best friend would explore the valley and canyons on their horses and camp out under the stars. He would know Tweed and Buster Wilson, Paiute Indians, who lived at what is now Spring Mountain Ranch, and ride his painted-up horse as an extra, playing an Indian in a western movie being filmed at Red Rock. He may have even met and had lunch with Howard Hughes.

Ed recalls moving to Oliver Ranch:

> My mom, my dad and my sister, who was two years younger than I, moved to the Oliver Ranch right after the war stopped in Germany because I remember that distinctly. We lived there as far as I can tell from 1945 to about 1952, midway through my senior year of 8th grade. My dad's job title was Cattle Manager, but it was not a cattle ranch. We would see the Olivers about twice a year. They kept a 1946 Mercury convertible in the garage for their use. Chauncey Oliver was

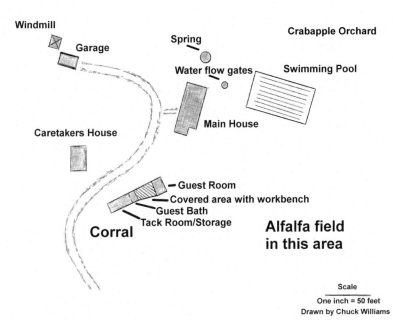

Water Cistern on top of the hill

Windmill

Garage

Spring

Crabapple Orchard

Water flow gates

Swimming Pool

Caretakers House

Main House

Guest Room

Covered area with workbench

Guest Bath

Tack Room/Storage

Corral

Alfalfa field in this area

Scale
One inch = 50 feet
Drawn by Chuck Williams

Oliver Ranch Layout c. 1948 from a sketch by Ed Price

a big man, very blustery and braggadocio. He was always a 'presence' wherever he was but always very kind to me and told me I could use the library whenever I wanted. Mrs. Oliver was a great storyteller and had a 'dramatic' memory.

Ed thought one of the reasons CB wanted a residence in Nevada was that he felt his two sons, Robert and Bruce, had a better chance to receive an appointment to Annapolis from Nevada than in Illinois. "Both boys went to Annapolis. I remember them staying at the ranch in their white navy officer uniforms."

According to Ed, the main house was beautiful and set back in the shade of a little knoll. It had an extensive library which included Paiute artifacts and parts of the crashed DC 3 that killed Carole Lombard and others at Mt. Potosi. He tells of being able to use the main house bathroom when the Olivers were not there as it had a shower, which he thought was a special treat.

Ed remembers helping his father and Mr. Oliver install solar water heaters for the bathrooms on all three houses. The water was gravity-fed to the roof and heated; it worked quite well, the water never becoming less than lukewarm even in the winter months.

Ed writes about the spring:

> The ranch spring came out of the south side of the hill to the north [the one the water tank was on]. A pipe fed the pool and another pipe ran to the windmill and then up and down the hill producing water pressure to the buildings. Most of the water fed into a ditch from the spring between the main house and the pool running east [behind the guest house and corral] feeding the alfalfa field and eventually just fading into the ground to the south. One day Mr. Oliver and my dad tried to measure the output of the spring using a gallon bucket. Mr. Oliver measured, I believe, 200 GPM. My dad thought this was a gross exaggeration. I do remember the spring source as coming out from underneath a large rock in the side of the hill. It was delicious and crystal clear and for a long time I thought any other water tasted 'funny.' There are many areas where the water would appear for a while then fade back underground.

Early on there was an alfalfa field to the northeast of the guest house/corral and Ed remembers:

> The ranch had an International Harvester Tractor, a red one. My dad and I would pull a mower and we would mow the alfalfa and store the hay in the tack room. The Olivers had a Model A truck, but

about 1949 or 1950 my dad bought an International Harvester two-ton truck for personal use. We used it for trips to Pahrump for hay and at least one trip to Blythe, California. We also had a 55-gallon drum we used to haul gasoline back from Las Vegas for ranch use.

There were several movies filmed in Red Rock, and Ed remembers:

I was an extra in a western movie filmed out where the viewpoint is today. I can't remember the movie. I was a redskin warrior riding my horse, whose name was Cinco because my dad said, teasing, that she wasn't worth a nickel. They painted me red and gave me a wig; they also painted Cinco as an Indian horse. Pay was great and the food was beyond anything I had ever experienced; I was in awe. Many years ago I saw myself on TV in the movie very briefly and still can't recall its name for what it's worth. The reason they hired me was that I could ride Cinco full speed without a saddle or bridle. We learned to watch for film crews and ride out to see if they needed any kind of help. They paid outlandishly and fed you incredibly well. We could not believe the Hollywood crowd; they were like space people to us.

Ed related another incident where he thinks he may have met a Nevada legend:

Toward the end of our time here, just before we left, within the year we left—so somewhere around 1952, my sister and I were in the crab-apple orchard or maybe we were at the edge of the swimming pool when a guy came wandering in from the north through the crabapple field, a tall, skinny guy with a mustache. He had a fedora on and suit and tie. He asked for some water and we gave him water and my mom fed him. In retrospect, that was Howard Hughes. And we got him a ride into Las Vegas. He had crashed some sort of experimental airplane out on the dirt strip at Bonnie Springs. The next day or later that day, there was a whole flurry of response to that. It was a big deal that no one could talk about. We went up on the hill and saw it from a distance. My Dad wouldn't let us go out there—that is my sister and I. It was a shiny aluminum job. It had two motors. The Bonnie Springs Ranch was off and on some sort of brothel or some sort of bar or restaurant. It never was successful while we were there. The airstrip was used off and on.

Ed also recalled how the wash would flood after a rain making it difficult to get in or out of the ranch (Price, 2012).

GLENN RICHARDSON AND RUBY RICHARDSON RANKIN

Glenn and Ruby's parents were caretakers after the Price family circa 1952-1954. Glenn remembers:

> We were just caretakers there on the ranch. The Olivers lived in Chicago and came out a couple of times while we were there. They weren't there very often, but we would get everything ready when they come out. It was a nice place, a really beautiful place. My mother was an old farm girl, so to speak, so we had a cow and we had chickens. And actually we sold some milk and eggs and stuff down to the village.

Glenn and Ruby said the solar heaters were not working when they moved there. Glenn can still remember helping fix the system and how it worked:

> I'm going to guess, about a fifty gallon maybe a little bigger tank. And on that tank was like pads on the side of it. Kind of like a tank-within-a-tank, a solar collection system that circulated water. The collector set at about a 45 degree angle and the tank itself was level with this collector, so just [a] thermal syphon I think you probably call it. As the water heated in the collector, it would flow over into these pads. This tank on the roof was insulated to keep if from freezing in the winter time. But the collector part of it needed anti-freeze in it to keep it from freezing in the winter and it actually worked.

Ruby said the windmill system worked well when there was wind, but someone needed to crank the windmill by hand if the wind was not active.

Glenn recalled when the fence that surrounded the ranch property was built:

> I think it was my junior year during the summer; Mr. Oliver hired me to make some fencing. He had bought about a thousand fence posts, somewhere along that line. Cedar post. We had a little tractor there on the ranch. He bought a posthole digger for it. And I actually built about two miles of fencing that went around the Oliver Ranch…it was beneficial for us to keep the horses in, they weren't just running the range all the time. I think, if I remember right, I got about $600.

Glenn remembered when the root cellar and room additions were added:

> Yes, it was kind of a dugout underneath the end of the house…but while we were there, my dad dug it out a little bit more and he actually wanted to put some concrete stairs down into the thing so he

could get underneath the house…to enlarge it a little bit. But anyway, we did make a stairway down into this dugout portion underneath the house.

We did add on to the house, the caretaker's house, on the south side of it. We added a kitchen and like a dining room area there. The front part of the house was just a big screened-in porch which was basically my bedroom during the summer time.

Ruby's husband Bud, who grew up in Blue Diamond and was a friend of Ed Price, remembers that he and Ed rode out to watch a Roy Rogers movie being filmed at Red Rock. Most likely "The Bells of San Angelo," filmed at Red Rock in 1947; but this was not the movie Ed was in (Richardson, G, 2013 & Rankin, R, 2012 & Rankin, B, 2012).

Susan Logan Smith and Nancy Logan Denman

Susan and Nancy, whose parents were caretakers 1965–1975 and 1978–1981, have many fond memories of the ranch.

Susan writes:

> I was younger when Mr. CB Oliver and his wife visited; but when they did, they often visited with my parents and Mrs. Oliver usually brought a little gift for me. When Bob Oliver's family came for their summer retreats, I would help with the horses and getting them saddled up, etc. and ready for daily rides, and usually would visit with the youngest child at that time, which was Julie. She was closest to my age and we would play and etc. In later years Bob Oliver remarried Barbara and they came out a little less regimented. But generally they would call in advance so my parents would have property ready, i.e. the house cleaned and all beds ready, pool full and ready for use, and all areas kept up.

When asked if CB still drove when he was at the ranch, the sisters laughed and said, "Yes, which was a little scary." The Logan's had electricity and a phone but no air conditioning.

The Logan sisters remember the plane parts and Indian artifacts, but said the library was mainly used as a bedroom with at least four beds and a painting by Barbara Oliver over the fireplace. The center room had a flagstone floor and contained chairs, beds, and the dining table. There were bars on the kitchen window which was part of the original building: they were told this was because that is where they kept the liquor.

Larry and Kathie Clinesmith live in Blue Diamond and Kathie boarded her horse at the ranch for many years. They became friends with the Logans and Robert Oliver. The spring always had good water and generally it would run across the road (SR 159) according to the Logan sisters and Clinesmiths. Larry Clinesmith felt that perhaps the flow has been restricted in later years because of modifications made to the spring area after the Bureau of Land Management purchased the property.

Kitchen wall mural assume painted by Barbara Oliver. This wall was demolished sometime after May 2006 when the photo was taken.

The sisters remembered that the Olivers held company "retreats" at the ranch and seeing the Olivers and staff sitting in chairs in the yard between the house and pool. The pool was never warmer than 58 degrees F and their mother had photos of the girls in the pool with their lips blue from the cold. They can remember that Bruce Oliver, along with his family and friends, would run from the house deck and jump in the pool. The Logans could hear the screams and laugher at their house.

Susan related that her family was always more alert when Bruce Oliver's son, Neal, was visiting the ranch. Neal had a habit of finding trouble, or having trouble find him. She remembers the time he fell through the large glass windows at the back of the house and another time when he fell and hurt himself when swinging on a rope out by the swimming pool.

The garage and windmill were located south of the main house. The pillars next to the concrete foundation where the garage was located are what's left of the second windmill. The first windmill was located higher on the hill below the water cistern.

Rooms were added on the south side of the caretaker's house after the Logans lived there, as were the concrete slabs east of the guest house / corral and southeast of the caretaker's house. The sisters pointed out the locations of the root cellar and well (after electricity was available, a well replaced the windmill and gravity fed water supply) on the east side of the caretaker's house and cactus garden next to the main house. Kathie Clinesmith and the sisters remember where an old tractor is buried south of the caretaker's house.

Susan Logan said that there were ten to twelve horses on the ranch when they lived there. The sisters remembered some of the horses' names. Flash, the mustang, escaped a lot. Sky, a white mare, had a palomino colt named Thunder, whose father was said to have been a wild stallion who had broken through the fence. Susan remembered that the Las Vegas Review-Journal printed a story about the event as Sky was over thirty at the time of the birth and that it was rare for a horse that age to survive the trauma. Other horses were named Belle, Big Red, Prince and Smoky. The alfalfa field was gone by that time, and the Logans purchased hay from Bowman's in Pahrump for $25 per ton.

The Logan sisters beside the main house after a snow storm. The garage can be seen in the background c. 1971

Nancy Denman and Susan Smith

Susan remembered her first day of school at Blue Diamond after moving to the ranch; it rained and the wash was impassable, so her father drove her to school on the farm tractor.

The Logan sisters stated that their father always wanted to be a cowboy and loved living at the ranch. When he died, the family spread his ashes on the hill near the cistern/windmill with Oliver family permission (Logan-Denman, 2012 & Logan-Smith, 2012-2013 & Smith, 2012 & Clinesmith, K., 2012 & Clinesmith, L., 2012, Denman, 2012).

LaMoyne Hinricksen

LaMoyne and his family were caretakers 1976-1978. LaMoyne remembers that the screened-in porch on the north end of the house was converted into a living room and bedroom when they lived there. Other than that, he just did normal maintenance on the house; he remembers having to repair the flat roof on their house when it leaked and they had to dig out the spring a couple of times so the water would flow better. He related that, "The spring was the only source of the water. The well was in but the pump set so long it froze up. So while we were there, we just used the water out of the spring." The fence was always in need of some type of repair. "One year I got the boys a pair of barbwire pliers and a key post driver for Christmas so they could go horseback riding and check the fence line and keep it fixed up."

Robert Oliver always visited with the Hinricksens when he was at the ranch:

> I know one time Bob and I was talking and he was saying that the state was trying to buy it from him and he didn't want to sell it. So they would get price from him and since the state legislature only met every two years it would be two years before they would have the money. Well it's been another two years so the price is up. So he kept doing that he said, 'I just don't want to sell it.'

He recalls Robert Oliver as being very personable and he always had stories to tell:

> He was telling me when he went into the service and in boot camp he was shooting a Thompson Automatic Rifle, the 45 caliber. And Bob is pretty good size guy and he was watching another guy shooting and how the gun would rear up. So when it came Bob's turn, he kind of leaned down into it and he tore up that target they were shooting at. The guy said, 'Wow! So you have shot these before.' Bob never had but he just looked at the guy and said, 'Yeah, I'm from Chicago.'

Robert Oliver did consulting work and LaMoyne remembers that the only phone on the ranch was in the caretaker's house. "He was a very nice guy, a very sharp guy. Like we had the phone in our house. And while he was there he was on that phone all the time. The people were after him and he would have to call back and he was very busy." LaMoyne said Robert Oliver and his sons came out several times, but he did not meet Bruce Oliver.

LaMoyne recalled the horse Prince Noble, "Prince, he was pretty much of an artist and he could get out whenever he wanted to." Once they received a phone call that one of the Oliver horses had been hit by a car. When they went to investigate, they found a carload of kids with the car's windshield shattered, "Prince was laying on the road with his head bleeding. We brought a halter… and kind of got things quieted down… and took him over to the house." They had a veterinarian come out but the horse was not hurt at all. "He had a hard head, a big head. Yeah, he was a big-headed old horse" (Hinricksen, 2013).

Jim Wilson Jr. and George Twison "Tweed" Wilson were the adopted half-Indian sons of the senior James (Jim) Wilson who founded the Wilson ranch with his one-time partner George Anderson (who was said to be the father of Tweed). Tweed would marry an Indian woman named Anne who was born at what is now Oliver Ranch. They had a son, Russell, who was better known as Buster, in 1908. Jim Jr., Tweed, and later on Buster, would be involved in the early history of the Las Vegas valley. Jim Jr. and Tweed helped survey the original town site of Las Vegas in 1905. All three Wilsons would live their life in Red Rock Canyon and are remembered by all the families that lived at the Ranch (Nevada State Parks, n.d.).

April Edner remembered that Mrs. Oliver did not like her son, Robert, riding with Jim Jr. and Tweed Wilson because they were drunk all the time. Robert, who used to play with Tweed's son Buster, recalled having several "wild rides" when Jim and Tweed would insist that he get in their convertible for a ride to the ranch after "hanging one on" in Las Vegas. Jim Wilson Jr. died in 1943, but Tweed and his son Buster continued to visit the Oliver Ranch until their deaths in 1959 and 1972 (Oliver, R., 1993 & Edner, 1996).

Ken Frejlach remembers coming out of school and seeing Tweed and Buster Wilson having a good time.

> They would have a few dollars as they were supposed to paint the aluminum sections of the TWA plane [to keep them from glistening in the sun] that crashed up on Mt. Potosi that killed Carole Lombard and crew. They would stop and buy the liquor before they went up there, and some days never made it to the crash site. I always got a chuckle out of them. They never created a problem, just neat people I thought. From memory, I think that they were given a 'life estate' to live at the Bar Nothing (Frejlach, 2015).

Ed Price recalls that Tweed and Buster were generally shunned by most people because of their drinking and general appearance, but his father thought they were interesting.

> We fed them many a dinner. My dad would ply the two Indians with liquor trying to get them to tell us about a secret cache of silver they claimed to know about. My mom and I thought all they wanted was a decent meal and the liquor. They would get drunk and sleep out in the guesthouse or out in the tack room on the hay. We never did find the silver cache, let me put it that way. My dad was kind of a hopeless romantic. It was fun for me as a kid to think, oh boy, I may find

a fortune one of these days (Price, 2012).

Ruby Richardson Rankin remembered the Wilsons having dinner with the family, but she was too young to be included in most of the conversations. Glenn Richardson remembers Buster from when the root cellar was added to the caretaker's house, "My dad had hired old Buster, Wilson I think his last name was, to actually do some of the work, but I know it seemed like it took him forever to get it done. My dad would pay him and then you wouldn't see him for about two weeks until he used up his money" (Richardson, G, 2013 & Rankin, R, 2012).

LaMoyne Hinricksen worked at the Wilson Ranch when he was a teenager living in Blue Diamond and remembered the Wilsons:

> This was in the early part of the summer. And it was pretty warm when Buster came in. Swed (the foreman) asked him where Tweed was. And Buster kept scratching his head; "Where is Tweed." And he finally remembered...they had got drunk and Tweed had passed out in the pickup with the windows rolled up. And Tweed was just about dehydrated, but he came out of it fine.
>
> I kind of enjoyed him. One time my grandmother was out visiting when we lived in Blue Diamond and about two o'clock in the morning there was this loud banging on the back door.
>
> Grandma said, "What in the hell is that?"
>
> I said, "Be quiet, that's Buster."
>
> She said, "What's Buster?"
>
> I said, "A drunk Indian."
>
> She said, "A drunk Indian?"
>
> I said, "Yep."
>
> She said, "Shoot him!"
>
> Yeah, he was a character. I kind of liked Buster. He was a talented person, very talented (Hinricksen, 2013).

By the time the Logans were caretakers, Tweed had passed on; but Susan remembers, "Buster would come by about once or twice a year and visit with my father and Mr. Oliver if he was in town. They would just catch up on the latest area happenings. I do recall he would usually be slightly intoxicated or

Foundation of structure at unnamed spring west of ranch in 2015

would be having a beer with my dad" (Logan-Smith, 2012-2013).

HANGING QUESTIONS

There are remains of stone structures at two locations on the ranch property. One location is next to an unnamed spring approximately 600 yards west of the ranch house. It consists of a structure with low stone walls and an excavated area on a hillside 25 yards east of the structure which was most likely a dugout.

The other location is at Mormon Green, about 600 yards southwest of the ranch house. These structures are somewhat of a mystery as no one is quite sure who lived there. According to April Edner, "miners" lived at the springs. There is an abandoned mine located 600 yards from Mormon Green Spring which has been described as "the old Turquoise mine." According to Robert Oliver, the mine operated in the 1880s. Ed Price remembers exploring the mine and thought it extended 30–50 feet, but he had the good sense not to enter. Larry Clinesmith remembers visiting the mine with Robert Oliver (who asked him to keep the location secret) and that it had a low entrance but extended quite a distance into the hillside. The shaft entrance is now inaccessible. In checking with the State of Nevada Division of Minerals, there is no state or federal record of any mine at that location (Edner, 1996 & Oliver, R., 1993 & Clinesmith, L., 2012 & Price, 2012).

The Harry Reid Center at the University of Nevada Las Vegas conducted an excavation of the Mormon Green Spring foundation structures in 2006. Based on the artifacts collected, they concluded that a male and female occupied the structures in the 1920–1940 time frame. The site consisted

Foundation of structure at Mormon Green Spring in 2015

of a residence, shed with enclosed yard/garden and a dugout.

This time frame matches the period when the Morgans lived at the ranch; however, the foundations are 600 yards west of the core ranch area. A moonshine raid in 1928 mentioned a dugout located west of the ranch house but no evidence of moonshining (bottles or equipment) was found in over 5,000 artifacts recovered from the Mormon Green Spring dugout site. The second dugout and structure area have not been excavated.

Susan Logan Smith related that CB Oliver told her that the foundations were the residence of early Mormon settlers. These may well have been homesteaded by people who never completed the patent process.

Another interesting question, based on Mary Hurtado's oral history that she and her husband lived on the Morgan Ranch 1934-1938 is, "Where did the Morgans stay when they were at the ranch" (Wedding & Winslow & Joye & Smith & Riddle, 2008 & Logan-Smith, 2012-2013 & Hurtado, M., 2006 & "One of Six Caught in Federal Dry Raid out on Bail," 1928).

The spring located adjacent to the ranch house is known as Indian Ben or Whispering Ben Spring. Ben was a Paiute Indian who lived in a house in the area. The exact location is not known, but some records indicate he lived at Mormon Green Spring about a quarter mile west of the ranch house. Ben's house would later become the first Blue Diamond School, so some feel that the house may have been located closer to the present town of Blue Diamond (Wedding & Winslow & Joye & Smith & Riddle, 2008).

However, April Edner related a conversation that might indicate that Ben's house was located at the ranch site:

> I understand that an old Indian woman had come out at one time. It was Don Carter [caretaker of the ranch in the early eighties] told me about it. He happened to be here that day and she just drove up or

someone drove her up. I believe she was in her 90s. I guess she was not in good health and wanted to see where she was born. And she did point out the trees she remembered (Edner, 1996).

THE LAST RIDE

Kathie Clinesmith writes about a horseback ride with Pam Vossler in August, 1993:

Nine was really too late in the morning to start out on a horseback ride in August, but we grabbed extra water and went anyway. This would be our last ride as the Ranch was being sold. Pam met me at the gate riding Thunder. The palomino had been born on the Oliver Ranch and was a favorite of hers. Her father was a friend and business acquaintance of Robert Oliver and her family had been coming to the Ranch for a few weeks every summer for as long as she could remember. I had been boarding my horse on the Ranch for more than fifteen years and we had enjoyed riding together. There wasn't a lot to say, so we just enjoyed the heat and the sound of the hoof beats on the sandy wash. As the canyon narrowed, we moved into the shade and stopped when it ended in a high rock waterfall. The silence was broken by the loud buzzing of a hummingbird and we finally saw her going back and forth, up and down at the end of the canyon. Unusual, until we realized she had a nest in a small bush growing out of a crack in the wall. But why all the fuss? We were far enough away not to disturb her. An owl hooted softly in the background, not what you'd expect at this time of day. And then the call was answered! Keeping the horses quiet so as not to disturb the hummer, we finally spotted a fluffy and obviously juvenile owl on a rocky ledge across from her nest! The hooting was repeated and we saw an adult owl fly up the canyon and light on the wall opposite the baby. After several more calls, the juvenile launched himself toward the adult and they both flew off down the canyon. The hummingbird hovered for a minute, then went back to her nest. It was quiet. We felt that we had been given a very special goodbye from a very special place (Clinesmith, 2013).

ENDNOTES

In January 1999, I signed up to be a volunteer at Red Rock Canyon and was scheduled for Natural Resource training at Oliver Ranch. The main house was still complete and the class was held in the living room. I recall the bathroom was still functional. Over the next few years several volunteer events were

Oliver Ranch—Friends of Red Rock Canyon meeting. November 2001

held on the back lawn beneath the large cottonwood trees. I remember how beautiful and peaceful it was and that it would be a wonderful place to live. I wish I knew then what I know now. I would have paid more attention and taken photos.

What a pleasure to meet and talk to people who lived there or visited on a regular basis. My heartfelt thanks for allowing me to use your memories in this chapter.

(top left) Main house from the back yard. Center portion of the house has been removed c. 2015 (bottom left) Caretakers house c. 2015 (top right) From left to right are the stables, tack room, covered area and guest room c. 2015 (bottom right) Pool area c. 2015

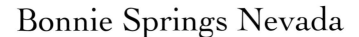

CHAPTER 8

Bonnie Springs Nevada

By Dan Wray

INTRODUCTION

Bonnie Springs Old Nevada has become one of the major tourist attractions in the area both for tourists and Las Vegas residents. As a replica of a Wild West Town, it offers a taste of the West as it is generally perceived to have been.

This chapter attempts to trace its development and reveal something of the glitzy Hollywood connections, of the colorful characters who each in their way contributed to it and of the trials and tribulations involved.

This chapter will add further details to an oral history interview undertaken by Gretchen Schroeder of the Blue Diamond History Committee on February 11, 2004 with Bonnie Levinson, founder of Bonnie Springs.

BEFORE BONNIE ARRIVED

Today's Route 159 into Las Vegas traverses a valley bordered to the west by the colorful sandstone escarpment known as Wilson Cliffs (named for the highest peak in the range, Mount Wilson) and for James Bernard Wilson who was an early rancher in the area. It was originally part of the original Old Spanish Trail, a major route for wagons going to California.

The combination of a scenic location on a major transport route, together with a ready supply of water from springs along the valley, encouraged numerous people to establish homesteads there.

It was, however, the establishment of the Hardy Gypsum Mine which gave impulse to major development. Blue Diamond, now a desirable residential area, was established initially as accommodation for workers at the mine. On March 24, 1917 the *Las Vegas Age* reported that Jack Coyle, the foreman of the Boss Mine, had purchased an eighty-acre ranch near the Wilson Ranch where he had built a comfortable house and was making further improvements (Bought Ranch, 1917).

Homesteading in the area continued to develop. Bill Morgan was homesteading 80 acres in 1927 and received the patent on May 12, 1939. He added to his holdings when Orren Naylor received ownership of 40 acres adjacent to his 80 acres and subsequently sold them to a Frank Wait who sold them on to Morgan. Morgan then sold the combined 120 acres to T.S. Thebo.

In the 1940s the Chambers family was leasing the ranch and two-room house which was later bought by a Dr. Fortier, who obviously had no penchant for ranching and allowed the property to dilapidate until it became little more than a junkyard (BLM Records).

It was at this point that a young lady enters the scene. A lady who was to indelibly stamp her name and personality on the property and on the map.

BONNIE'S STORY

She was born Bonnie McGaugh in 1921 on Wilcox, two blocks off Hollywood Boulevard in Hollywood, California, to Wilbur F. McGaugh (who worked for Universal Studios) and his wife Gladys. Wilbur had started out with ambitions as an actor but fate determined otherwise. Instead, he became a stand-in actor and eventually a film director.

Universal Studios recruited John Boles, who although he had trained as a doctor and served as a U.S. spy during the First World War, decided to embrace music as a career. Boles made his name initially on the New York stage, but it was Hollywood which gave him his first big break when he starred in "The Love of Sunya" opposite Gloria Swanson. When "talkies" arrived, Boles, with his fine operatic voice, was in great demand for roles in musicals. Because Bonnie's father had a close resemblance to Boles and was a skilled horseman, he was frequently called on to act as a stand-in, particularly in roles requiring riding. Playing stand-in did not match up to Wilbur McGaugh's ambitions, and he turned to directing where he had a distinguished career up to the time of his death on January 13, 1965 in Hollywood. John Boles retired in 1952 and died of a heart attack on February 27, 1969 (Internet Movie Database).

At first, life must have been hard for the McGaugh family as Bonnie's mother Gladys, who was an accomplished seamstress, augmented the family income by sewing tailor-made shirts. The family moved to Lincoln Heights when Bonnie's grandmother died and left them property there.

Besides being a skilled seamstress, Mrs. McGaugh was an excellent cook and hostess which was probably to the good as her husband would often call home at short notice to say that he was bringing home

Bonnie Springs Ranch

Bonnie and her father-Unknown date

this director, this star or that star for dinner. Bonnie met many of the famous movie stars of the day. She recounts that she came to know Red Skelton very well and found Cary Grant cute, friendly and with a nice personality; but the visitors were too many for Bonnie to recall each and every one of them. Grant had a pet name for Bonnie and would greet her with, "Hi, McGoo."

In spite of his busy work schedule, Wilbur McGaugh was a caring father who devoted as much time as possible to his family. Bonnie recalls going on frequent fishing trips with him.

Unfortunately, her mother and father separated when she was in her early 20s, and it was not until later that he and Bonnie were reconciled.

Bonnie was athletic from an early age and loved to dance, but it was not until she was twenty that she took up skating. Her grandmother and mother were accomplished pianists, but there was no history of skating in the family. Her

Bonnie as a skater-Unknown date

first recollection of skating was with her friends. She modestly says that she was not very good. "Well, I could skate fine going forward and I could skate going backward but I couldn't do a Mohawk to turn around, so I would have to stop and turn around." Perhaps this is another example of Bonnie's modesty. The Mohawk is one of the first movements a beginner learns; but even if she couldn't execute that, she confesses to being able to do a "real nice spiral."

Even as a tyro skater, Bonnie had plenty of confidence; and when auditions were advertised for a tour with the Olympic ice dance champion Sonja Henie, she and her friends applied. At the close of the auditions, the director told her that she had got the job, not because she could skate, but because she was the right size and had a nice smile.

Bonnie found Sonja's mother "quite nasty" and reluctant to allow her daughter to mix. She thought Sonja was friendly, very cute and smiling. This does not accord with the biography "Queen of Ice, Queen of Shadows" written after her death by her brother Leif in conjunction with Raymond Strait. In the book, Sonja was described as "obsessed with money and sex, had a vile temper when crossed, and used her family and others shamelessly to advance her own ends." Bonnie obviously took her as she found her.

As a newcomer, Bonnie was not exactly welcomed by the established members of the cast. She recalls that the old-timers would go by her and as if talking to themselves say, "Yes, I hear they are sending all the bad skaters home." Bonnie thought, "They aren't going to send me home, and I'd skate and practice until my heels would bleed and stick to my boots; but they didn't send me home." Bonnie's determination paid off and she was soon given a couple of numbers in which she was able to show off her skills in lifts and adagio dancing.

After touring extensively with Sonja, she took up a six-month engagement in a "tank show" at the Adolphus Hotel in Dallas. Bonnie explains that a tank show is a show skated on a portable ice rink approximately 20 feet by 24 feet in area. This was followed by work in several of Sonja's films.

Bonnie recalls that when she went for the interviews for the films, the director would say, "Oh well, if she can't do it now, she'll do it when we shoot, that's OK." She says, "The director didn't like me to begin with, and I always loved yellow and green, and he'd say 'That girl with the yellow shirt.'" If he didn't like Bonnie, he at least recognized in her the ambition and determination to succeed.

Her next engagement was in a new ice show backed by Clyde C. Fisher and called "Folies Bergere." It was a successful show with a large cast of around 125. Six months in San Francisco was followed by a move to Seattle. One day Bonnie overheard Fisher say something about horses. She pricked up her ears and told him, "Oh sure, I've been riding all my life. My dad was a good horseman." She ended up "with a very good spot with a high-schooled horse and about 75 girls dancing behind me." But the riding she was about to do was far different from the riding she had been used to. It was dressage. She was sent to "a school, well, a trainer, because I had no idea how to rein a horse to do all of his prancing and side-passing and everything with one hand." Soon she was guiding the horse through waltz turns, high Spanish marching with his front feet, and rearing and bowing. Bonnie loved her horse and thought him very pretty especially when the groom would caparison the rump of the coal black horse with alternating squares of satin and velvet.

Mrs. McGaugh sold their home in North Hollywood and moved to Laguna. When the show closed, Bonnie joined her temporarily in rented accommodations. After touring for around ten months and possibly seeking some respite from the hectic life of show business, Bonnie made the move, telling only one of her friends where she was. They had no telephone but one day when they returned home, there was a note pinned on their door asking her to telephone a particular number. Her mother liked to use playing cards to tell fortunes.

Bonnie says, "My mother used to lay out the cards and it kept saying that I was packing my suitcase and was going to sign papers with a blond man and a brunette man and I was leaving the state and we'd laugh because no one knew where we were." She made the call and was offered a contract by George Arnold who, along with his brother, was to stage an ice show at the Last Frontier. It was the first ice show ever in Las Vegas. Bonnie was pleased to accept the offer as George was no stranger to her, having previously skated with him in New York and at various military bases. Coincidentally, George was blond and his brother brunette.

Bonnie recalls that, "The Last Frontier was beautiful. It had a huge three-way fireplace and great big long beams and all leather furniture." Her engagement ended after some ten months and Bonnie returned to Laguna to help her mother with a small shop they had opened there.

While she was there, Bonnie evidently kept in touch with her friends in the film industry as she recalls that "everyone around Columbia Studios was getting a five-acre tract around Twenty-Nine Palms." So she bought a small trailer and followed suit. She started a small dancing school and worked Friday and Saturday as a waitress at a local restaurant. Then Bonnie bought about 100 turkeys and together with a young man she met there who had 1,000 birds, embarked on a career in turkey farming and smoke-curing them. It was short-lived. Bonnie found the area too hot and during the height of the summer everything closed down; so, she resolved to return to Vegas. "I was going with a fellow then and we started driving over here." She bought a new station wagon and started delivering produce to Vegas. The business grew and she bought a one-and-a-half-ton truck. According to Bonnie, there were only two other firms delivering to Vegas at that time.

It was Gene Christian, who owned a large drive-in on the corner of Las Vegas Boulevard and Charleston, who told Bonnie about a property out near Blue Diamond. He told her, "I know just the property you would love, but mow down the buildings. There are (sic) lots of water and lots of big trees." She says that she "drove out early in the morning and saw the mountains behind aflame with color. It was just beautiful." It was to be a fresh start for Bonnie in more ways than one as she made up with her estranged father who came out to help her.

It took almost a year to find out that the property was owned by a Dr. Fortier. It was in a complete mess; but Bonnie persuaded Fortier to grant her a three-year lease with option to buy and in evidence of her good faith, she paid him $1,000.

Bonnie describes the site as follows: "Dr. Fortier had added from this beam over to that wall, a kitchen, it was like three rooms. The place was in a mess.

And there was just a little tiny, well, you couldn't call it a barn but it had a generator plant which we only turned on once a week. When I started, I didn't have any electricity for twelve years. I had kerosene lamps and Coleman lanterns."

Bonnie set about renovating the place. She soon put her one-and-a-half-ton truck to good use hauling out loads of rubbish not only from the surroundings but from the former bar itself. There was so much trash in it that Bonnie surmised that the previous proprietor had simply let empty beer cans be thrown anywhere.

According to Bonnie: "There were two little rooms down there and I could never find out. They weren't lined inside or anything. But at that time Blue Diamond was so busy that people were living in trailers over by the spring across the road there, this side of Blue Diamond. So I had these two little rooms. I put a wood stove in one of them and rented them. Now they weren't a bit fancy. Blue Diamond (the mine) it used to be, all of their plasterboard if it was an inch too long, they threw it away. So they piled it all out on the slope down from the mill there and somebody said, 'Why don't you go down there and get some of the plasterboard, they're just throwing it out there.' I didn't have any money, so I went down and I started getting it and lined those couple of rooms and then I rented them."

Bonnie had plenty of help with the renovations. The men from the mine helped her with the plasterboard although Bonnie took her fair share of the labor, "I was in better shape and much younger," she says. Further help came from neighbors, in particular from Buster Wilson, son of Tweed Wilson, about whom Bonnie tells more later on in her interview. Buster helped lay the flagstone floor and build a fireplace using material from the nearby Tilghman Rhea Quarry (more information about the Rhea Quarry can be found in Chapter 12). Unfortunately, according to Bonnie he was not a reliable workman. He would arrive with a barrow-load of cement, only to disappear for two or three days armed with a box of crackers and a bottle of vodka. This resulted in the waste of a barrow-load of cement. That was an expense Bonnie could ill-afford, so she got Buster to show her how to mix the cement to do the job and completed the restaurant floor herself.

Buster may have been unreliable but he passed on many Indian skills to Bonnie. He taught her how to cut young spears off Spanish spear cactus or agave, pound them and soak them to produce shampoo. He showed her how to pick Mormon tea plants and brew tea from it and how to make eyewash out of "Snake Eye." It is unclear as to what plant Bonnie is referring. It may have been *Agermone intermedia*, which according to the *Encyclopedia of American Indi-*

ans Contributions to the World was used by the Shoshone. They pulverized the seeds and mixed them with water to make a poultice, while the Comanche extracted the sap and applied it to the eye.

Buster and his father helped Bonnie gather a collection of artifacts from the surrounding area; arrowheads, even a gun with notches on it, petrified wood and fossils were retrieved. Bonnie was surprised to find something which looked like fossilized feet. According to her, they were initially identified by the university as camel feet; but later in her oral interview she says, "And when I took the bones down, from out here where I found them, the university said that they were from these big-headed lizards that were here." Perhaps Bonnie means dinosaurs, in which case the fact that dinosaur remains have recently been found at Spring Mountain Ranch and dinosaur tracks identified within the Red Rock Canyon Conservation Area in the summer of 2013 would confirm her statement.

About a year and a half after she arrived in Blue Diamond, a young man called Al Levinson started to come out to the ranch. According to Bonnie he heard of a "dingy blond out in the boondocks running a bar and he got stuck coming back for 40 years." They married in 1954 and together set about making the property commercially viable.

Fortier's bar had a bad reputation and had been closed for eighteen months when Bonnie arrived. Her friends repeatedly urged her to reopen the bar, but to do so she needed a license. Bonnie feared that because of the previous reputation of the bar she might have difficulty being approved for one. However, a friend of hers named Frank Burke who was bar manager at the Sahara, vouched for her at the meeting. At a cost of $250, she not only got the license but managed to stock the bar.

The water Gene Christian had told her about came from a natural spring. Bonnie recounts how she would get excited as it bubbled. She would move rocks and it would bubble more. "We'd rake it all clean and sprinkle a little chlorine around the mud around the edge so the water always tasted fine." She was so proud of her springs. One day, however, an inspector came to check on the water quality. He found that the spring was not covered and that animals could drink there, so the spring had to be enclosed. The resulting brick enclosure had a redwood lid covered with roofing paper as a roof and the water was piped. On his next visit the inspector lifted the lid only to find a dead mouse in the tank, so an enclosed tank had to be installed. Buster built some pools fed from the spring and Bonnie's husband raised bait for a bait shop.

Once Bonnie and Buster had dug out the rubbish from the unused swimming pool, they found it had a sound cement base. Bonnie realized that when water from the spring was piped to it, the whole area could be developed as a picnic and recreational area.

Water supply was not usually a problem, but there were times when too much of it caused difficulty. Bonnie had to take her children to Blue Diamond School each day; but in times of heavy rain, the floods would wash out the access road much to the delight not only of the children who couldn't get to school, but also to that of Bonnie who valued the extra time they could spend with her. "I guess I was bad," she says. Bonnie recalls the sweet nature of the teacher at the school who would line-up the children and kiss them hello in the morning and kiss them goodbye at the end of the school day. She was evidently very caring of each of her charges and would telephone Bonnie and say, "You know, I think Robin has been here long enough today." It says something about Bonnie's community spirit and her relationship with the Blue Diamond School that she established a custom of inviting the children over for a picnic and swimming on the last day of the term.

Further exploration of the spring area revealed a cave about 50 feet long with water dripping continuously from the ceiling. It had evidently been part of a bootleggers' tunnel judging by the coils and old barrels Bonnie found when she first explored it. Bootlegging evidently took place in the area. The *Las Vegas Age* reported in the June 8, 1928 edition that six men had been arrested and tried in connection with bootlegging activities on the neighboring Morgan Ranch ("One of Six Caught in Federal Dry Raid out on Bail," 1928).

Bonnie took a personal interest in her customers. Tweed Wilson, Buster's father, was one of them. She recalls: "He was so cute. He was a little man and his feet had been frozen off. Up to the instep on one foot and all his toes on the other and his little boots curled up in the air. He had a herd of cattle over the mountain and down on the Sandy Valley side and he couldn't get back, there was so much snow over the mountain. And Tweed used to come over and the more he would drink, he was so cute, he was so afraid he'd be loud and he got so quiet that you couldn't hear what he wanted because he whispered his order (Levinson, 2004)."

More About the Wilsons

According to his granddaughters Gloria Wilson Shearer and Marie "LuLu" Wilson, Tweed Wilson was born on October 21, 1876, the son of George Anderson and a Paiute woman named Kayer but known as "Annie," a generic name for Paiute women. Word got out that he needed a cook; so Annie, who came from the Panamint Mountains, answered his advertisement, started cooking for him and ended up marrying him. Annie died in 1878 but perhaps her spirit lives on. There is an image in the rock at Black Velvet Peak which some people say looks like an image of the Virgin Mary. But others, noting the direction in which the image is looking, say that it is Annie protecting Spring Mountain Ranch.

George Anderson was a furrier and lived at Sandstone Ranch which is now Spring Mountain Ranch State Park. Gloria Wilson Shearer recalls a reunion in 1970 when family members told her that because of his flaming red hair, one could see Anderson from miles away whether he was walking or riding. He left Sandstone Ranch, leaving his son Tweed behind to be adopted by James Bernard Wilson.

Tweed and his son Buster built two cabins in Lovell Canyon in the late 1930s or early 1940s. One was of adobe in which Buster and his friend Jake Stone continued to live through the late 1960s. The other was later converted to a concrete structure and was inadvertently razed by a forest service fire crew in 1998. According to an article by Keith Rogers in the *Las Vegas Review-Journal* on Sunday, November 5, 2000 entitled "Archeologist charting cabin's significance," Jake staked mining claims with the Bureau of Land Management (BLM) throughout the 1960s. Etched into the door of the cabin are the words "Take Little Leave Much" and there is a reference to a mining claim, "Jake Stone Exploration Co. Inc. barite 1, 2, 3, 4. Feb 27 1974."

BLM records confirm several lode claims at that site which were closed in 1981. There certainly is barite, sometimes called "white lead," on the site. "White lead" is a misnomer. Barite is barium sulphate and is used in the manufacture of paint from which the "white lead" term originates. There is no record of Jake having marketed the barite, but he filed a mill site claim to support his lode claims.

Bonnie correctly thought that Tweed was possibly of Scottish ancestry but continues the story saying that after being brought up by a family downtown, he went to Loyola, California where he stayed for fifteen years. According to her, he was not only a rock mason but also a skilled silversmith who made her girls "little delicate things for chains." He was also a terrific baker and made his own whole meal bread.

It is fairly certain that it is Buster and not Tweed who Bonnie is referring to in connection with Loyola. According to the Spring Mountain Ranch archives, Buster lived with the Lake family in Las Vegas when he started grade school and was sent to the Sherman Institute in Riverside, California in 1919 when he was eleven. The Sherman Institute was opened in Perris as a school for Native Americans in 1892. Initially called Perris Indian School, it assumed its present name in 1902 when it relocated to Riverside. Although the school taught mainly agriculture to the Indian boys, Buster must also have been tutored in Art because his first job after graduation was painting scenery for film sets (Trafzer, 2012). Painting was a pastime which endured throughout his life, and some of his works can be seen at the Red Rock Canyon Visitor Center where they are on temporary loan from the University of Nevada, Las Vegas.

During his time in the film industry, Buster must have also picked up an interest in photography; Bonnie recounts the following story. One day Vera Krupp and a group of press photographers descended on the ranch, and she told Bonnie that one of the photographers had gotten into a conversation with Buster about modern photography. "That photographer was just stunned to think that this little old Indian, with his feet all curled up, with a tooth here and a tooth there, you know, and a little old handlebar moustache, would answer all these modern questions about modern cameras." Here again, Bonnie is confusing Buster and Tweed.

It becomes evident that Buster was well read as Bonnie describes Buster's cabin saying, "There were two rock and adobe cabins on the Spring Mountain Ranch, one of which was home to Tweed (Buster)." Bonnie describes it as: "Just rock and adobe and probably not as big as my kitchen...and had shelves lined in it. Then his little old cabin that he lived in had a little old wood stove that he cooked on all the time, a little old wood cooking stove, and his bed and a little old table and a couple of little chairs that were very antique." She adds that the shelves in the cabin were lined with books. Buster was killed in a vehicle accident in 1972 (Wilson Shearer, 2010).

BACK TO BONNIE'S STORY

Bonnie's interest in her customers was reciprocal; they were protective of her. On opening the bar she immediately set standards for behavior. For example, there was to be no swearing and transgressors were immediately removed by other patrons.

The rather isolated situation of the bar and the fact that arrests had been made in respect to bootlegging in the area prompted the sheriff to give Bonnie a gun which she hid behind the bar. One of the regular customers, baby-faced, blue-eyed and with curly hair, as Bonnie recalls him, saw the growing takings of the bar, and over a period of several months weighed the possibility of a robbery. A year or more elapsed before he showed up again, this time with three others. He must have looked young as Bonnie asked him for his ID. Bonnie's husband was occupied setting up a newly acquired generator when they arrived. The leader of the gang, having previously seen where Bonnie kept the gun, took it from behind the bar. Although Bonnie's German shepherd dog was with her, it didn't react.

The old-fashioned registers with their golden scrolls were bulging with a very good day's takings. The thieves emptied them before clearing all the shelves of liquor. The five slot machines proved more of a problem and resisted attempts to open or remove them. When Bonnie managed to alert her husband, they found that the thieves had immobilized their car but had not seen the old truck parked behind the house. Bonnie and her husband were able to drive to the nearest telephone and raise the alarm.

The thieves were eventually caught, and it emerged that they were from Utah and Arizona where they had police records for previous robberies. After this, Sheriff Lamb suggested that she should have a portable telephone.

It must have been a traumatic experience for Bonnie as she was expecting their first child. The situation was made worse by the police who were investigating the robbery suggesting that she had served minors. Bonnie protested that she had served only the man who showed her his ID. Nevertheless, she was charged. There was confusion as to whether they could restock the bar immediately or the shelves would have to remain empty until after the trial.

Despite her doctor pleading that the trial should be delayed until after the birth of her child, the trial took place two weeks before the baby was born. Bonnie was fined $500 and given one year probation but was allowed to keep the license and restock the bar.

Bonnie recalls that she "got so upset I swelled from 105 to 185 lbs. I couldn't lay down at night because my heart would stop beating." The natural birth which Bonnie had hoped for did not materialize. She was rushed to the hospital and after a labor lasting some twelve hours, she had a successful caesarean operation and gave birth to a healthy girl.

The local newspaper ran a story under the heading "Horse trading still goes on" and gave only a brief, incidental reference to the birth. "Oh, by the way, Mrs. Levinson just had her first baby girl." Despite that, Bonnie felt "very flattered." Bonnie and Al, happily married, were to see their family grow over succeeding years.

Bonnie and Al didn't always see eye-to-eye about the property. As the property developed, word got around about Bonnie Springs and the owners of the Fremont Hotel made an offer for the property. Al wanted to sell in order to pay back Bonnie's mother and anything they had borrowed, but Bonnie refused to sell. She felt that after all, this was where the children had been born. According to Bonnie, Al was so mad that he didn't speak to her for about two months but came around to her way of thinking even though bigger and better offers came in. The final test was when Howard Hughes, who quite often dined there, sent them a blank check and Al still said "no" to selling. Bonnie's account has to be taken at face value, but the consensus of opinion seems to be that once Hughes settled into his apartment at the Desert Inn, he never left it.

Besides starting a family, Bonnie was building-up a herd of riding horses. She had around a dozen horses initially and her father brought up three or four more from Universal Studios. Her husband added three more when he traded an old car for them.

As the business grew, more help was needed. Bonnie's mother moved from Laguna to help in the bar where she was popular because she had read extensively about mining and could talk with the miners on equal terms.

Word got around about Bonnie's horses, and dancers from the Dunes and the Tropicana started to come out. They caused quite a stir with the men as they would ride around dressed more appropriately for their shows than for riding.

Some bees made a nest in the back of the bar wall and Buster was able to relieve them of their honey which Bonnie's stepmother then strained and stored in an old-fashioned wash tub. So, when the showgirls asked, "Don't you have something to eat?" she was able to give them biscuits, coffee and sage honey.

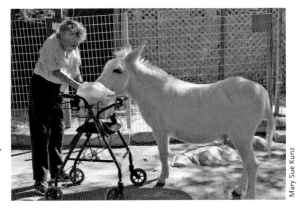

Bonnie feeding burro c. 2008

Bonnie continued to add to her collection of animals. She had five dogs and acquired another when she rescued a puppy from the middle of Charleston Boulevard and bottle-fed it. Her first pygmy goats were given to her by Wayne Newton, and someone else brought her an Anglo Nubian kid which had been left outside their office. Anglo Nubians are ideal for desert conditions as they can tolerate high temperatures. She bought a couple of deer and an old llama with a funny twisted back leg which she got very cheaply and had for 22 years. The deer started to breed and the herd grew. Bonnie bought a bull calf, Ferdinand, for $45 from a local dairy and two pigs, Hansel and Gretel, from a pig farm on Craig Road. She bottle-fed them and even taught Hansel to shake hands and would walk him out on a leash. The cowboys were amused by the bottle-feeding and used to give the pigs a drink and then pretend they and the pigs were both drunk.

Bonnie is proud of her petting zoo. "Grandma," as she is known to the many children who visit it, considers it important for them to appreciate animals.

Not only were the foundations being laid for the present petting zoo but for new buildings on the site. Bonnie and Al would go around old ghost towns and take the measurements of aged buildings so that they could build replicas. Al did the building, the plumbing and the electrics, while Bonnie laid the floor, did all the rock work and built the tables. They would go up to Big Bear and bring back rough slabs of red cedar which they cut with a chain saw. Buster taught her how to wield a double-edged axe and helped her cut down small pine trees which they used in the picnic area.

Bonnie recalls a succession of neighbors who owned the neighboring Spring Mountain Ranch. First Chet Lauck of "Lum and Abner" fame, then Vera

Bonnie Springs Ranch

Bonnie and Al placing the last spike in the Old Nevada Railroad-Unknown date

Old Nevada c. 2008

Krupp, followed by Howard Hughes and finally Fletcher Jones, who to Bonnie's dismay wanted to build condos on the site. Actually, according to Spring Mountain Ranch Archives, Fletcher Jones' zoning application was to permit the development of a planned "equestrian oriented" community capable of supporting a population of about two thousand. However, it was withdrawn in the face of public opposition.

Although Bonnie and Vera Krupp were friends and frequently talked with one another, theirs was not a particularly close relationship. "I don't know why we were friends, but funny friends; she'd have something strange happen and she'd call me to come look."

Bonnie Springs Old Nevada was not developed without more than its fair share of difficulties.

There were two fires. According to Bonnie, the first was caused by Fortier's caretaker who Bonnie had allowed to stay on after she bought the property. The old generator in the barn was causing problems. While smoking a cigarette, the caretaker went out to check whether it still had gas and burnt the barn down. The second was again caused by a cigarette. The cook went out to check on four colts and dropped the cigarette on the straw bedding, resulting in the deaths of the colts. Wild fires in the area were always a threat, but luckily Al was watchful; with the help of the local fire department, nearby fires were extinguished before they got too close.

The lamps which Bonnie placed at the entrance to the property proved attractive targets and were regularly shot out. There was the robbery and there were development disputes. Bonnie said that Al was in a dispute with the BLM at the time of his death. She is referring to his planning application for a

There's a new sheriff in town c. 2008

recreational vehicle park and campground and his dispute with the commissioners. As Fletcher Jones found out, there is concern in the community about development in what is considered an environmentally sensitive area. Public concern was reflected in the coverage of the County Commissioner's deliberations by both the *Las Vegas Sun* and the *Review-Journal*. On April 4, 1978, Levinson's application was refused by the commissioners. On May 17, 1978, the commissioners were divided on the issue; but at their meeting on June 7, 1978, despite objections from state park officials and the BLM, the application was approved on a split vote ("Recreational Vehicle Park," 1978).

There can be unanticipated problems in any commercial enterprise. Although horse riding is a relatively safe activity and riding at Bonnie Springs is both popular and well established, there can still be problems as when a fall from a horse by a client led to litigation.

Bonnie Sums Up

In spite of everything, Bonnie was able to say of her life: "I think it's been better than almost all of the average people. I had a very exciting time growing up. I was raised in a studio, met a lot of famous people, knew them. Then I started skating, travelled all over the country and ended up skating in a tank show at the St. Regis in New York and the Adolphus in Dallas, the St. Francis in San Francisco, a lot of big hotels. I don't think I can complain. Then I found the place I wanted to live and had my babies and that's what I did. I have been working for it ever since, but I think that is okay, kept me going (Levinson, 2004)."

CHAPTER 9

Calico Basin

By Chuck Williams

The present area of Calico Basin, also known as Red Springs, was used by Native Americans for hunting and farming. Several springs in the area provided year-round water and the ground gently slopes away from the sandstone outcroppings. Rock shelters, roasting pits, grinding slicks, metates, pottery sherds and lithics have been found in the area. But best of all, the Indians decorated the boulders and cliff faces with petroglyph rock art.

After the Europeans arrived, the basin was used as grazing ground for the Wilson Ranch. The Wilson brothers filed stock watering rights for their herd of 400-500 cattle on the four springs which were later identified as Red Springs 1 through 4, running north to south along the base of the Calico Hills. On the current topo maps they are identified by different names. I will list both names when discussing the springs to help eliminate confusion.

Red Spring 1 – Ash Spring

Red Spring 2 – Well (AKA Little Spring on the Wilson water applications and 1914 map)

Red Spring 3 – Calico Spring

Red Spring 4 – Red Spring

There may have been earlier attempts to settle the area, but there is no record of land ownership prior to 1915.

ELLA MASON

Ella Mason was born in 1867 and listed her birthplace as Can-English in the 1910 Census Records which we can assume means that she was from the English speaking portion of Canada. Other individuals on the same census page indicate their birthplace as "Can-French." She immigrated to the United States along with her parents in 1874. In November 1909, the *Las Vegas Age* reported her move to Las Vegas:

> Miss Ella Mason, of Goldfield, has taken the Cottage Hotel, corner of First and Carson Streets, and is fitting it up as a first class rooming house. The interior is being newly painted and nicely furnished. Miss Mason was formerly the proprietor of the Lick House in Goldfield ("Local Notes," 1909).

Sometime over the next few years, Ella developed an interest in Calico Basin. On January 25, 1915, she made a homestead entry for 160 acres of land on the western side of the basin which included all the above springs except Red Spring 4/Red Spring. The homestead acreage would sit to the north of the present Red Spring parking lot and westward to include Red Spring 1/Ash Spring ("Notice for Publication," 1921).

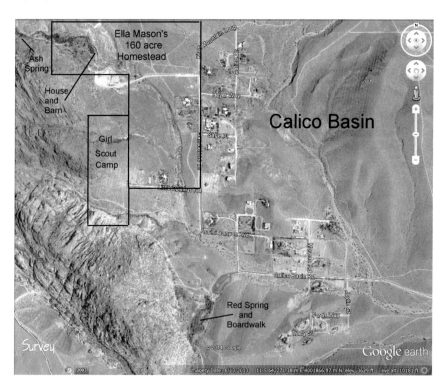

Google Earth map showing the boundary of Ella Mason's 1915 homestead.

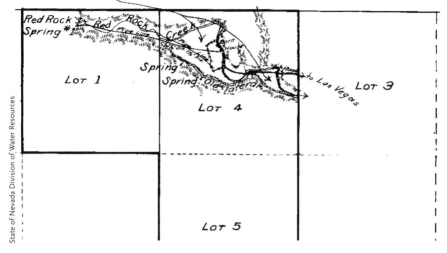

Irrigation map drawn by Fred Rodolf dated Oct 20, 1921 showing completed irrigation features at Red Spring 1/Ash Spring.

Two days earlier, on January 23, 1915, she applied for permission to appropriate water from all four springs by the means of dams, iron pipe and irrigation ditches with the water used to irrigate alfalfa fields and for domestic use. One dam would be located in the Red Spring 1/Ash Spring steam bed. The second set of dams would pipe water from the other three springs ("Notice of Application," 1915). She may have been a bit overzealous when calculating the amount of pipe needed as she later advertised for sale 5,000 feet of used one-inch water pipe ("Local Notes," 1915).

Both applications were approved with the provision that there would be no conflict with the preexisting stock watering rights held by the Wilson Ranch on all four springs. Ella provided proof-of-work and maps for both applications in 1921. The documents show she was irrigating 7.5 acres of alfalfa and had built a house and barn on her property east of Red Spring 1/Ash Spring.

The other application, covering the three remaining springs, indicated she would be irrigating 2.5 acres of alfalfa to the northeast of Red Spring 4/Red Spring on what would be open range.

The application for the three lower springs was cancelled in 1921 by the Nevada Division of Water for failure to comply with the provisions of the permit, and it doesn't appear that the dams and irrigation ditches were ever completed. The permit for Red Spring 1/Ash Spring was not cancelled until 1972, thirty-five years after she sold the land. There were problems with the Wilson

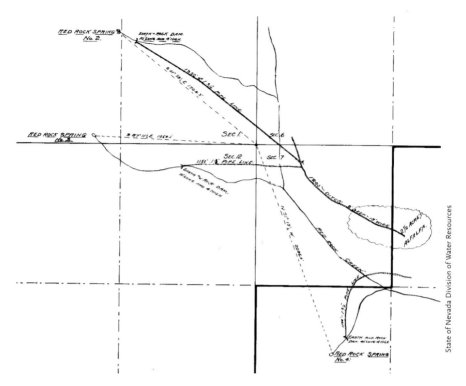

Map drawn by C. E. McCarthy dated Jan 28, 1916 showing proposed irrigation plan for Red Springs 2, 3 and 4.

Ranch when Ella fenced in some of the springs and an ongoing battle with the Nevada Division of Water over the permits that lasted into the late 1930s.

Ella appears to have been a feisty woman and one of the people I would have liked to meet. It wouldn't have been easy to start a homestead while keeping the hotel going. She had some issues remembering when she was born, listing her year of birth as 1867, 1871 or 1873 in various census reports. Certainly not the first or last time someone fibbed about their age.

In the 1920, census Ella still owned the Cottage Hotel where she was the landlady. Her mother Angelina lived with her, so she may have stayed in Calico Basin only part-time or rented the property to others. Ella also bought and sold several pieces of property in Las Vegas which she may have rented for additional income.

About 1924 she married Frank Marvin, and in April 1924 they sold a Las Vegas property that was recorded under the names of Frank and Ella Marvin (Clark County Recorder Book 10, Page 140).

By the 1930 census, Ella had become a widow, keeping the last name of Marvin. She was living in her own home in Riverside, California with her mother

Two views of the Ash Spring area from the spring of 1962

and renting out some of the rooms. She lived in the same Riverside house in the 1940 census but listed her occupation as a café owner.

Ella finally sold the 160-acre Calico Basin property to S.H. Milligan and Murry Wollman in April 1937 after several years of correspondence with the Nevada Division of Water (Clark County Recorder Book 23, Page 434).

We don't have information if anyone was living on Ella's land or irrigating and raising cattle after she moved to California. The State Water Rights Surveyor noted that the seven acres were "formerly irrigated" but not under irrigation during his visit in October 1921. As noted above, the water application was not cancelled until 1973.

Ella's property was purchased by various individuals and investment groups over the years, some of which announced plans for subdivisions. As late as 1991, developers were proposing to build 27 houses on 49 acres of Ella's former property ("Red Rock Canyon reels under big visitor crush," 1991). None of the proposed subdivisions materialized, a lack of water and other utilities being a contributing factor. The Bureau of Land Management now owns most of the 160 acres. There are currently only five homes on her former property, all built after 1995 and none located where Ella's house and barn stood.

LATER DEVELOPMENT 1940–1960

There were no additional homestead patents awarded in the Calico Basin area until 1953; however, individuals could build and make improvements on the land if they filed notice that they intended to apply for a patent. George Heyer appears to have made such an application in 1949 for 75 acres to the east of Ella's property. Heyer never received a homestead patent for the property which later became the core developed area. He later bought and then sold most of the land but jokingly called himself the mayor of Calico Basin. At one time he envisioned building a western village on the property (Werner, c. 1987).

Between 1953 and 1959 there were 34 land patents recorded in Calico Basin. However, there was limited development until the late 1950s.

Don Triolo lived in Calico Basin from 1955-1957 and still has vivid memories of his time there. He remembers their home and the seven other families that populated the little community:

> We moved there, it would have been the summer of 1955. My mom and my stepdad homesteaded five acres out there for $200 per acre! And all you had to do for improvements in a two-year period was sink a well and put up a building, any kind of building, just some kind of building. So we did and we put in a well and obviously there was an outhouse. My stepdad and Ted Kalain put it up, it was just 1 by 12 pine boards and a tarpaper roof and a door with a lock and hasp. That was it for improvements. There was no electricity and just dirt roads. The three of us lived in a 16-foot trailer the whole time we were there.

> We heard about Red Rock Canyon from George Heyer. He and his wife Billie had a lovely home for the time out here. Ted and Nicky Kalain had another nice home. Ted was a concrete mason. To the left of our property was a hill with a real cute house that belonged to a family named Mayes. They only came out three or four times a year for the weekend. Ozzie Kraft had the major pool company in Las Vegas in the 50s and 60s. He had a nice weekend home. Ollie [Victor] Olson and his wife had a big long house trailer; he was stationed at Nellis. Dick [Richard] and Mary Gardener had a home in town as well as their house in Calico Basin parallel to George and Billie Heyer. And they turned out to be very good friends. I remember when my folks would go over to their house and they would play cards, pinochle, poker and all that stuff.

So there was just a handful of us here. We hadn't been here too long when a family from Ohio, Zack and Pauline Steed and their two kids Bobby and Sandy, moved in. Sandy was my age; Bobby was younger. George Heyer had his ranch just west of our property down a little dirt road. He had horses and cattle. There was an old trailer on it and stuff. Anyway, he rented that to the Steed family. So that was part of my solace, having the Steed kids to play with (Triolo, 2013).

Don recalled that life was rougher then, but as a young boy of 10 he enjoyed growing up in Red Rock:

So you know what? For ten to twelve years old it was very different but what a wonderful lifestyle. There would be a lot of kids who would never have that chance and if you told them [how we lived] they would probably look in shock and [think] what on earth are you talking about? When I mention to people now that we didn't have electricity, they find that absolutely impossible to believe. We had Coleman lanterns and a butane tank for a little two-burner range in the little trailer. And my parents, who were entertainers at the Golden Nugget, would get a 25-pound block of ice from Market Town and that was what we kept in the refrigerator to keep the food cold.

Don Triolo

Don Triolo standing on the gravel road leading to their trailer c. 1956

George Heyer had what you called a jet water pump. He would fire that sucker up with a gas motor and he had running water. Well we had a hand pump and our well was 400 feet deep. My stepdad could handle that hand pump, but mom and I couldn't do it. So Ted Kalain said, "Here we can fix that." He took a five-foot piece of galvanized pipe and made a sleeve to put over the handle so my mom and I could work the handle up and down.

When it got hot, we rolled up the crank windows on the trailer and my stepdad would take the burlap feed bags that my mare's feed came in, stick them in a tub of water and then hang them on the windows and [with] the breeze through the canyon, there was your air conditioning.

After I started going to school in Blue Diamond I met a classmate, Ned Londo, and his dad "Swede" was the ranch foreman at the Krupp Ranch. Vera Krupp had a working cattle ranch. Ned and I, we just hit if off right away; so every weekend for months I would jump on my horse, he would jump on his horse. We knew what time to leave and we would meet halfway or I would go over and spend the weekend at his place. One day Mrs. Krupp (and that woman was gorgeous, a stunning blond), anyway, she invited Ned and me to come in and have lunch. And we walked into this home and I mean I was just aghast. It was a beautiful old ranch house obviously from the 30s and 40s, and when we went into the kitchen all the appliances were copper. I mean restaurant style, they were huge. And she was always so nice to us.

Aside from that, my life consisted of going to school at Blue Diamond. I had Bobby and Sandy Steed for friends and Ned over at the ranch; and in the summers, Mrs. Steed would take us kids into town and we would go swimming for ten cents at the twin lakes.

A lot of times when school was out, my mom or Mrs. Steed couldn't get to the school because the roads were washed out. So we would stay with Mrs. Radtke who [was] the sixth grade teacher. And sure enough the next day the roads would be better and you could get home (Triolo, 2013).

Don recalled capturing a wild horse he named Cherokee:

I had gotten for my tenth birthday this little horse named Cindy. And there used to be a band of wild horses, a palomino stallion with about four mares that would wander over. Well I'm ten years old, I don't know anything about the birds and the bees. And my folks were not horse people. So my little horse Cindy was in this little corral [and] of course he [the stallion] was coming over at night trying to get her out of there. Well I didn't look at it like that. I'm thinking I want a palomino. So within a period of about two months I made a plan, and I didn't dare tell my parents because I knew they would just go nuts and say you are going to get killed, blab, blab, blab. So I

Don on his horse Snow with his dog Scottie practicing for the circus after seeing the movie "Trapeze" c. 1956

started putting out hay and I would just move it about five feet closer each day. This went on for about three weeks. And the last day I tied Cindy up to a railroad tie inside the corral, put hay inside, then [hid] behind the trailer that night, at night mind you. Sure enough here comes Cherokee and he followed that hay inside the corral and I flew out of there like a crazy person and closed the gate and that was how I got him. I had him for about three months and then some horse people came out with someone from the Sherriff's office and also a couple of people from BLM and I had to turn Cherokee loose. And I was just devastated. And I was mad. I ranted for six months [that] I had it in my calculated mind that the BLM should give me back the eight dollars that I had spent feeding him. (Triolo, 2013).

As much of Calico Basin was still open range, I asked if he remembered seeing cattle in the area:

Yes, it would have been [open range] because George Heyer had his property fenced in to keep wild horses or stray cows from getting to his hay. Of course, it didn't make a difference then, but I know for a fact that Ted and George both shot more than one [cow] and everyone had beef for the winter (Triolo, 2013).

Don and his parents left Calico Basin in 1957 and sold their land to George Heyer. He remembers the figure of $1,500 per acre which was a lot of money back then.

Red Spring picnic area c. 1966. Damaged structure can be seen in the background. Note the spring-fed pond and dump truck on the road. The pickup truck parked by the pond looks to have stones or trash. This photo may have been taken on one of the Red Rock cleanup work days.

GIRL SCOUT CAMP

The Frontier Girl Scout Council purchased 80 acres south and west of Ella Mason's property in 1966. The scouts had first approached the Bureau of Land Management (BLM) in 1956 when Mrs. Paul Warner filed for 80 acres of land at Red Spring 4/Red Spring to supplement the Fox Tail Camp in Lee Canyon. In 1958 the Bureau announced their intention to sell the land to the scouts. However, the process was held up for eight years when Vera Krupp protested the action, feeling it would limit her grazing rights and access to

the spring. In addition, the League of Women Voters was pushing for Red Rock to become a recreational area and archaeologists wanted to protect the area because it was used as a prehistoric farming site.

Mrs. Thaila Dondero, then the Frontier Girl Scout Council Executive Director, eventually contacted Senator Allen Bible who worked with the BLM to secure 30 acres of land about one mile northwest of Red Spring 4/Red Spring. Since it was a homestead patent, the cost to the scouts was $2.50 per acre. In the end, the scouts liked the new location better than Red Spring 4/Red Spring because it was more isolated and less worn (Levin, 1966).

I attended the March 19, 2012 meeting of the Las Vegas Media Group where Thaila Dondero spoke. She remembered that Vera Krupp remained defiant about the Girl Scouts camping on her grazing ground. When she found out the scouts owned the land, she brought her biggest bull over to graze near the camp thinking that it might intimidate the group into leaving. However, the girls just thought he was cute. The scout area is no longer utilized.

The Howard Hughes Corporation owned land west of Las Vegas that bordered the east and south side of Calico Basin. In 1988 this land was acquired by the Bureau of Land Management through a land transfer of 5,000 acres, providing a buffer zone between the city and the Red Rock Canyon Recreation Area.

Calico Basin became an inholding within the Red Rock Canyon Recreation Lands and no additional public land will be offered for sale. The Bureau of Land Management has purchased several private properties including 147 acres of Ella Mason's original 160-acre homestead.

Red Spring 4/Red Spring became a popular picnic area for Las Vegas in the 1960s, as well as a rock climbing and bouldering site in later years and remains so today. In 2005 the Bureau of Land Management constructed parking areas, picnic shelters and a boardwalk to protect Red Spring 4/Red Spring and the associated desert meadow.

Hanging Question

A concrete slab lays inside the Red Spring Boardwalk area, the remains of an earlier structure. The interpretive sign attributes the structure to Ella Mason, but this area was not part of her land and was never homesteaded. Photos from the 1960s show the structure with partial walls of concrete and stone. One wall contains a window opening and in the background cattle can be seen grazing on what must have been public land. The same group of photos show a man-made water pond between the spring and the structure, so it is possible that the structure was built by the Wilson Ranch, which maintained grazing rights until the 1960s. Buster Wilson, in particular was known for his masonry work. However, at this time I have been unable to document its history.

Red Springs 4/Red Spring in October 1963

Red Spring meadow with structure in April 1962.
There are cattle grazing in the background most likely belonging to Vera Krupp.

CALICO BASIN TODAY

Calico Basin now mostly consists of newer, expensive homes mixed in with run-down or vacant properties. Lots, when they do become available, are extremely expensive.

In early 1964, two of Don Triolo's former neighbors, George Heyer and Ozzie Kraft, along with three other individuals, formed an ad hoc committee called the Red Rock Archaeological Association. The group lobbied state legislators, asking that Red Rock Canyon become a Nevada State Park ("Red Rock Survival Plan Here," 1964). Other groups such as the Sierra Club and League of Women Voters were also involved in the issue. Thanks to everyone's efforts, Red Rock Canyon Recreation Lands became a reality in 1967.

An inholding is privately owned land inside the boundary of a national park, national forest, state park, or similar publicly owned, protected area. Inholdings result from private ownership of lands prior to the designation of the protected park or forest area, which then end up grandfathered within the legally designated boundary.

In the United States, the main causes of inholdings are checker-boarding due to railroad land grants under the Pacific Railway Acts beginning in 1862, homestead claims under the 1862 Homestead Act, and mining claims patented under the General Mining Act of 1872, along with the more recent Alaska Native Claims Settlement Act of 1971. The railroad checker-boarding primarily affects national forests, while inholdings due to the other types of claims occur frequently within national parks and national forests throughout the western United States. Over the last several decades, conservation groups have lobbied the United States Congress to acquire inholdings especially within designated wilderness areas, either by direct purchase or via land exchange which trades the inholding for other federal lands located outside of national parks or wilderness areas (Wikipedia).

CHAPTER 10

Mountain Springs

By Chuck Williams

The mountain pass has always been a gateway between the Las Vegas and Pahrump Valleys. When European explorers arrived in the 1830s, the pass became part of the Spanish Trail, a trade route between Santa Fe and Los Angeles.

Explorer John Frémont camped there on May 1, 1844. Frémont noted that overcoats were needed in the cold air, "We encamped at a spring in the pass, which had been the site of an old village. Here we found excellent grass, but very little water. We dug out the old spring and watered some of our animals. The mountain here is wooded very slightly with the nut pine, cedars and a dwarf species of oak." Frémont's cartographer, Charles Preuss, would write about the stop, "Raw weather but clear, dark-blue sky. When will that eternal wind stop? We've had it almost incessantly for more than a month now." After Frémont's report was published, the route became more popular and the pass was one of the stops on the Mormon Trail between Salt Lake City and Los Angeles (Fremont, 1845 & Preuss, 1958).

On May 18, 1860, Major James Henry Carleton attempted to lure Paiute Indians into attacking his wagon train in the pass during the "Pah-Ute Campaign" but no Indians were present (Casebier, 1972).

Lt George Wheeler's party passed through the area in August 1871 on their way to Cottonwood Springs (Blue Diamond) from the Pahrump Valley and wrote, "An excellent pass near Mountain Spring, where we found plenty of wood, grass and water" (Wheeler, 1872).

Mine claims were filed in the Spring Mountains and miners surely camped near the springs for a water source. Cowboys from the Wilson Ranch used the mountain area for a summer cattle range, and in 1911 the Findlay Copper Chief Mining Company filed a claim for 20 acres on the mountain above the pass. In 1943 the Malcomb family developed four claims on the mountain northwest of the community which are still active.

But it would be almost a century after Frémont made his camp before the pass was homesteaded.

THE MOUNTAIN SPRINGS COMMUNITY

The earliest record of a homestead was for William A. Wood who filed on June 26, 1934. The patent was approved in 1937 ("Notice for Publication Department of the Interior," 1937). Edith Morgan (see Chapter 7), wife of Bill Morgan, was one of his witnesses. His eighty-acre parcel was located on both sides of what would become State Route 160 and is now the center of the Mountain Springs community.

William was born in Oklahoma in 1902. According to the 1930 census, he was living in Phoenix, Arizona, working as the manager of a pool hall. He was married with one daughter and living in a rented house. The 1940 census has him living in a "flop house" in Phoenix and looking for work as a pick-and-shovel laborer or doing road construction. He indicated he was married, but his wife and daughter are not listed as living in the same house. The 1940 census asked where you lived in 1935, and William indicated he lived in Las Vegas, Nevada. William may have come to Las Vegas looking for work during the construction of Hoover Dam, or he may have been prospecting and decided to homestead. I didn't find any record of mine claims in his name. As part of the homestead process, William would have had to furnish proof that improvements were made on the land. At this time, we don't know what William planned to do with the land or what improvements were made.

William sold the 80 acres to Ray Dewar in July 1938 for $500. It doesn't appear that Dewar made many improvements on the land as he turned the property over within two years, selling to F.W. Leadbetter in July 1940 (Clark County Recorder Book 25, Page 13 & Clark County Recorder Book 27, Page 18).

Again, we don't have a record of what improvements, if any, were made on the land. We do know that by the late 1940s Otto Baker was living in a log cabin on the property and raising chickens, perhaps renting from Leadbetter.

Google Earth map showing Mountain Springs with William Wood's 80-acre 1934 homestead noted

Paul Warner was the next owner, purchasing the 80 acres from Leadbetter in April 1949 (Clark County Recorder Book 60, Page 2). Paul was born in Oklahoma in 1901. According to the 1930 census, he was married and working as an automobile salesman while living at a boarding house in Los Angeles. His wife is not listed as living in the same house, so he may have been working away from home at the time. In the 1940 census he was living in his own house in Las Vegas, Nevada. He was married with an 11-year-old son and working as a bartender at a nightclub.

We are fortunate to have the oral history of Raymond (Ray) Trousdale, who provides some insight into this time frame. Ray was born in Oklahoma in 1934. His parents moved to California later that year, and when he was six they moved to Las Vegas. Ray remembers:

> We arrived in Vegas late in the evening October 30, 1940 at my Grandma and Grandpa's on the west side of town. They came from Oklahoma a couple years before us. Anyway, we got a small house a couple blocks away and lived on the west side for 14 years. I went to school on the west side through the fourth grade, then to Las Vegas Fifth Street Grammar School through the 8th grade then to Las Vegas High.

A lot of the old-timers lived on the west side. Mrs. McWilliams, she was a French lady, they settled the area [and] she and her husband built the first house in Las Vegas. She had a large orchard in the backyard surrounded by grape vineyards. She would always give us neighbor kids all the fruit and grapes we liked (Trousdale, 2012).

Mrs. McWilliams husband was J. T. McWilliams (see Chapter 11) a surveyor, map maker and founder of McWilliamsville which later became known as "Westside."

In the summer of 1949, the family drove to the summit of Mountain Springs to visit a friend of theirs, Otto Baker. Ray really liked the mountains and told his mother he wanted to stay there that summer:

He [Otto] had a chicken farm. He lived in a cabin about 1,000 square feet; it was built out of railroad ties; it was old but clean with plenty of room for two people. No electricity or running water. He had an outhouse and had to walk up to a spring about 100 feet or so and dip his bucket in a pond and carry it back to the cabin. There were two springs on the property and some meadow springs north of the area about one-half a mile [away] and evidence of an old mining camp around the area. I went up there that summer after school, and I spent all summer with him. I went back to school in September but dropped out in November. My mom was upset to say the least (Trousdale, 2012).

In the end his mother agreed to let him move to the mountain and work with Otto Baker. Shortly after Ray arrived, he met Paul Warner who was then the manager at the Bar Nothing ranch (Spring Mountain State Park), Buster Wilson and three cowboys whose names he didn't remember. They were driving cattle up from the west side of the mountain:

Paul came up to the place and told Otto he was the new owner [Mountain Springs] and said he was going to build a house and motel and asked if we wanted to stay and help him. So we did. He said I can't pay you but you'll be welcome to stay in the cabin rent free. He said I'll buy all the food. We agreed, it took us about six months to complete his house. I sawed every board in the place by hand, there was no electricity or power for electric saws. I took woodshop in school and worked summers on the railroad for B and B builders in their wood shop, so carpentry was not new to me. The hardest part was the cement floor. We poured it a wheelbarrow at a time. But it was all fun being in the mountains. Paul lived in a trailer while the house was being built. The house set on a knoll about 75 yards above [north] the bar and about 20 yards to the left [north] of the green cabin we lived in. During the rest of the year we finished the bar and three units of the motel which connected to the back of the bar building. Then a couple of Paul's friends came up and started to build two houses. I didn't work on them [as] he had a couple of carpenters and block layers come up from town. I hunted a lot of rabbit and deer for meat during the winter months. His wife [Paul Warner's] was a Girl Scout leader and worked downtown (Trousdale, 2012 & Trousdale, 2014).

Ray has fond memories of Buster Wilson:

We hit it off right away and he said, you know, we can go hunting someday if you want. I said that would be great. I had hunted a little downtown where it was desert, hunting rabbits and stuff. When Buster stopped at Mountain Springs he would stay the night as it was a pretty long journey from there to Pahrump, 40 miles and you just didn't drive that in one day on rough roads. So we would go hunting once in a while and he would get a deer. He was a hell of a deer hunter and tracker; he could track anything. I really learned a lot from him, and he showed me where several different Indian camps used to be. Buster was very intelligent. He was a mechanic in World War Two, I think on the Mustang airplane. And he was an artist, he could draw your picture setting right here, and it would amaze you. He was really good at that. Buster at that time was between 45 and 47, I believe he told me. He was probably born in 1905. Tweed, his dad was born in about 1885, he looked to be seventy when I first met him (Trousdale, 2012).

Ray stayed on with Paul Warner until joining the Navy in 1952. After leaving the service in 1956, he worked for six months at the Bar Nothing ranch, then owned by Vera Krupp, and became reacquainted with Buster Wilson. "Swede" Londo was the ranch foreman at that time.

Ray's mother Clara Mae, sister Jane and Buster Wilson at Mountain Springs c. 1950

World Famous Saloon c. 2014

Warner would remain owner of the bar and motel until 1979. The bar is still in business as "The World Famous Mountain Springs Saloon." I know this because the sign says so.

The interior walls of the three motel rooms were removed by new owners to expand the size of the bar.

Paul Warner subdivided and sold-off the rest of the property between 1973 and 1978; most of the original 80-acre homestead is now two or three acre lots. Other homestead patents were issued on the surrounding property between 1954 and 1960; but the community is now landlocked from future growth, surrounded by the Red Rock Canyon National Conservation Area and U.S. Forest Service land.

Google Earth map showing the bar, pond and homes in 2015

The pass is no longer a place where travelers stop to rest. Now impatient drivers hurry by on their way to Las

The Mountain Springs Saloon in 2014

Vegas, Pahrump and Death Valley. The bar continues to draw customers, especially on weekends.

Pond (left) and inscription c. 2014

Ray and Geraldine Trousdale November 12, 2014 Mountain Springs, Nevada

ENDNOTES

On November 12, 2014, I visited Mountain Springs with Ray and his wife Geraldine. We walked around the area and Ray showed me the cabin he lived in, Paul Warner's house and the pond that he helped build in 1951.

We went into the bar where Ray and Geraldine enjoyed a nice visit with the current owner, his son, the bartender and three customers. Ray said that was only the second time he visited the property since he left to join the Navy. It was a beautiful fall day in the clear mountain air with the trees turning color and many memories rekindled.

CHAPTER 11

The Sandstone Quarry

By Chuck Williams

The spring of 1905 was an exciting time to be in southern Nevada. How often does one get to witness the birth of a new town? The San Pedro, Los Angeles and Salt Lake Railroad was nearing completion. The company had decided that Las Vegas would be a division point and the site of workshops and storehouses promising to employ several hundred men. The railroad had purchased 1,800 acres of the old Stewart ranch, laid out a townsite and advertised an auction for business and residential lots. This "new" town of Las Vegas would be located to the east of the railroad tracks.

To the west of the tracks, J.T. McWilliams, who surveyed the townsite for the railroad, saw an opportunity to purchase 80 acres from the Stewart ranch. He completed the purchase in 1904, subdivided the property and advertised lots for sale "In the Real Townsite of Las Vegas" in Las Vegas and Los Angeles newspapers. It was estimated that the McWilliams townsite population approached 2,000 by the time the railroad was completed on May 1, 1905. The mostly tent city contained three newspapers, three hotels, four restaurants, a store, a bakery, a meat market, a theater, horse stables, and a dozen saloons and gambling houses. J.T. also developed Lee Canyon at Mt. Charleston and produced more than 3,000 maps of Clark County and its subdivisions.

Hundreds of people began arriving in Las Vegas before the May 15 auction date, setting up another tent city with a post office, saloons, merchandise stores and two banks.

It was the largest sale of lots at one time ever known – 1,200 lots were sold over two days for an aggregate of $265,000. On the morning of May 17, the new owners began a search for stakes that marked the location of lot corners, the streets not yet cleared of brush. By nightfall, buildings were under construction with some being used before their roofs were on ("Untitled ad," 1905 & Squires, 1912 & *McWilliams Townsite*, 2008 & Hopkins & Evans, 1999).

Twenty miles west of town, at what would become Red Rock Canyon, another development was already in the works.

SANDSTONE QUARRY

Newspapers were published in the McWilliams townsite months before the railroad was completed. Volume one, Issue one of the *Las Vegas Age* was published on April 7, 1905 and carried this story on page one:

EXCELSIOR STONE QUARRY

> The Lyon-Wilson Construction Company of San Francisco is now operating the sandstone quarry eighteen miles northwest of Las Vegas. The stone is of superior quality, red and white in color. The company has built a good wagon road to the railroad and has purchased a traction engine and three strong wagons, capable of hauling twenty tons each down the grade from the quarry to the railroad. From three springs in the vicinity of the quarry water has been piped and from fifteen to twenty men will be employed in the quarry this spring getting out stone for buildings in Los Angeles and San Francisco. A channeling machine is used in the quarry with which blocks of stone ten tons each are cut. Manager J. Rinner says it is a shorter distance from these quarries to San Francisco than from the Ogden quarries now shipping stone to the Pacific coast ("Excelsior Stone Quarry," 1905).

There are five springs within three miles (straight line) of the quarry; but two, Red Spring and Ash Spring, are located at an elevation below the quarry which would make them unsuitable. The closest (1.8 miles) is White Rock Spring and local legend has it that the route of a pipeline from this spring to the quarry could at one time be seen from Turtlehead Peak. The other two possibilities are Willow Springs (2.8 miles) and La Madre Spring (3.2 miles). Piping water from any of these locations would require crossing several ridges and washes before reaching the quarry. It would have been an impressive engineering and construction feat.

Channel Machine used to drill holes for
removing blocks of sandstone c. 1905

Overview of quarry operations showing cable crane used
to lift and move ten-ton blocks of sandstone. Iron anchor
bars are still in place on both sides of the quarry. c. 1905

By mid-May *The Las Vegas Age* reported that W.C. Pidgey, superintendent of
the Sandstone Quarry, was in town looking after the shipping of stone ("Las
Vegas Brevities," 1905). The same issue announced the arrival of the company's steam engine:

BIG DEVIL WAGON

The big traction engine or steam wagon—or whatever it is—to be
used in transporting rock from the Excelsior Quarry to the railroad arrived in Las Vegas yesterday and started on its journey to the quarry
Friday evening. The machine is higher and looks bigger than a railroad locomotive, and it presented a weird and rather thrilling spec-
tacle as it plunged along the street and headed out across the desert,
regardless of track or tie ("Big Devil Wagon," 1905).

A photo in the October 3, 1906 *Las Vegas Age* shows the engine and attending
wagons in profile.

Big Devil Wagon steam engine and trailers October 3, 1906

Lee Fosburgh of the Caterpillar Corporate Archives could not say for sure, but based on its shape, he felt it was manufactured by the Best Manufacturing Company in San Leandro, California.

On August 26, 1905 the *Las Vegas Age* announced that the first baby was born in the

Best steam engine owned by the Oakland Museum

new town, a girl to Mr. and Mrs. J.A. Lytle (Vegas's First Baby, 1905). The same issue also provided another promising update about the quarry:

> Supt. W.C. Pidgey of Las Vegas Sandstone Quarry says a large force of men will be employed October 1, when they will begin to turn out 200 tons of stone per day. The stone is taken to San Francisco in the rough and sawed. Channeling machinery for the quarry will soon arrive. Being 2000 feet higher than Las Vegas, the temperature at the quarry is comfortable ("Stone Quarry," 1905).

The summer and fall of 1905 saw the new town experience growth and infrastructure development at a rapid pace. The Age newspaper transported its presses to the Las Vegas side of the tracks in May, shortly after the town was established. Many other McWilliams townsite businesses relocated about that same time and in September a fire swept through that tent city, destroying most of it. It became part of Las Vegas when the city was incorporated in 1911 but continued to be called "Old Town," "West Las Vegas" or "Westside." A portion of the old town site became the local segregated community (McWilliams Townsite, 2008).

September also saw construction begin on the Las Vegas and Tonopah Railroad and the Nevada Rapid Transit Company's chartered automobile road from Las Vegas to Beatty had reached Indian Springs. In Las Vegas buildings were being put up at a record pace and eight miles of street had been graded, curbed, oiled and graveled (Las Vegas and Tonopah Railroad, n.d. & "Nevada Auto Road," 1905).

There were no additional updates about the quarry until the following July when the newspaper ran a photo of the traction engine and reported that the quarry had closed after falling on hard times:

The monster traction engine and train of the Sandstone quarry in Charleston Mountain near Las Vegas, designed to haul the rock from the quarry to the railroad, now sits idle because high transportation charges on the railroad make the industry unprofitable ("Harriman Jealous," 1906).

More bad news about the quarry was reported in October 1906:

An agent from Los Angeles has taken back the traction engine and wagons from the stone quarry west of Las Vegas. The red and white sandstone has been used for building in Los Angeles and San Francisco, but is too far from the railroad. From the Salt Lake [railroad] to the quarry is about 20 miles, and the haul is too expensive, in connection with the rail freight to the coast. A good quality of sandstone exists north of Erie on the Salt Lake, 20 miles from Vegas ("Taken Away," 1906).

Erie is a railroad siding between Sloan and Jean on the San Pedro, Los Angeles and Salt Lake Railroad. The quarry mentioned is still in operation by Las Vegas Rock outside of Goodsprings, Nevada.

The company was unable to pay its bills and some merchants, such as Kuhn Mercantile Company, filed suit for $241 in outstanding balances ("Summons," 1906). However, the steam traction engine found a new home as reported on November 24, 1906:

R. H. Elsey, a professional engineer, has delivered the traction engine from the sandstone quarry to the Lincoln County Lumber company's sawmill in Charleston Mountains. The huge machine will be used to haul lumber from the mill to Owens siding on the L.V. & T [Las Vegas and Tonopah Railroad]. The running of the big engine from Las Vegas to the mountains was a difficult task. From Owens siding to the mill there is a good road, but from Las Vegas to Owens, poor roads and desert sands presented serious obstacles. Mr. Elsey has received considerable praise accomplishing the feat ("Traction Engine," 1906).

Owens siding was located where Lee Canyon road intersected with the railroad. By the fall of 1906 the railroad had reached Rhyolite and supplies and lumber were being shipped by train from Las Vegas to the Bullfrog Mining District (Las Vegas and Tonopah Railroad, n.d.).

As far as the quarry, there was some positive news at the end of 1906 when another company announced plans to reopen it.

1908 photo of the quarry buildings

The Age learns that the Lincoln Stone Co. will commence active development of their quarries early in the spring. This company owns the red sandstone deposits, which can be seen from Las Vegas, in the foothills of the Charleston Mountains. The quarries were closed last year after an unsuccessful attempt by another company. The company, of which J. A. Byrne is president, proposes to open the quarries in a practical way ("Stone Quarry," 1906).

However, "active development" of the quarry would not take place for over two years as Las Vegas went through a downturn. One reason was the completion of the Tonopah & Tidewater Railroad from Tonopah to the Santa Fe Railroad at Ludlow, California. This line built by Francis Smith, the "Borax King," provided competition with the Las Vegas & Tonopah Railroad, bypassing Las Vegas for goods and services (*Tonopah and Tidewater Railroad*, n.d.).

Also in 1907, a financial panic affected the entire country and heavy rains washed out the San Pedro, Los Angeles and Salt Lake Railroad tracks in the Meadow Valley Wash. Rail traffic was suspended for six weeks.

Las Vegas began to experience real growth again in 1908. One of the main reasons for this growth was that the San Pedro, Las Vegas and Salt Lake Railroad started construction of the promised machine shops and warehouses.

In January 1909, additional information about quarry operations was published in the following article from the *Las Vegas Age*.

QUARRIES MAY BE OPENED IN THE NEAR FUTURE: CAPITALISTS INVESTIGATING THE IMMENSE LEDGES OF BEAUTIFUL RED BUILDING STONE

J. A. Byrne of San Francisco has been in the city the past week looking after the property of the Lincoln Stone Co. in which he is the principal owner. These properties consist of immense bodies of red sandstone of a quality ideal for building purposes. The color is rich and particularly attractive for large structures. The quantity is unlimited, the great sandstone cropping showing up in a blaze of color from Vegas, 20 miles distant. An immense amount of money was expended in building roads, piping water and opening up the quarries four years ago, but owing to lack of capital to build a railroad to the property it was necessary to abandon the enterprise temporarily. Capitalists are now investigating the proposition and it is highly probable that a spur will be built from the railroad and operations begun on a large scale within the next few months ("Sandstone," 1909).

Evidently other issues arose, as it would be another year before there was another announcement about the quarry reopening. Clark County, with Las Vegas as the county seat, was created out of the south half of Lincoln County on July 1, 1909. On New Year's Day 1910, flash flooding wiped out 110 miles of railroad from just north of Moapa to 35 miles north of Caliente. This time it would be almost six months before rail traffic resumed ("Railroad Situation," 1910).

Finally in March 1910, J.A. Byrne was back in Las Vegas announcing the formation of a new company and singing the praises of Red Rock Sandstone while exaggerating a bit on the size of the deposit:

SANDSTONE QUARRY BEING OPENED BY REORGANIZED COMPANY WITH PLENTY OF CAPITAL

The Nevada Sandstone Company is the name of the reorganized company which has succeeded to the interests of the old Lincoln Sandstone Co., in the quarries west of Vegas. The new organization is under the management of Mr. J.A. Byrne and has ample capital for opening the quarry and marketing the product. Eight men are now at work doing the necessary work preliminary to installing the machinery. Machinery consisting of channeling machines, gadding machines, hoists, derricks, etc., with the necessary power to operate the same has been ordered and will be on the ground within thirty days. When the machinery is in place, about 20 men will be employed and the force later increased to 30 men which is estimated as the normal force for the operation of the quarry. The machinery ordered is of a capacity to handle blocks of 24 tons weight. The deposit is so exceptionally free from seams that blocks may be taken out larger than any machine will lift or any car carry. This quarry is about 20 miles almost due west from Vegas and is said to be the largest known deposit of sandstone in the United States and the only one where both red and white may be taken from the same quarry. Tests of this stone made by the University of California at Berkeley, California, show this to be the purest sandstone, chemically, in the market, and also that it stands a more severe crushing than any other known deposit of sandstone. The density and fineness of grain of the stone adapts it perfectly to the most ornate architecture, lending itself as readily as it does to hand carving and machine work. These many advantages will be sufficient to create a demand for this stone for building purposes which will in a few years put the product of the Nevada quarries at a premium in competition. Orders have already been received for stone for buildings in Los Angeles and contracts will be filled just as soon as the machinery is in place. For the present the stone will be hauled to the railroad by teams. It is expected that a spur track will be built to the quarry as soon as the conditions will warrant it ("Sandstone Quarry," 1910).

J.A. Byrne traveled to California in April to purchase machinery for the quarry while J.T. McWilliams completed the survey for a road from the railroad to the quarry. The road was being pushed with the road gang working out from Bracken siding. A new manager, James G. Neish, arrived to take charge of the quarry work ("Local Notes," 1910, April 2, April 9, April 30).

Bracken is a siding on the Los Angeles and Salt Lake Railroad (formally known as the San Pedro-Los Angeles-Salt Lake Railroad and nicknamed "The Salt Lake Route" or "The Salt Lake") located between Tropicana and Flamingo. The route is part of the current Union Pacific Railroad.

In early May the new tractor for hauling stone to the railroad arrived and was reported in the newspaper:

CATERPILLAR ORDERED BY NEVADA SANDSTONE
COMPANY ARRIVES AT BRACKEN

A caterpillar weighing 34,980 pounds seems about the limit for crawling things. Yet this is just what the Nevada Sandstone Company has at Bracken for the purpose of transporting its product from the quarry to the railroad. The concern is really a gasoline traction outfit built by

Holt Manufacturing Company Model 40 Caterpillar Tractor

the Holt Manufacturing Co., with three 12-ton platform wagons for trailers. The reason the machine is called a caterpillar is that it carries its own track which it lays down ahead of the wheels and picks up after, furnishing a much more substantial contact with the ground than in the old type of traction engine and, it is claimed, doing away with many of the disadvantages of old-style machines. Work on the road has progressed rapidly. Considerable machinery and appliances for handling the stone have arrived and in a few weeks the new industry will be taking out and shipping stone ("Caterpillar," 1910).

The Holt Manufacturing Company merged with its main competitor, C.L. Best, in 1925 to form Caterpillar Inc. (*Company History*, n.d.). I contacted Caterpillar to see if they could identify the tractor being used and received the following from Lee Fosburgh in Corporate Archives, "I have found your request very interesting and if I had to guess, the tractor used was a Holt Manufacturing Company, Model 40 Caterpillar Tractor that was made in Stockton, California. I cannot verify that, but that would make the most sense to me. I have attached a photograph of a Model 40 for your display."

At the end of May, the tractor made a return trip to Las Vegas and made the front page of the newspaper:

Sandstone picnic, unknown date

BIG BUG--CATERPILLAR WEIGHING 35,000 POUNDS CRAWLS
INTO VEGAS

The big four-cylinder gasoline traction engine belonging to the Sandstone Company made its first trip to Vegas Thursday evening. The
big bug seems to work perfectly and is doubtless a great improvement over the old type of traction engines with large drive wheels.
The machine will make a speed of four miles per hour over rough
roads and haul a load of from 30 to 40 tons. The object of the present
trip is to secure supplies ("Big Bug," 1910).

In June the County Commissioners approved the establishment of a 60-foot-
wide county road running from Bracken station to the sandstone quarry

("Commissioners," 1910). This is the road being built by the Nevada Sandstone Company and was a nice development for the company because now the county would be responsible for road maintenance. This new county road followed the old wagon road (now Flamingo Road which connected to what is now the Moenkopi Road going through the Red Rock Campground) and on to the Quarry. Work and improvements at the quarry continued over the summer, with the Las Vegas Hardware and Plumbing Company receiving a contract to build four 300-gallon tanks on the site ("Local Notes," 1910, July 16).

A newspaper snippet in January 1911 reported, "J. McGown has returned from Nevada Sandstone Quarry after completing $500 worth of annual labor. He has been reappointed agent for the Nevada Sandstone Company for the coming year" ("Local Notes," 1911, January 6).

This was the last newspaper mention of the quarry and it appears that the company was out of business by 1912. However, people continued to visit the quarry and it was a popular spot to picnic.

The boom town of Las Vegas would soon experience another economic decline and slowdown in growth. The mines in Goldfield were shutting down and by 1914 the Las Vegas and Tonopah Railroad discontinued service from Beatty to Tonopah. Demand for lumber had fallen to the point where the mill in Lee Canyon quit operations. The railroad discontinued all service in 1918, and by 1919 the track had been abandoned and scrapped. (Las Vegas and Tonopah Railroad, n.d.).

In 1924 the old quarry would stir up excitement once again. This time around it wasn't about quarrying stone, but about black gold.

LAS VEGAS OIL REPORT HOAX—TONOPAH, MARCH 27

Through inquiries from Carson City stating that people were filing on lands around Las Vegas for oil drilling, it became known here that an oil excitement was brewing with the center of Clark County for its axis.

Nobody here had heard anything of oil prospects and Frank Rapp began investigating with the result that the story blew up in short order. It appears that some joqers [sic] had removed a slab of sandstone from an old quarry and shipped to friends in Reno as a sample of the oil-bearing sandstone of Clark County.

There was plenty of oil in the stone, in fact the oil oozed from every pore, but the inquiry developed that the oil came from a seepage left

Engraved boulder at Calico Basin c. 2010

when the quarry owners removed an oil burning steam boiler ("Las Vegas Oil Report Hoax," 1924).

While the quarry would no longer operate as a functional business, people continued to remove sandstone for building purposes. Don Triolo, who lived in Calico Basin in the mid-1950s, remembers, "Ollie Olson used to go up there [the quarry] and cut flagstone for somebody. And we kids would go up and watch him. There was, I guess you would call it a conveyer belt that he worked by hand" (Triolo, 2013).

There were two areas where stone was quarried. The largest quarry is located adjacent to the Sandstone Quarry parking lot. The second, a much smaller area, is located approximately 550 yards northwest of the parking lot and may have been part of these later quarry operations.

There is an interesting engraved boulder, approximately two miles away, on the ridge above the Red Spring Boardwalk with the words "Old Quary" [sic] followed by faint indentations that have been reported to read "2 Mile." It is unknown if the stone was engraved during the time the quarries were in operation or after Calico Basin was established.

The Sandstone Quarry continues to be a favorite destination for people visiting Red Rock Canyon and draws hikers and rock climbers from around the world. The buildings are long gone, leaving only a bit of foundation to mark their location. Large blocks of cut sandstone remain in place, quietly waiting for orders that never came.

The Sandstone Quarry in 2014

Chuck Williams

ENDNOTES

After I finished compiling reference material about the Sandstone, I listed the material in chronological order to determine the chapter outline. Since most of the reference material was newspaper articles, I included article text along with the published date. As I began to read the entries, it hit me that the chapter was already written – I just had to fill in some background and provide flow between articles. I couldn't see where I would improve on what the reporters had already written. I liked their writing style and the fact that they sometimes painted a mental picture using just a few words. An example would be a short item in the "Local Notes" column of the *Las Vegas Age* on August 13, 1910, "The 'caterpillar' galloped in from the sandstone quarry Wednesday."

Just nine words, but the image brought a smile to my face. Had I been on the street that day I would have stopped and watched the "Big Bug" until it disappeared from view.

CHAPTER 12

One Man's Dream

By Dan Wray

It was a parade to celebrate the liberation of Paris and a World War II G.I., a veteran of the Battle of the Bulge, marched proudly around the Arc De Triomphe with his colleagues. The G.I. was unaware that also in Paris on that day was a red-headed Army nurse who had spent the war years serving throughout Europe.

Tilghman Palmer Rhea, or T.P. as he was better known, was born on October 26, 1915 in Blue Mountain, Mississippi and moved to Las Vegas after his discharge from the Army on October 12, 1947. Geology and mining fascinated him and he built up a comprehensive library on the subject. Red Rock Canyon, not then a National Conservation Area, gave him ample opportunity to indulge his passion. He took pleasure in the rocks with their vivid colors, with the plants and with the vistas. He hiked and climbed extensively, Mount Wilson being one of his conquests. T.P. obtained a post at the Blue Diamond Gypsum Mine and was soon promoted to foreman. He was a handsome man with a fine physique as some of the ladies still living in Blue Diamond recall.

One afternoon, after a hard day's work at the mine, T.P. was relaxing at the bar in Bonnie Springs when in walked that beautiful little red-headed former Army nurse, Mabel Grace Randell. It was love at first sight, and they were married one month later.

Stories still abound in Blue Diamond as to T.P.'s kindness and concern for

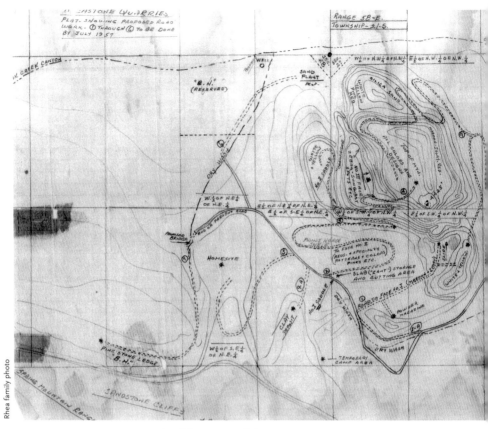

T.P.'s hand drawn map of the quarry site

his fellow workers. One lady tells that when her husband could not get time off work to visit his out-of-town family whom he had not seen since he had returned from the war, T.P. arranged for him to be laid off temporarily and rehired on his return.

T.P.'s kindness, however, eventually cost him his job. A new superintendent was appointed at the mine and began to verbally abuse the workers. T.P. remonstrated with him and was fired. As only workers employed at the mine were allowed to live in the settlement, T.P., his wife and their four-month-old daughter, Joy, had to leave. They went to California where he worked in the roofing trade and where a second child, Faye, was born to them. Three years later the family was blessed by the birth of twins, Pam and Becky. Becky later died tragically in a car accident.

On the family's return to Las Vegas, T.P. was able to resume his interest in Red Rock Canyon. Even before he met his wife, he had started surveying an area that he thought could provide an idyllic site for a homestead in which to bring up a family and for a stone quarry that would provide the livelihood to

enable him to do so. He was determined to stake a claim and initially marked the boundary using Prince Edward Tobacco tins. The claim was submitted on March 1, 1955.

T.P.'s love of the rocks and their beauty was reflected in the survey documents. Areas that contained "white, yellow, pink and red; zebra, sunburst and spots and maroon, ivory and red" were all carefully pin-pointed.

T.P. was under no illusions as to the difficulties involved in setting up the quarry. He acknowledged that. "The Quarry cannot be put in sensible and/or profitable operation on a shoestring nor with a few strong hearts and bare hands. Had this been possible, it would have been done years ago." He set out his proposals for incorporation of the enterprise stating that the quarry consisted of seven placer mining claims approximately five miles north of Blue Diamond. Discovery, location, development and 100% interest had been maintained by him since the fiscal year 1953. T.P. had already committed $1380 of his personal money for the hire or purchase of equipment, mainly for the construction of access roads. Now additional financing was required for further development. He proposed to incorporate the venture with an initial share offering of 100,000 shares at $1 each, 51% of which would be retained by his family.

A certain amount of equipment was already available, including various vehicles, some of which would need some modification—a compressor, generator and a skill saw. T.P. identified a guillotine, electric rock hammer and a jack hammer as major items required.

The initial operation called for the development of two claims; another three claims would be used for "access roads, hoisting sites, cutting and storage space, fabricating and equipment sheds, cookhouse and dormitory and other uses pertaining directly to the operation of the quarry and/or housing quarry personnel."

For the purpose of estimating production, T.P. adopted a very conservative assessment of the depth of the deposit. He had initially estimated it at 150 to 400 feet but now took 100 feet as the base figure. With a five to eight man crew producing eleven tons per day, six days per week, 52 weeks a year, the cash return would be $102,960 based on a price of $30 per ton.

T.P. envisaged that "in the foreseeable future with proper production facilities, skilled and cooperative workers, adequate management and marketing methods, it is not inconceivable that the quarry can produce and sell fifty tons per day for a gross of $468,000 per year." T.P. was looking forward but at the same time trying to be realistic when he assessed that fifty tons per day was the limit which could be absorbed by the marketing area. He also foresaw later expansion into the eleven western states.

Perhaps it says something of T.P.'s kindness that one of the first uses of stone from the quarry was in the construction of a new fireplace and swimming pool area for Bonnie, a family friend. The first building to be constructed using the stone was the former Stuckey's on Boulder Highway.

Buddy Rhea with his father Tilghman working at the quarry.

As with so many fledgling businesses, not enough income was generated to allow the quarry to function on a full-time basis, and T.P. had to take various jobs to keep his dream alive and support his family. He worked at the manganese plant, the test site and with a paving company. It was while working on a project with the latter in Goldfield that he had a heart attack and died at the early age of 55. His widow Mabel, with four children to provide for, struggled to keep the

Truck load of cut stone going to Fresno, California

dream alive. However, the conditions attached to the claim were too much and the claim lapsed.

In its relatively brief existence, the quarry may not have produced the quantity of stone nor the amount of income which T.P. had envisioned, nor did it provide a permanent homestead for his family. But in retrospect, the wealth generated lies in the happy memories which his family has of the time spent at the quarry site.

Let Joy, the eldest daughter, tell that story:

> I remember Dad saying that an unusual smooth rock I was looking at was where early Indians had ground acorn nuts in earlier days. The area

has a seasonal creek and I remember how wonderful it was sometimes to find water in it and how wonderful it was to find pine nuts the birds hadn't discovered. I still remember the exquisite taste of those nuts!

I remember Dad saying that he soaked corn kernels in whiskey and left them out for the quail. He was hoping that they would eat the corn, get drunk and then be easier to catch. Maybe he was hoping that they would pass out as I don't remember Dad ever having a gun. Anyway, he said that the plan didn't work out because the quail never seemed to feel the effects of the liquor. Lucky for them I guess.

Once when we were having much difficulty finding a certain size rock to ring a campfire, Dad dissolved in laughter. I asked what was so funny and Dad said that he thought it was so funny that we were surrounded with untold rocks and we couldn't find the exact size we needed for the campfire.

Pam recalls building a snowman and their dog Cubby eating the carrot intended for the nose. The children soon learned that campfires and snowmen don't live happily together when their masterpiece melted all too soon.

Faye says:

I remember always picking up lots of small rocks and stones and taking the time to hold each of them up to the sun to see the color hiding within. I still do that. Dad would break open certain rocks and show us the beautiful centers that had been hiding beneath the drab surface. We carefully carried all of these rocks back home because they were treasures! I remember climbing and running all over the 'quarry' and not wanting to come back to camp to eat because I didn't want the day to end. I remember getting annoyed and losing patience with Mom because she was always so worried that we would get lost or hurt or bit by a rattlesnake. In our minds nothing bad was ever going to happen to us there.

We always brought home our Christmas trees from the quarry. I remember hiking all over to find the 'most perfect' one and Dad suggesting trees that were closer to our vehicle as we went along; but he always allowed us to pick out the one we wanted, no matter how far away from camp it was. Now I realize that Dad was trying to get us to choose one that he didn't have to carry a long distance.

T.P. built a two-room cabin at the quarry, complete with a potbelly stove. The cabin was never locked. He wanted any hikers who found the quarry to be able to go in, sit down and get warm. Friends, neighbors…it didn't mat-

Faye matching her hand with her childhood handprint imbedded in concrete in 2010.

ter who. T.P.'s philosophy was that, "We are all God's children, aren't we?" Visitors responded by leaving little thank you notes. One visitor left a clean pair of white bobby socks. On one was written "CU soon" and on the other "Thank U."

After T.P. died, his wife and Joy had a meeting at the Bureau of Land Management (BLM). Joy recalls the sick feeling she had upon realizing that they were not going to be able to fulfill the requirements stipulated by the BLM in order to keep the quarry, such as a permanent dwelling, a fence around the entire claim, subsistence work, etc.

Boulder with drill hole c. 2010

Today, as T.P.'s daughter Faye and the Cultural Resources Group of Friends of Red Rock Canyon found on a visit to the quarry, little or nothing remains of the project other than a few stones showing evidence of having been concreted together to form part of a boundary wall and others with holes drilled ready for the black blasting powder.

Some things, however, had not changed; and it was with a tinge of sadness for everyone in the group that the locations were identified from various old photos showing T.P. at the quarry. It was easy to see why T.P. had chosen that particular site for a homestead and quarry. The bright sunshine brought out those vivid colors and patterns which T.P. had documented in his survey, and the towering Wilson Cliffs seemed to want to protect and preserve the tranquility.

Faye matching the background in a photo of father with the quarry landscape in 2010.

Faye sitting on petrified wood at the quarry site c. 2010

T.P. would have been pleased that the documentation of the quarry has been restored and preserved mainly through the efforts of his daughter Faye and the University of Nevada Las Vegas. He would also have been pleased that even if he did not provide his family with the homestead he had hoped for, he gave them a happy childhood and perhaps more importantly, lasting memories. He would have been equally pleased to know that the quarry with his beloved rocks and plants is now part of the Red Rock National Conservation Area and preserved in perpetuity for all to enjoy.

CHAPTER 13

Stone of La Madre Quarry

By Chuck Williams

Five members of the prominent Foley family and their partners in Stone of La Madre, James Hogan and Thomas Bodensteiner, filed a claim on a one and one-half square-mile terrace of sandstone that overlooks the Las Vegas valley. The land would later become part of Red Rock Canyon National Conservation Area but was open to mining at the time of the filing. The Bureau of Land Management suspended action on the claim in June 1992 stating that the sandstone was a common variety and did not meet a requirement that the rock must be unique.

Stone of La Madre challenged the suspension, claiming the rock was an uncommon variety, and that there was a market in Las Vegas for its use as decorative landscaping material that would otherwise have to be hauled from Arizona (Rogers, 1993).

Had Stone of La Madre been able to establish that it was truly "unique," they then could have asserted that their claim should be considered as a "locatable" rather than a "saleable" claim under the mining laws. Sandstone, gravel and other common mineral items are normally sold by the Bureau of Land Management on a per cubic yard basis as opposed to "locatable" minerals (such as gold and silver) where the claim holder could apply for a patent (ownership) after establishing the validity of the claim.

Acquiring a mining patent would force the Bureau of Land Management to sell the land at $2.50 per acre, the fair market value of public land according to the mining law of 1872. Stone of La Madre would receive surface rights to the land, and it would also remove the acreage from an ongoing Wilderness Area Review (Rogers, 1993).

There was public concern that the quarry operation would present an eyesore visible from Las Vegas or that the company, once ownership was established, would use the land for residential development. The terrace is not only visible from the Las Vegas valley, it also contains prehistoric features such as rock art, roasting pits and rock shelters.

IT IS GOOD TO HAVE A FRIEND

On January 18, 1993, Friends of Nevada Wilderness conducted a public meeting at the Nevada State Museum calling for a boycott of decorative sandstone from the Red Rock Canyon area in an effort to derail plans to mine a scenic terrace next to the canyon.

The group presented a draft petition asking landscape architects, designers, contractors, nursery wholesalers and retailers not to purchase decorative rock from the area. The petition also asked for support for a national recreation area in the Spring Mountains.

Pat Dingle, the group's state chairman, said the plan was to eliminate the profit from any potential mining of the land so the Bureau of Land Management could deny the claim because it did not meet a profitability requirement of the 1872 Mining Law. Dingle stated, "We are in a position as a friend of the court (to convince) a judge that this is not a profitable operation" (Rogers, 1993).

When the Bureau of Land Management mineral examiner reviewed the application, it was determined that the sandstone was no different than all the other Aztec sandstone in this area. Therefore it could not be considered a "locatable" mineral under the mining laws, thus eliminating any possibility of obtaining a patent (ownership) of the land. Following the validity exam, Stone of La Madre abandoned the claim as the company would not be able to develop the land and there would be no profit in starting another quarry in the Las Vegas area.

Chuck Williams

Chuck Williams

Quarry overview and detail of drill hole c. 2014

ENDNOTES

There is evidence of some quarry operations in the area which I assume was done by Stone of La Madre, perhaps as part of their claim documentation; but it may be from historic operations. The quarry is now within the boundaries of Red Rock Canyon National Conservation Area

The quarry did not disturb a large area, but it is located adjacent to several prehistoric features. The site is located in a remote section of the conservation area. This makes it difficult to protect the site from campers and off-roaders who find the scenic location ideal as it offers a spectacular view of the Las Vegas Valley. Not all of these visitors respect the historic features nor do they practice leave-no-trace principals.

CHAPTER 14

Blue Diamond Mine

By Linda Carlyle McCollum

THE FIRST 30 YEARS 1900-1929

The Blue Diamond Materials Company of Los Angeles was founded by J.W. Jamison in 1900 with the company being named for the high quality lime being mined in the quarries at Tehachapi, California. The quality of the gypsum which was in the lime deposits at Tehachapi was said to be comparable to the blue diamond among gems, thus the name of the company. Jamison opened the first plaster mill in Los Angeles in 1922 with his partner William Hay, with whom he had patented their ready-mix mortar process in 1915.

The Blue Diamond Materials Company purchased gypsum rock from the Imperial Gypsum & Oil Company in Imperial Valley, California (now the U.S. Gypsum Company) and the Mammoth Gypsum Company of Cedar City, Utah (Leavitt, 2011).

NEVADA DEPOSIT FOUND

In the spring of 1923, W.G. Bradley joined the firm and helped locate the Nevada deposit on the hill northeast of the Cottonwood Springs area to which Peter Buol and Vincent Matteucci owned the mining rights. After a great deal of consideration and determining it was "one of highest grade gypsum deposits known," Bradley negotiated the deal and acquired the 1,000 acre Buol Gypsum Deposit in November of 1924 (Bradley, 1932). Bradley mentions

(left to right)
Mr. Bradley, Adelma King, Unknown person

negotiating with an Italian family named Matteucci. This purchase did not involve the Cottonwood Ranch. "Vic was the older brother and negotiator....We finally paid them $75,000 for it and proceeded to patent it" (Bradley, 1932).

For approximately six months immediately prior to starting operation of the present mine, Blue Diamond produced rock from a small deposit at Bard, Nevada, four miles south of Arden and two miles off the Union Pacific Railroad (Leavitt, 2011). Some of the company's mine workers in Tehachapi, California were transferred to Arden, Nevada in 1924 to mine in the foothills at Arden before coming to the mine site in Blue Diamond.

About October of 1923, the company started making plans and ordering equipment, planning to produce 200 tons in a ten-hour day and hoping the deposit would last for 20 years. Because of the distance to markets in California and the difficulties and expense connected with the development of the new mine site, actual work did not start until January 1925.

Bill Rogers, the mine manager, explained how the mine got started:

> Before they could open the mine they had to put in eleven miles of standard gauge railroad track to the Union Pacific Railroad at Arden. They needed eight miles of road built to bring in heavy machinery and supplies and a mile long aerial tramway to transport gypsum from the top of the bluff to the railroad terminus.

> Water was pumped to the top of the hill for industrial and domestic purposes. A large diesel engine was hauled to the top to generate power for the crushers, conveying equipment and compressors.

> Houses were built for all the workers at the top of the hill. A refrigeration plant was constructed for the storage of meats, vegetables and fresh fruit. A private electric light plant provided illumination for all areas of the camp.

> Shipments of gypsum to the company's plaster mill in Los Angeles

started in July, 1925. I.E. King, a mining engineer, was the first super-intendent of the Blue Diamond Mine (Rogers, 2005).

A Thousand Acres

In October 1925, the Blue Diamond Materials Company applied for a mining patent on a thousand acres, half of which was covered by gypsum deposits, making it one of the world's largest gypsum mines. Mining began using underground tunnels, then converted to open-pit mining with drilling and blasting over the years.

The gypsum deposit consisted of four separate beds. Numbers 1 and 2 did not have hanging walls or sound footing and were not considered important, but some rock from Number 2 was obtained in a stripping operation. Most of the rock came from Numbers 3 and 4 whose seams were about eighteen and fifteen feet thick respectively. The rock was exceptionally pure with some clay and anhydrite intrusions.

Mining was first done by hand, loading the ore into one-ton narrow gauge cars which were pushed to the crusher by men. Various methods of extracting the gypsum were used over the years. Both underground and open pit equipment, as modern as possible, were in use increasing extraction to seven-and-a-half times its original capacity. To reduce man-hours, electrical controls were used to a maximum (Bradley, G., September, 1932).

Work Falls Off

In 1926 there was a problem with the gypsum market. Cutthroat competition with severe price cutting eliminated all profit in the western segment of the industry. In 1929 construction work had fallen off, so the mine needed to operate efficiently. People working the mine mention occasional shutdowns during the depression.

THE SECOND THIRTY YEARS 1930-1959

The company's application to the Nevada Division of Water Resources for water rights in 1932 shows the company name had changed to the Blue Diamond Corporation. The company considered a plaster mill and sacking plant at the site. By 1934 the mining operation was well underway with two hundred tons a day being mined for the first six to seven years. (The mine may have supplied gypsum which is used as a retardant in cement to the Boulder Dam project.)

The Mining Camp

The mining camp had two diesel generators for power; a cook house, commissary, office and bunkhouses for laborers; three apartments and three houses for some of the more prestigious positions. In a few years, some of the miners moved their families up to the camp.

The miners lived in bunkhouses on top of the hill in Camp One near the mine.

Eventually Camp One had a mess hall, recreation hall, timekeeper house, a couple of small houses where the schoolteachers lived and the maintenance shops.

Number Two Camp at the mine had a house for the superintendent of the mines, one for the foreman and then one for the family of the man that ran the crusher or the shovel operator. They also had triplex apartments where some families lived. A total of seven families lived at this campsite (Leavitt, 2011).

Extracted from oral histories, the next few pages give additional insights into how the families lived during this period.

Homes

Ray Phelps described the mining camp:

> In the main village where families lived, the homes have been designated as A through G. There was a second and smaller residential location, and those homes have been designated H through J. The rough distance between the two villages was two miles.

> In the main village area, A-G was for families. ABC was an apartment house consisting of three apartments, each having three rooms—a kitchen, living room and a bedroom with a shared bathroom. DEFG were houses with two or three bedrooms and private baths. These were luxury places compared to all other living quarters for the family employees. In these days, all quarters were owned by the Blue Diamond Corporation.

> Though times were good and enjoyable at Blue Diamond, life styles were limited. For example, the use of electricity was rationed. In those days, we only had DC current and the generators had limited capacity. There were no electric refrigerators, washers, dryers, air conditioners, etc. Those who could afford refrigerators had bottled gas-operated units. The others made their own water coolers by stretching burlap over a wooden frame, with dripping water on top of this fabricated assembly. The water would evaporate, cooling the

Camp One, c. 1930s

Recreation hall is the larger building in back, the small building in front was used for a residence

School house and playground

Camp Two, c. 1938

inside of this ingeniously designed unit, enabling us to keep milk, butter and meats for a little longer period. For cooking, wood/coal stoves were used. Water jackets were placed inside the stoves, so when they were in use, we had hot water.

Another location of importance, in addition to the main village and second village, was the administrative office area, which was located about one mile from the main village. Points of interest here included: three bunkhouses which housed approximately 30 men; a cook house where meals were served to the miners who lived in the bunkhouses; administrative offices; mechanical repair shops; an entertainment hall for playing pool, dancing or putting on school plays; a teacherage which was a small apartment provided to the teacher if she were single; and the commissary or company store.

Because the company store was only able to handle emergency supplies, the villagers had to travel to Las Vegas at least once a week to stock up on food. This was usually done on Saturdays, as stores were not open on Sundays. Church services were not held at Blue Diamond and so to go to church on Sunday meant an extra trip to town. Since money was in short supply, we did not often get to church.

Times were hard in 1928-1932 because of the depression. Jobs were very scarce and people considered themselves lucky to have a job. As such, the miners' jobs were important, so people worked hard to keep their jobs and to support their families (Phelps, 1978).

Tent Houses

The Bogdanovich and Hurtado families lived up on the hill past the crusher in tent houses. Sophie Bogdanovich Roman (whose father worked the mine), her sisters Angie and Nina and brother George remember living off by themselves on a hill down below the crusher, away from the other two camps. Their father set up a big tent and over the years eventually built around it, adding on rooms to make it comfortable for use. But it was still quite a walk to the other camps and the school.

Mary Hurtado, whose husband worked at the mine while they were living at what is today's Oliver Ranch, recalls moving up the hill to the mine:

Mr. King asked my husband if he wanted to live up at the mine. My husband told him yes. Mr. King told my husband that he didn't have a home, but he had a tent that needed a roof. It had the flooring and everything in it. It just needed a roof. My husband went and bought the lumber and he put a roof on it instead of canvas.

That was my first home up at Blue Diamond. The Bogdanovichs were already living there. They already had a home there. I guess George must have built it. I don't know, but they had a nice home there with a lot of ivy growing around it. He had his own little garden there.

As my family grew, my husband made me a kitchen. We made the tent into a bedroom, just the beds. We had a kitchen made out of railroad ties. It had a dirt floor….Although it was dirt, it was clean. We really had a nice time (Hurtado, 2003).

THE SCHOOL AT THE MINE SITE

The small frame schoolhouse at Cottonwood Springs was moved up to the mine site in the mid-1930s and placed at the base of Indian Hill, about one mile west of the main village at the mine site. It was a one-room, one-teacher schoolhouse with all eight grades in one room and about twelve or fourteen students attending. There was no electricity or running water. Drinking water was supplied in five-gallon bottles placed in a clay jug by the front door and each student was required to have their own drinking glass. Waste water was drained into a container and used for washing hands after recess (Phelps, 1978). There was a fuel-burning stove on the left-hand side of the room. In the back of the room, on either side of the front door, there were cupboards for storage of books and materials.

Just below the school in a small valley to the north was a small corral and shed to hold the horse one girl rode to school. A baseball field/playground was just in front of the school with a girl's outhouse to the left and a boy's to the right (Delong, 2008).

After the eighth grade, students were bused to high school in Las Vegas on a company bus or moved into Las Vegas and lived with friends or relatives or made other arrangements.

RECREATION

For recreation the mine residents played badminton and volleyball. Down by the springs was a "duck pond" to which the men would later add cement walls so they could go swimming.

Every year there was a Christmas play put on by the students and a party in the pool hall. Some years there were at least three plays put on by the students with bed sheets used as curtains and all the people in the camp attending the performances (Wolters, 2009).

Stella Phelps, whose husband worked at the mine, recalls going into town every two weeks on payday. "It was just a dirt road, then, full of washboards, and we'd take turns on whose car we'd use, and we'd all go in together. It would take the whole day just to get into town, shop, and get back. It was fun. And living on the hill was fun. The Company was always so good to their employees. You can tell that by how long most of them have stayed" (Phelps, n.d.).

Some of the mine workers' children had some inventive recreational pursuits. Jackie King Appledorn, the mine superintendent's daughter, remembers riding her bike down the hill to the spring and spending the whole day at the Cottonwood Ranch swimming and playing. The road went alongside Bitter Spring where she would go into the wash and dig the clay out, play in the water and make mud pies with the clay (Appledorn, 2007).

George Bogdanovich's son George recalls how he and his friends would play in the abandoned mine tunnels:

> We used to play in the tunnels. Even when we were very young my mother used to take us to the tunnel near our house because it would be nice and cool in the summer. As we grew older we became more adventurous. Because they went to strip mining in the mid-40s a lot of tunnels were abandoned. The main tunnel we played in was about a mile long with a small incline. It still had the rail tracks, ore cars and two dinke engines stored there. We used to push an ore car up the incline, jump in and ride it through the tunnel like a roller coaster. Pitch black. When we got to the end it would crash into the other cars so you either bailed out or hung on (Bogdanovich, 2009).

Nina Bogdanovich Wolters recalls how as kids they would go into Las Vegas once a month:

> I remember that as we got older, the school bus took us into town. About once a month we would ride the bus into town. And we would spend all day Saturday. We went to at least three movies that day in town, the nine o'clock one at the old Western Theatre on First Street there. And then we would sell newspapers. And then we'd make the next movie in the early afternoon at the Palace Theatre there on Second Street right across from the courthouse. And then we'd sell some more papers and then go down to the El Portal (on Fremont and Fourth) and catch that movie. But we did the movie thing. And at that time the courthouse was just a little building in the middle. And it had grass all the way around, trees and sidewalks up each corner up there and that's where we met the bus. But when we got through

running around town, which was not very many blocks, we ended up there at the courthouse. That was the going-to-town thing. That was a lot of fun (Wolters, 2009).

Mary Hurtado's son Al shared memories of living at the mine. "Our sole entertainment [was] either listening to the radio or listening to stories the adults used to tell us. We used to spend time outside. I mean this was our entertainment. We had big old beds outside. Dad would tell us stories," (Hurtado, 2003).

They were outside telling stories on January 16, 1942, the night the airplane carrying Clark Gable's wife Carol Lombard crashed into the mountains killing her and 21 other people on board. "[Dad] was telling us a ghost story when the plane came over. We saw the actual plane. It looked like one of the engines was on fire. Somebody said, 'Look there goes the witch!' And when it hit the mountain, it just scared us all. You know we were young kids (Hurtado, 2003).

EARLY MINE OPERATIONS

Ray Phelps describes the power source for the mine and the mining jobs in the early days:

The original power source was a three-cylinder 180 H.P. Fairbanks Morse diesel engine driving a line shaft which furnished power to the crusher, compressors and tram drive. There also was a small hot-head engine driving a generator for lights. This worked some of the time, but more often did not.

Rock from the mine was hauled to a tipple six miles below the plant as the railroad was complete only to this point. The day after the railroad was completed there was a violent cloudburst which washed out the last one-and-a-half miles.

One entry-level mining job was that of a "mucker." The mucker loaded gypsum into mine cars in a tunnel. A mucker's job was so demanding that at day's end, he was completely exhausted. If one was a good worker, after a time he could work up to a better position. Other workers were locomotive operators, truck drivers, crusher operators, office personnel, supervisory personnel and others, all of whom labored together making Blue Diamond prosperous.

The process of mining the gypsum and transporting it to Los Angeles began with the muckers who loaded the gypsum rock into small railroad cars. The locomotive operator would take several loaded cars

Tramline hauling gypsum to plant in background. The tramline was replaced with a covered conveyer belt system that ran to the plant and can still be seen today. Photo c. 1940s

Loading truck for trip to crusher c. 1940s

Tramline entering bunker for the mill then into the plant c. 1940s

(top left) Crusher with the Bogdanovich family dog in foreground c. 1940s

(bottom left) Slusher operation c. 1940s

(above) Dumping gypsum into crusher hopper c. 1940s

out of the mines passing the bunkhouses and administrative offices on the way to the crusher. Later this was done by powered shovels and trucks from open pit quarries.

The gypsum rock, of literally boulder size, was dumped into a receiving bin where the boulders were crushed into small rocks from 2″ to 4″ in diameter. After the boulders were crushed, they were conveyed upward into a large hopper and then loaded into aerial tramway cars that ran on steel cables over the cliffs and through a small canyon.

The tramway cars later dumped the boulders into a bunker at the bottom of the hill. The drop in elevation from the crusher to the bunker was approximately 3,000 feet and the overland distance was an estimated one-and-a-half miles.

The crusher served four purposes. One was to crush the boulder into rocks. The second was to load the gypsum rock into tramway cars and transport it to the bunker. The third purpose was to provide braking of the loaded tram cars because they descended with a full load and came back to the crusher empty. The pull of gravity on the loaded cars necessitated some braking power. This braking power was provided by three huge Fairbanks Morse single-cylinder diesel powered motors. In other words, this was an overhauling application, and some means had to be used to prevent the cars from running out of control. As the years passed and new technology developed, electric motors with dynamic braking were utilized.

Later these aerial tramway cars were replaced by a covered rubber conveyer belt running over the cliffs and downhill just above ground level. Gypsum, when rained on, could be a sticky nightmare for those who worked with it. Because of this, the covered conveyor belt has reduced labor problems.

The fourth function of the crusher was auxiliary, which was to generate electricity for daytime use. Since the crusher did not operate at night, another generator located between the main village and the administrative office came on in the evenings to supply the nighttime electrical power.

The last stage of the mining operation was the bunker into which the gypsum was dropped from the passing aerial tramway cars. Railroad cars were located beneath the bunker waiting for the gypsum to be loaded into them and then transported to Los Angeles by the Union Pacific Railroad.

The bunker area also served as the water pumping station to pump water to the "hill" area. Two such artesian wells existed at the bottom of the hill and provided the water for our desert community. The water was fed to the pumping station by gravity, held in a covered cement reservoir and then by a reciprocating engine, pumped up the hill into two storage tanks. This provided all the water we needed, sometimes even a surplus of water which ran across the land (Phelps, 1978).

PLANT EXPANSIONS

In the 1940s gypsum sales were stimulated by the building boom as people geared up for the war and emergency housing was needed. The mill in Los Angeles was moved to the mine site in 1941. That same year the Blue Diamond Corporation leased the Cottonwood Ranch for 25 years from the Union Pacific Railroad with an option to buy. The Union Pacific Railroad retained the water rights and leased them to the corporation, pumping water from Cottonwood Springs to Arden.

A COMPANY TOWN

After leasing the Cottonwood Ranch in 1941, the Blue Diamond Company began building a company town to provide housing for married supervisory and key employees. Some employees still lived on the top of the hill at the mine site. A trailer court was added to the original camp for men.

When the post office was officially established in the village on December 1, 1942, the company town became Blue Diamond. In 1946 and 1955 additional homes were built, as well as a school, store and other installations to ensure the workers a "key personnel supply" (Leavitt, 2011). The town was laid out in the shape of the state of Nevada.

The village on top of the hill was eventually torn down and the inhabitants moved to the new location. The bunkhouses, cook house, dining hall, and main administrative offices were relocated to the new plant site.

MINING OPERATIONS IN THE 40s

In 1946 an additional roller mill and calcining kettles were installed and the boiler plant expanded. The wallboard plant's output doubled and a tramway was reworked to increase capacity.

Bill Rogers' interview:

> Plant production facilities were substantially enlarged in 1947. Plaster mill capacity was increased by one-third and the wallboard plant was

Aerial view of the plant c. 1960s. The buildings on the left side of the photo are dormitories for the mine workers.

expanded by more than one-half. All phases of production, including the mining and quarrying of gypsum and its transportation, were expanded to conform with output from the plant.

The location of the mine with respect to the plant presented unusual transportation problems. Transportation involved a truck haul of about one mile down a grade averaging five or six percent to a crushing plant, followed by belt conveyor delivery to a dispatching station for an aerial tramway. The gypsum dropped 600 feet in elevation along the 1700 foot long tramway.

Gypsum rock was excavated by a combination of underground mining and open quarrying. Mining took place in the 3 bed and the 4 bed. The two beds averaged 16 feet in thickness. Underground mining employed the room-and-pillar methods. The open quarry method employed power shovels. Open pit was used until the striping became sufficient to dictate going underground. The bulk of the high grade gypsum was recovered from the underground workings. The extent of excavation from either the underground or from the open pit was dictated according to the products being manufactured at any given time.

Previous to the expansion, 10 to 12 hours of mining were required to produce enough rock to keep the plaster mill supplied for 24 hours.

(top left) Tipple feeding wall-board into kiln

(bottom left) Bundling and stacking machinery c. 1950s

(right) Inside view of the plant

Slushers were used to a great extent for loading cars on narrow gauge rail which were hauled away by diesel locomotive to the tramway dispatching tower. After the 1947 expansion, rail haulage was abandoned in favor of trucks. The slushers were then limited to the opening of the portals, then were followed by a Joy Loader and shuttle cars. This made for a very flexible operation. Production of the plant requires that an average of 800 tons of gypsum be delivered to the plaster mill in eight hours. Rock is dumped into a steep hillside hopper. The Lawon automatic tramway, supplied by Interstate Equipment Corporation, delivers the rock to the mill.

The tramway was a bottleneck in the expansion program and the capacity was increased. This was accomplished by installing heavier cable and adding more buckets. Each of the 44 buckets carry 18 cubic feet of rock.

The plaster mill has been unchanged except for increased equipment to step up capacity. A 20 foot by 120 foot addition was made to the building to house the equipment. A third Raymond Mill and a fourth calcining kettle were added, along with additional packing equipment.

The biggest expansion was in the board plant which was rebuilt to more than double the original capacity. The expansion program was completed under the supervision of W. G. Bradley, vice-president of Blue Diamond Corporation; H.I. Waldthausen, works manager; Jack Lafever, plant superintendent; Marion Brooks, mine superintendent and Floyd Day, maintenance superintendent (Rogers, 2005).

A wallboard plant was also built just in time for construction of the Gunnery School which became Nellis Air Force Base in 1949.

CONSTANT GROWTH THROUGH THE 1950s

By 1950 the company was producing nine hundred tons a day. The mill wallboard and roller plants ran twenty-four hours a day with three shifts while the mine operated six days a week with one shift. By 1953 there were two hundred employees at the mine and mill. A second wallboard plant was added to the original plant in 1954. By 1955 there were 352 employees. The rest of the 50s had between 250 and 275 employees. In 1959 the Blue Diamond Corporation was the sixth largest producer of gypsum in the United States.

FLINTKOTE MERGER

In 1959 the Blue Diamond Mine merged with Flintkote Corporation. Flintkote acquired the water usage of the wells as well as the three aggregate plants in California and eight cement products plants with the purchase.

When Flintkote acquired the mine it did not want the responsibility of maintaining a company town and the village was sold to the Castella Corporation who specialized in buying company towns and selling the real estate to individuals. By May of 1966 all the homes were sold.

TO THE PRESENT DAY

The mine and plant changed ownership six times over the next thirty-five years.

The plant was sold to Genstar in 1981, which was taken over by Imasco, which sold the plant to Domtar in 1987. The same year, James Hardie Gypsum, an Australia based company, purchased the mine site and continued mining operations through 2004.

The Quarry Closes

Late in 1999 James Hardie Inc. offered the mine site for sale as it wanted to divest itself of U.S. properties. Early in 2002 James Hardie Gypsum, wanting to concentrate on its fiber cement business, closed the quarry at the Blue Diamond plant site and sold the properties. British Plasterboard (BPB) acquired the plant along with James Hardie's three U.S. plants located in Nashville, Las Vegas and Seattle. It later sold the Nevada plant to Certain Teed, a Canadian Company.

Developers and the Mine Today

In 2001, after a land swap with the Bureau of Land Management to create a more continuous developable property and remove land occupied by the endemic Blue Diamond cholla from development, the Australia-based home builder John Laing Homes entered into an agreement to purchase the property from James Hardie.

In November of 2001, John Laing Homes released a plan to build a residential development on the property for 20,000 people. To implement the plan and make it profitable for the developer, the land would need to be rezoned to allow for higher housing density. When John Laing Homes was unable to convince the majority of commissioners to rezone the property, they withdrew the project and developer Jim Rhodes' Gypsum Resources, LLC, leading a group of investors, began negotiations and purchased the property in 2002. They attempted to rezone 2,600 acres in order to build a housing development for 21,000 people (8,400 homes) along with a business community.

There was a great deal of opposition from the people of the Las Vegas area on the impact such a development would have on the Red Rock Canyon National Conservation Area. Chapter 19 gives details about the struggle to protect the area from future residential development. Finally in 2013, with insufficient water and the lack of a road to support his original plan, Rhodes decided to convert the acreage to a land conservation area and trade it for a less controversial property in Southern Nevada. The property was, and still is, zoned for rural use which restricts development to no more than 1500 homes (Mower 2013).

The mine is basically closed. The plant still operates with ore being transported to the site from out of state. In 2014 Rhodes negotiated with CertainTeed to provide gypsum from the existing stockpiles. Ore is currently transported by truck to the plant.

GREAT WESTERN GYPSUM COMPANY

Great Western Gypsum Company was an Arizona corporation which mined in southern California and Nevada. The company sublet property at Cottonwood Springs, today's Blue Diamond, in 1921 and set up a tent community for its employees who were mining in the area.

ARDEN PLASTER MINES

The Arden Plaster Mines operated in the southwest Las Vegas valley in the Desert Hills region from 1907-1930. Ore was hauled over a five-to-eight-mile long three-foot gauge railroad operated by the mining company southeast to the Arden Plaster Mill, a station on the Union Pacific Railroad. In the spring of 1912 the mill was almost totally destroyed by a fire and was rebuilt. In 1919 the Arden Plaster Company operation was purchased by the parent owner, U.S. Gypsum Company. By 1930 ore beds were deemed to be exhausted and the entire operation was shut down and abandoned.

SUPERINTENDENT'S HOUSE

Jackie King Appledorn (whose father was the superintendent of the mine) remembers Buster Wilson (of today's Spring Mountain Ranch) having done the rock work on their home in Blue Diamond: "...(He) did beautiful rockwork... when they built the big house for us at Blue Diamond, the one you called the 'White House,' all the rock work in that was done by Buster. He built the fireplace. He built the patios. Everything...all the sandstone. He was a very talented man, very talented man."

STELLA & REED PHELPS

Stella Phelps and her husband Reed moved to the mine in 1932 and lived at the top of the hill:

> It was right after the Depression. My husband Reed and I had moved from Idaho to California years before. He was a railroad man, but then the hard times came. There was no work. We had two children and a friend told him he could get him a job with the Blue Diamond people.
>
> Reed went to work climbing the hill to check the tramline. He did

that every day for six-and-a-half years for fifty cents an hour, and we were grateful to get it...No one can believe that he used to climb up it every day.

MINING TERMS

TIPPLE was a device used to screen the size of the ore being mined before it was loaded into mine carts known as hoppers. When a mine car entered the upper level of the tipple, the contents were dumped down a chute leading to a railroad hopper car positioned on a track running beneath the tipple. Since each car tipped over, the name was tipple. Today conveyer belts, frequently known as a Tipple are used to load ores into railroad cars.

SLUSHER is a mining method or equipment used for removing ores. Slushers have a double drum hoist and may have either an electric or compressed air motor. One cable is attached to the front scraper so it can be pulled toward the slusher and ore passes through. The other cable goes around a block securely fastened at the far end of the slusher's drift or pillar and is attached to the back of the scraper. Pulling this cable brings the bucket toward the end of the drift or pillar as the scraper is dragged across the muck pile and the ore is pulled into an ore pass or into an ore car.

JOY LOADER was invented by Joe Joy in 1919 and was the first fully mechanized loader in the mining industry. It revolutionized ore loading because shovels were no longer used to manually shovel loads into mining cars.

RAYMOND MILL is a highly efficient, closed-cycle grinding mill/pulverizing machine used for small or medium mines. Its low power consumption and small size makes it a lower investment than a ball mill.

CALCINING KETTLE is an apparatus comprised of a kettle, a heating chamber for heating the outside of the kettle, a stack for exhausting gas from the heating chamber and a duct connected at one end of the stack.

ROOM AND PILLAR, also called pillar and stall, is a mining system that extracts mined material in relatively flat-lying deposits on a horizontal plane resulting in arrays of rooms and pillars. The process is done in two phases. Pillars of untouched material are left to support the roof overburden and open areas called rooms. The pillars are then partially extracted in which the mined material is removed across a horizontal plane, creating horizontal arrays of rooms and pillars. The ore is extracted in two phases. In the first, pillars of untouched material are left to support the roof overburden; open areas or rooms are extracted underground. The pillars are then partially extracted.

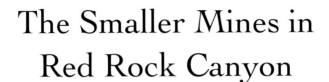

CHAPTER 15

The Smaller Mines in Red Rock Canyon

By Sharon Schaaf

The first mining in Clark County was done by Indians in the Muddy and Virgin River Valleys at the beginning of the Christian era. They found salt, soapstone and turquoise. Franciscan monks were followed by Spanish explorers in the mid-1700s; a little mining was done during that time. The oldest mine in the state was the Potosi Mine in Goodsprings. Discovered by Mormons in 1855, it produced lead.

It wasn't until 1905, when the San Pedro, Los Angeles and Salt Lake Railroad came through and established the town of Las Vegas, that mining became important to the area. Gold, silver, zinc, lead and copper deposits brought lessees and small companies to the area (Vanderburg, 1989).

Many of these mines are located in the Red Rock Canyon National Conservation Area (RRCNCA). Blue Diamond Mine is the largest and is still active; Chapter 14 told the story of this mine. This chapter will share the history of the smaller mines and prospects in the area, a few of which are still operating.

Government records and reports give us information about the minerals that were found in the mines. Newspaper articles from the early 1900s tell us about the mine owners and their contributions to the Las Vegas economy and culture. Today there are abandoned mining sites and artifacts left behind when the mines proved unprofitable. Friends of Red Rock Canyon hikers have visited the sites and found them very hard to reach. Entry into the mines was done with ladders going into deep, dark holes. Their photos and experiences provide us with an insight into what life was like for the miners in Red Rock Canyon.

The mines of Red Rock Canyon—La Madra, Quo Vadis, Midnight, Smuggler, Oliver, Lucky Strike, Iron Age and White Beauty—are all unique and have their own story to tell.

La Madra Mine and Prospects

Upstream from the dam at La Madre Springs is a miner's cabin and four shafts for the La Madra Mine. The State of Nevada does not have any documentation about this mine, which is no surprise because its name, ownership and location was changed several times before W.E. Hawkins and J.R. Hunter got title to it in the early 1900s. It was known as the Excelsior when it opened in 1876, but was abandoned in 1883 due to a lack of shipping facilities.

Apparently Hunter and Hawkins found silver ore there in 1907 and built a one-hundred-foot tunnel ("La Madra," 1907). July 1907 is the last time the

Norm Kresge

Restored cabin c. 2014

actual mine is mentioned in the newspaper. Only the comings and goings of Hunter and Hawkins are reported after that.

Hikers have visited this "mystery" mine. The cabin had been vandalized, but volunteers have replicated and restored it. They aren't sure who put up the unsafe mine sign, but there are three or four more unmarked mine openings in the area (Pene Herman, Tom Hughes, Roger Kolar, Sue Kolar, Norm Kresge and Chuck Williams, interview by author, February 2014).

Norm Kresge

Unsafe Mine Sign c. 2014

The U.S. Geological Survey and the U.S. Bureau of Mines determined that the LaMadra Wilderness Area was important enough to conduct a mineral survey in 1984. Five mines were described in their report published in 1986. White Beauty Mine is still operating and hikers have visited the Iron

Overview c. 2014

Age Prospect site; they both will be discussed later in this chapter. The Emerald Prospect, Mountain View Prospect and Karen Placer Prospect contained zinc, lead, copper and silver, but apparently not enough to be profitable (U.S. Geological Survey, 1986).

Emerald and Mountain View Prospects are both located in Red Rock Canyon near Keystone Thrust. Karen Placer is near Box Canyon, just outside the wilderness area. Since Emerald and Mountain View Prospects are located near the La Madre Fault, it is felt that the fault was a conduit for metal-bearing solutions in the area (U.S. Geological Survey, 1986).

Six adits (a horizontal passage leading into a mine used for access and drainage) ranging from eight to 105 feet, one 72-foot shaft, one caved shaft and one pit were found for Emerald. One pit and one 20-foot inclined shaft were found for Mountain View. No pits or shafts were found for Karen Placer, but a sample from the area found a small bit of fine gold (U.S. Geological Survey, 1986).

The photo taken by hikers from the LaMadra mine site looking toward White Rock gives you a good feel for how remote the site is. There are no accounts for what it was like to work in these prospects, but digging a 105-foot passage into our rock-hard soil in the early 1900s must have been a monumental task. We can only imagine what equipment the men used and how they got it there to begin with.

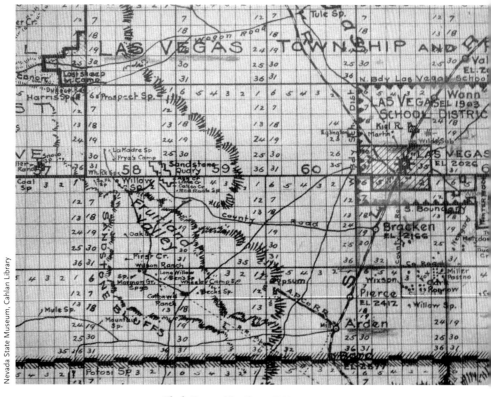

Clark County Map From 1914

QUO VADIS AND MIDNIGHT MINES

When looking for information about the Quo Vadis Mine, several names kept coming up: Arthur Frye, W.E. Hawkins, F.A. Doherty, George Garwood, the Caitlin Brothers and E.W. Clark. Only Clark was a Nevadan. Many of the *Las Vegas Age* articles about the others describe their visits to and from Las Vegas. Even county and state records for the time period are conflicting.

Newspaper reports from early 1907 show that the ore at the mine site did generate interest. In January of that year, page one of the *Las Vegas Age* reported that four tons of ore was found and that A.J. Frye was in charge of four men working the site. They optimistically predicted it would sell for $3,000 a ton ("Rich Ore," 1907). In March, the newspaper reported that two tons of "promising" ore was sent to a Salt Lake smelter (a plant that extracts metal from its ore by heating and melting) from a shaft 30-feet deep and 8-inches thick. The Caitlin Brothers and George Garwood were co-owners with Arthur Frye ("Ore Shipped," 1907).

Frye's name in connection with mining comes up again in newspaper accounts of shipments in 1911 from his Midnight Mine and the Panchita claim, co-owned with Hawkins and Doherty. It is possible that these are other names for the La Madra mine openings. One newspaper article states that the mines were located four miles west of the Stone Quarry, which would place them in the vicinity of La Madra Spring. In addition, the 1914 Clark County map indicates that Frye's camp was located adjacent to La Madra Spring ("Midnight Group," 1911).

Frye owned a lot of different businesses during his time in Las Vegas, but an incident at his First Street Saloon landed him on the front page of the October 7, 1905 edition of the *Las Vegas Age*. His night watchman, Joe Mulholland, was shot three times by saloon district "habitne" (a word not in any current dictionary) William McCarthy at 6:00 a.m. on a Sunday morning. They had quarreled the night before over a ring. Mulholland had arrested McCarthy but let him go because he felt the jail was too cold and damp for anyone to spend the night.

McCarthy got a gun from one Jack Quintell, returned to the bar and shot Mulholland when he came in. Drs. Martin and Renshaw were called but could not save him. The shooting was called premeditated and cold-blooded, and McCarthy was taken to prison in Pioche. Arthur Frye helped with the funeral arrangements for Joe ("Sunday's Killing," 1908). The incident shows that Las Vegas certainly was part of the Wild West.

The story of the Quo Vadis Mine gets confusing and sparse again. This time the mine is owned by E.W. Clark with five unpatented claims in 1915. Clark County records state that Quo Vadis produced several small shipments of high grade gold and silver from a 90-foot shaft (Vanderburg, 1989).

SMUGGLER MINE

Newspaper accounts from 1908-1909 mention the Smuggler Mine in the Charleston Mountains many times. Apparently A.L. Murphy owned the mine, and he and his wife were important to Las Vegas city life because their names pop-up four times in one year in the *Las Vegas Age*. With such a unique name, it is surprising that more wasn't written about the Smuggler Mine (*Las Vegas Age*, 1908 and 1909).

OLIVER MINE

Although there are no official government records for Oliver Mine, Oliver Ranch owner Robert Oliver and his caretaker's son Ed Price are sure that the abandoned site near Mormon Green Spring did operate in the 1880s.

Bill Durbin of the Nevada Division of Mines visited the site with several mem-

Mine opening c. 2011

bers of the Friends of Red Rock Canyon Cultural Resources Team. When Bill looked into the opening, he could see in about 20 feet where there were timbers and a cave-in.

Green-colored stone caused by copper ore surrounds the opening, leading to the rumor that Oliver Mine was filled with turquoise. Unfortunately, it wasn't. The mine opening will be closed for safety reasons (C. Williams, interviewed by author, June 10, 2013).

LUCKY STRIKE MINE

Located a little outside the RRCNCA, Lucky Strike Mine has left a lot of its history behind for us to discover. Numerous shafts, camp debris and newspaper articles tell us that this must have been a significant find for its time.

In 1907, the *Las Vegas Age* reported that C.P. Squires brought out two "great lumps" of solid galena (galena is the main ore in lead) weighing one hundred pounds each. They were on display in Judge Beal's office for all to see. The mine shaft is 100-feet deep and a drift (horizontal or inclined passage following a mine vein) would be run from the bottom as soon as a hoist could be sent to the site ("Lucky Strike," 1907).

Can dump c. 2014

The location is remote and the sample was very heavy; it was April in Las Vegas. This is another reminder of the difficult working conditions the miners faced. Friends of Red Rock Canyon hikers have found a can dump near the mine site. Since the tops are soldered, they know the cans are old. The lids have been cut open, so they assume that food and condensed milk were in them.

The mine openings have been closed with gates to protect not just people but also the wildlife in the area. The size of the gates shows how large and how deep the shafts were.

Protective gate c. 2014

The abandoned mines are now home to the bats in the conservation area and the Forest Service has put up signs reminding us of their presence. Since desert tortoises also occupy the area, some of the bat gates have special openings at the bottom so the tortoises can go in and out.

The size of some of the Lucky Strike shafts might be what put it on a unique list in 1969. That year the Civil Defense Department updated its list of national fallout shelters. Many Nevada mines were on the list and Lucky Strike was one of them. (Gypsum Cave and Blue Diamond were also on that list.) The survey included a guide with information on how to change the mine into an emergency shelter for human habitation and provide light, ventilation, water and sanitation in case of nuclear attack (Forgotten Nevada, n.d.).

IRON AGE MINE

The Iron Age Mine seems to be one that received a lot of government attention. The 1986 U.S. Geological Survey found lead and zinc in the dolomitized (dolomite is a translucent mineral made of calcium and magnesium and usually iron) limestone found at the Iron Age Prospect (a prospect is a place likely

Mine with identification number c. 2014

to hold mineral deposits). Samples in the area also found silver, tin, copper and other minerals. They also found one adit, two shafts, two inclined shafts and five pits (U.S. Geological Survey Bulletin, 1981).

The site of the mine is very hard to reach. In January of 2014, hikers Chuck Williams and Norm Kresge found seven mine openings. They have all been closed off by The Nevada State Bureau of Mines and identification numbers painted on them.

WHITE BEAUTY MINE

Located 1.2 miles off Kyle Canyon Road and covering 204 acres, the White Beauty Mine has stirred-up plenty of controversy since it started producing gypsum in 1972.

In 1986 the U.S. Geological Survey found one open pit at the site. It was 1,000-feet long, 500-feet wide and 20-feet deep. There is no report of how much gypsum came out of the mine during its three years of operation in the 1970s. Samples taken by the survey showed that the limestone was ten to 100-feet thick and about 95 percent gypsum. The original owner estimated reserves of 14 million tons and 22 million tons inferred (U.S. Geological Survey, 1986).

That kind of potential for making money explains what happened in 1994.

Jim Bilbray was a four-term congressman who had authored a bill that would include White Beauty Mine in an expansion of the Red Rock Canyon National Conservation Area. Bilbray's political consultant was Don Williams who had bought into ownership of the mine for $1 million. Williams' hope was that the Bureau of Land Management (BLM) would give him land elsewhere in a land swap deal to ensure that the site would not be actively mined. Williams wanted $8 million worth of land in exchange for the mine site.

Williams never got the deal, and his friend Jim Bilbray lost his bid for reelection. His opponent for the seat, John Ensign, made the controversy a campaign issue; and even though Bilbray said he didn't know his friend owned a mine there, he lost (Morrison, 2012).

The controversy didn't end there. The 2012 edition of the *Directory of Nevada Mine Operations* lists the mine having nine workers, operated by Las Vegas Crushing and producing gypsum (Nevada Department of Business and Industry, 2012). However, the Nevada Division of Minerals and the Nevada Bureau of Mining and Reclamation told *Las Vegas Review-Journal* reporter Jane Ann Morrison in September, 2012 that there is no record of gypsum production and not even a state mining permit for White Beauty Mine. The mine's website and Clark County assessor's records don't even agree about who owns the mine (Morrison, 2012).

The only thing that seems certain is that the current owners want to sell the land to the BLM for more than the BLM has budgeted. They are using the fear of actually mining the site to get a profitable deal from the government (Morrison, 2012).

CONCLUSION

Except for the Blue Diamond Mine, profitability wasn't in the cards for the other mines in the Red Rock Canyon National Conservation Area. Their stories are: dig a shaft and be disappointed with the findings; then abandon the site leaving behind deep holes, debris, cabins and equipment.

The U.S. Geological Survey concluded that the minerals found in the LaMadra Wilderness were the result of the faults in the area producing veins that are only pathways for metal-bearing solutions. Also, they are minerals that can be mined and shipped from locations much closer to where they are needed (U.S. Geological Survey, 1986).

Hikers Pene Herman, Tom Hughes, Sue Kolar, Roger Kolar, Norm Kresge and Chuck Williams have visited these mine sites. Most of the time they know where the site is located. However, sometimes they happen upon a mine

Filled in mine openings c. 2014

opening in an area they knew had been mined but aren't sure exactly where the opening is. Some of the mine openings are so difficult to get to, they wonder how the miners reached them along with their equipment. Using burros is their conclusion.

The National Park Service has identified more hazardous sites that need to be filled in, but that will take time and money. None of the open mines in the Red Rock Canyon National Conservation Area are listed to be filled in at this time. If there are no bats in the area, the State of Nevada or the National Park Service will close off the openings for safety (Personal interview with the hikers, February, 2014).

It is hard for us to imagine heavy equipment being hauled into Red Rock Canyon and deep holes dug into its mountains. But these mines and the people who owned them and worked in them are part of the history of Red Rock Canyon.

ENDNOTES

A special thank you to Pene Herman, Tom Hughes, Sue Kolar, Roger Kolar, Norm Kresge and Chuck Williams for sharing their experiences and photos with me. Their knowledge of Red Rock Canyon helped me understand the impact of mining in the conservation area. Thank you also to Sue Kolar, Norm Kresge, Chuck Williams and Dan Wray for permission to use their photos.

CHAPTER 16

Others Who Left Their Mark

By Norm Kresge and Chuck Williams

NAYLOR PROPERTY

Orrin Payne Naylor and his wife Ruth homesteaded 40 acres of land in the early 1900s that would later become part of what is now Bonnie Springs Ranch. They received the homestead patent on November 21, 1921. It is unknown if the Naylors used the property as a ranch or retreat.

In December 1922 the Naylors briefly sold the land to Richard Bosteed but repurchased the property in November of 1924 (Clark County Recorder Book 9, Pages 102-103 & Book 10, Page 361).

In December 1926 the Naylors sold the property to Frank and Della Wait (Clark County Recorder Book 12, Page 46). Based on newspaper accounts, the property was likely used for moonshining in the late 1920s ("One of Six Caught in Federal Dry Raid out on Bail," 1928).

Bill and Edith Morgan acquired the land from the Waits on February 28, 1939, adding the 40 acres to their existing 80 acre ranch (Clark County Recorder Book 25, Page 283). A week later the Morgans sold the entire property to T.S. Thebo (see chapter 6). The Morgan/Thebo property changed hands over the years and was eventually purchased by Bonnie McGaugh from a Dr. Fortier (see chapter 8) who developed it into today's Bonnie Springs.

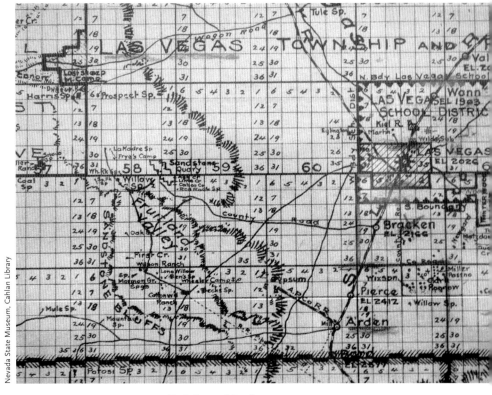

Clark County Map from 1914

La Madre Spring Dam and Structures - Las Vegas Archery Club

The La Madre Spring area was the site of several mining claims (see Chapter 15) and was identified as Frye's Camp on the 1914 Clark County map. Arthur Frye was one of several individuals associated with the claims. The exact location of the camp is not known but the 1914 map shows the camp located below the spring source and south of the mines.

Presently there are foundations a short distance from where La Madre Creek has been dammed. The dam itself has an inscription written in the concrete cap, "LVA 1968," indicating the Las Vegas Archery Club which used the site at one time. The area around the dam and foundations may well have been where Frye's camp was located as there is limited suitable building space upstream.

The foundations and dam site were homesteaded by Jerome Coleman and Nelson Noon who received a patent for 120 acres on August 18, 1937. The land was eventually purchased by Theodore and Jeannie Couch. The Bureau of Land Management then acquired the land by doing a land swap with the

Couches on November 3, 1972 (BLM Land Records).

We know a little of the Couch history from an email by Linda Nations concerning a phone interview she conducted when she worked at Red Rock Canyon:

> ...The man who told me about it was an employee of Southwest Gas Co. at the time and said his family had owned the old archery area, and his dad and uncle had built the houses that are now just foundations. The dad or uncle had worked for an asphaltic tile company and some of the asphaltic tiles he installed could still be seen covering at least one of the house foundations.
>
> He said his dad and uncle had each built themselves a house on the east side of the trail, above the ravine, and another house on the west side of the trail for their mother. She wanted nothing to do with living out there in the middle of nowhere and never moved in. The men dynamited one of the agave roasting pits thinking they'd find "Indian treasure" in it, but were disappointed. They left the other pits intact. They knew of the very old cabin (now a ruin) and mine shaft on the uphill slope.

Jim Cribbs, Red Rock Canyon Ranger, provided additional information in an email about the Couch's and the Archery Club:

> ...Mr. Couch did build and live in the homes, and he built the dam for their water supply. This was confirmed by Ms. L. Rigoni; she was one of

La Madre Dam c. 2014

Norm Kresge

Inscription on top of dam "LVA" (Las Vegas Archery Club) c. 2014

Norm Kresge

The dam was removed in 2014 because it was located in a wilderness area.

Norm Kresge

East foundation c. 2014

Chuck Williams

West foundation c. 2014

Chuck Williams

the original members [of the Archery Club] and her husband was president. Mr. Couch built the dam, but the club maintained it. One of their members did initial and date the dam. The lower house was still standing and they were using it. It was vandalized after they left.

At present there are only two foundations, one on each side of the trail. Above the foundation on the east is a small concrete slab that may have contained a water storage tank. An exposed water pipe seems to be leading to that location.

Gypsum mine prospect c. 2014

The old road bed c. 2014

Old Road and Gypsum Prospects
East of Blue Diamond

On the hill just east of the town of Blue Diamond there is an old road that has been bulldozed. What looks to be prospects have been cut into the mountainside at several locations. I asked George Bogdanovich, who worked at the Blue Diamond Gypsum Mine, if he knew anything about the road. He replied by email:

> In response to your question about the road, I remember Blue Diamond Corp. doing some exploratory work on the east side about the mid-1950s. They were grading a road on the top [that was] visible from the plant. Nothing ever came from it as far as I know.

We assume that gypsum was not present in enough quantity for Blue Diamond Corporation to pursue mining and the road is no longer accessible by vehicles. The land is now part of Red Rock Canyon National Conservation Area.

Inscription Rock

Near the base of the escarpment in the area of Spring Mountain Ranch, we have hiked to a promontory nicknamed Inscription Hill because a boulder is located there that has been inscribed. That boulder has become known as Inscription Rock.

Inscription Rock c. 2014

No one knows why the men whose names appear on the rock would leave the inscription except for the need of people to leave their "mark" and be remembered by those who come after.

On the rock is the date April 19, 1916. Then you have the two names and finally the words "saw minne hare." We have interpreted that to mean that on their walk to the promontory, the men saw a lot of rabbits. It appears the names on the rock are German, and this may have been their message to us. That is only a guess.

In less than one year, the message on Inscription Rock will be 100 years old—quite a milestone.

CIVILIAN CONSERVATION CORPS

There were three Civilian Conservation Corps (CCC) Camps in the Red Rock area in the late 1930s: Mount Charleston (F-4), Las Vegas (DG-122) and Fish and Wildlife (FWS-4).

The Division of Grazing (DG), which became the Grazing Service in 1939, operated the Las Vegas Camp which supplied the men and resources for projects in the Red Rock Canyon area. The Grazing Service would later merge with the General Land Office to form the Bureau of Land Management.

Construction of Camp DG-122 began in August of 1938 with a 40-man team from CCC Camp DG-45 out of St. George, Utah. The camp was located on property owned by Frank Beam adjacent to the proposed municipal airport (Warm Springs Road and I-15) on a "flat, arid and dust covered site." Local unions supplied the skilled labor, with the CCC providing the manual labor, to construct 23 portable buildings and a baseball diamond.

In November 1938, CCC Company 3542 from Xenia, Ohio arrived by train to the partially completed camp and began work on grazing-related projects. The placement of a grazing camp in Las Vegas was questioned by various officials and some locals. Special Investigator J.C. Reddoch was sent to Las Vegas in December 1938 to gather information. Reddoch found that the proposed camp was supposed to be built at Searchlight, Nevada. He surmised that politics had something to do with the Las Vegas location. His report to the Director of the CCC stated that the area within a thirty-mile radius of Las Vegas was wholly unsuited for grazing and that poor judgment was exercised in locating the camp in Las Vegas. Even surrounded in controversy, the Las Vegas Camp remained open.

That first season, the camp workers constructed 100 miles of truck trails, drilled 10 water wells with storage and pump facilities, installed several miles

White Rock Spring guzzler c. 2012

Chuck Williams

Lower Brownstone Dam after a rain c. 2012

Norm Kresge

Upper Brownstone Dam from above c. 2015

Norm Kresge

Upper dam from below c. 2015

Roger Kolar

Water trough upper Brownstone Dam c. 2015

of fence lines and developed numerous springs. There were three roads proposed in the work plan: one into Red Rock Canyon, a road from Las Vegas to Pahrump and another from Corn Creek Ranch to Mormon Wells. The Red Rock Canyon and Pahrump roads may have been tied together and became what is now known as the Rocky Gap Road which runs from Willow Springs to Lovell Canyon. The 1937 Clark County Map does not show a road leading to Pahrump, but maps printed after World War II show Rocky Gap Road designated as State Highway 85 with spur roads running to the Sandstone Quarry and White Rock Spring.

In April 1939, the camp celebrated the sixth anniversary of the founding of the CCC with an open house and baseball game against the Las Vegas Elks. Early that summer, Company 3542 was sent to White Pine County. That fall, Company 2557, consisting of men from Ohio and West Virginia, transferred to Las Vegas from Pipe Springs, Arizona.

During the next two years, work continued on the Red Rock truck roads, well-drilling and rodent control on ranches and other infested areas in the county. They established Spike Camps (temporary camps so the men did not have to drive back and forth to Las Vegas) at Corn Creek Ranch for biological surveys and in Searchlight for well-drilling and range improvements.

It is assumed that during the three years the camp was in operation, the concrete water guzzlers at Willow Spring and White Rock Spring were constructed along with the masonry dams in Brownstone Canyon.

On April 5, 1941, the men and officers of Company 2557 held another open house to celebrate the founding of the CCC eight years earlier. The general public was allowed to view the camp facilities and were served a light lunch. Weather postponed a planned softball game, but the men were able to perform a formal retreat for the guests.

Two months later, the Las Vegas Camp was closed and the men moved to Corn Creek for two months before transferring to Ruby Lake in northern Nevada in September. The Las Vegas community seems to have appreciated the work of Companies 3542 and 2557 according to an editorial in the December 13, 1940 *Las Vegas Age*:

> The prevailing opinion that CCC operations have in general been wasteful, inefficient and not well-directed is disproven by an inspection of the work done by Las Vegas Camp 122...Las Vegas certainly owes a vote of thanks to State Superintendent Tom Miller, Superintendent Jameson and Vegas CCC 122, which we must admit, have done something really fine and constructive for Clark County.

The CCC was formally disbanded on June 30, 1942 (White, 2003 and Kolvet & Ford, 2006).

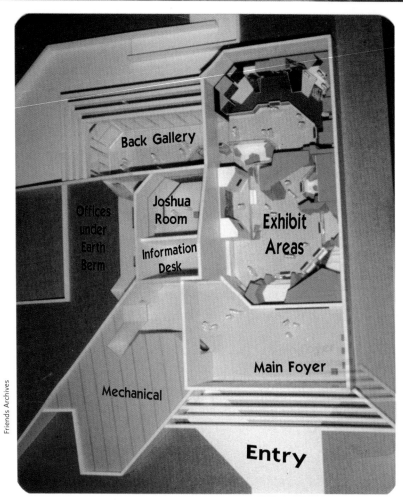

Back Gallery

Offices under Earth Berm

Joshua Room

Information Desk

Exhibit Areas

Mechanical

Main Foyer

Entry

(top) Visitor Center Front Desk c. 1982 (bottom) Visitor Center construction schematic c. 1981

CHAPTER 17

Friends of Red Rock Canyon

By Cam Camburn with Pat Williams

The mission of Friends of Red Rock Canyon
is the preservation and enrichment of
Red Rock Canyon National Conservation Area
and the public lands of southern Nevada.

Oh, the times they were a'changing for the Red Rock Canyon Recreation Lands.

A Visitor Center, the first of its kind within the Bureau of Land Management (BLM), opened on May 22, 1982 with great fanfare. The Visitor Center, intended to have ten full-time staff members, made do with a staff of five, resulting in the new building being open Friday through Monday. The BLM staff assigned to the new center was focused on a new era for the agency: interpretive programing, resource education and community engagement. Within the community, there were people who cared about the Canyon and would help with the BLM's new direction.

FRIENDS OF RED ROCK CANYON IS ESTABLISHED

In September 1984, the BLM and a dozen or so people assembled with the intention of forming a Friends group. Nothing like this had been attempted

Original Visitor Center under construction in 1981

within the BLM before, so there was much discussion and speculation on the purpose of the Society (FORRC was referred to as a "Society" in the original Articles of Incorporation and in the early organizational By-Laws). Joel Mur, Red Rock's first Chief Interpretive Specialist (and possibly the first Interpretive Specialist within the BLM), summarized that, "Friends of Red Rock Canyon (FORRC) would allow BLM to provide activities and information to the public that could not otherwise be provided" (Fleming, 1984). FORRC minutes and other first-hand accounts of this initial meeting show that their overall vision of *"what **could** be"* worked and has since served as a role model for more than 55 Friends groups.

Anga Rebane, FORRC President, and Joel Mur, BLM Chief Interpretive Specialist, RRCRL, signing first agreement in 1984

THE EARLY DAYS

The newly formed organization and the BLM immediately began planning for the group's sustainability via fundraising, bringing the Las Vegas community to Red Rock Canyon in an ownership role and establishing a plan for training the many volunteers needed to maintain and sustain the Recreation Lands. The BLM had a contractual agreement in place with the Southwest Natural and Cultural Heritage Association (SNCHA) to provide for the sale of interpretive material in the new Visitor Center (Hunsaker, 2012). FORRC immediately stepped up with t-shirt designs to be sold in the fledgling store. The merchandise sales agreements with SNCHA and later with Red Rock Canyon Interpretive Association

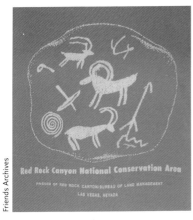

*One of the original Friends
t-shirt designs c. 1990*

(RRCIA) would prove to be one of the first major sources of income supporting Red Rock Canyon programs and services. The sales agreements generated funds ranging from $20,000 to $50,000 annually between 1984 and 2014 when the sales agreement ended. Donation boxes, first placed in the Visitor Center and later expanded to the Scenic Drive, would eventually generate over $100,000 in direct aid for Red Rock Canyon.

Another early priority was training the volunteers desperately needed for staffing the visitor center, leading hikes, providing interpretive programs, maintaining the trails and helping coordinate and staff community events. The founding members and the BLM staff created a Volunteer Manual that included an overview of the Society and the BLM, as well as information about the (then) eight volunteer activities, the six active FORRC committees and a synopsis of the history of both Red Rock Canyon and Las Vegas. Also included in the manual was information on the flora and fauna, area geology and material about the Canyon's archeology, cultural resources and Native American history. The FORRC volunteers were encouraged and trained to be an extension of the limited BLM staff.

The last part of the equation, getting the community involved at the Canyon, began almost immediately with a FORRC sponsored Mother's Day 10K Fun Run drawing over 700 participants. There

1985 Fun Run

Moenkopi sign installation in 1994 with John Lennon and Kathy August (BLM) and Harley Decker (FORRC)

Kate Sorom (BLM) and Maria Lolich (FORRC Volunteer) at the Front Desk in 2002

were also Star Watch programs with over 500 attending, school groups making field trips to Lost Creek and Fossil Ridge, volunteer-led hikes and the photo and art contests. The Visitor Center began staying open five days a week—Friday through Tuesday—in March 1985 due to the additional volunteer staffing. The Visitor Center, thanks to volunteer support and budget increases, would finally be open seven days a week in July 1988—slightly over six years from its grand opening in 1982.

FORRC was making a positive impact on the Canyon. The volunteer driven organization was funding things such as trails signage, front desk remodeling in the visitor center, new carpeting for the Joshua Room and purchasing needed supplies and equipment for the BLM. The members were also donating thousands of hours of their time and talents to sustain and improve the Recreation Lands. The vision of the founding parents was beginning to come true: there was financial and volunteer support and the community felt ownership and responsibility for Red Rock Canyon. How could this get any better?

GROWING WITH THE CANYON

Visitors continued to flock to Red Rock Canyon—over 80,000 people came through the gates in 1987! How could the Canyon sustain this visitation boom? The BLM decided that Red Rock Canyon needed another site-based nonprofit dedicated to fundraising and education. Red Rock Canyon Interpretive Association was created with a start-up loan of $10,000 from FORRC.

In 1990, the Red Rock Recreation Lands became Nevada's first National Conservation Area and the Red Rock Scenic Drive was designated a Scenic Byway.

Senator Harry Reid dedicating the Conservation Area – April 1991

The BLM received additional appropriated funding to add more staff to the increasingly popular area, including two law enforcement rangers. With the increased popularity, the need for FORRC volunteers went up exponentially. Graffiti was being reported in areas such as Lost Creek and Brownstone Canyon resulting in Brownstone Canyon having entry barriers installed by the Seabees. The archeologically and geologically important Cave Canyon area was being heavily damaged by graffiti. The damage resulted in multiple clean-ups with the solution being the installation of metal gates intended to prevent

further damage to the fragile caves. Sadly, most of the metal gates were forcibly removed and the graffiti continues through the present day.

More and more visitors were coming to the newly created and expanded Red Rock Canyon National Conservation Area. FORRC expanded their funding to include BLM staff and volunteer training, publications such as the Lost Creek/Children's Discovery Trail Guide as well as additional Visitor Center remodeling and upgrades. The Homer Morgan Bicycle Pavilion, funded by FORRC, the Las Vegas Bicycle Club and the BLM, was constructed and eased some of the congestion in the Visitor Center. The Pavilion would later be the main staging area for community events such

Irreparable damage in the Cave Canyon area
c. 2000

(top) 1993 construction of the Homer Morgan Pavilion
(bottom) Utilizing the Pavilion for a FORRC meeting c. 2005. Left to Right – Barb Jorgensen, Lorrie Vavak, Dale Kavula, Pat Williams

as the Tortoise Trot, Red Rock Day, Make a Difference Day and Harvest Fest.

FORRC provided majority funding for the much-needed remodeling and expansion of the Visitor Center in 1997 and 1998. The Friends Room, which increased the public space by one third, was constructed and utilized for classes, meetings, contests and eventually office space. The former Joshua Room's conversion to sales space for the RRCIA Gift Store was made possible by a $10,000 donation from FORRC to cover their funding shortfall.

The Tortoise Habitat was opened in March 1995, and FORRC members played a key role in providing both staffing and visitor education for the

Registration for the Tortoise Trot Trail Run in 2004

(top) Dan Wray (FORRC) and Max c. 1996
(bottom) Vera Wray (FORRC) and Maxine
c. 1996

Sue Kolar (FORRC) measuring Hugo in 2014 as
part of the tortoises' annual check-ups

The girls dining in 2014

A 2014 field trip includes a visit with the desert tortoise.

threatened species. The current habitat is home to ten desert tortoises consisting of eight females and two males – the females live in a harem-like enclosure; and the males, Max and Hugo, have their own kingdoms separated from the females by a metal wall. FORRC provides all funding for the care of these gentle reptiles, lovingly referred to as the "Rock Stars," as well as scheduling the dedicated team of caretakers.

In 1997 the FORRC Environmental Education committee expanded its scope to fund the Explore the Great Outdoors teacher workshops and provide funding for bussing at-risk schoolchildren to Red Rock for educational field trips. To date, over 60,000 children have been able to visit Red Rock Canyon due to the FORRC funded bus grants.

FORRC developed and funded a project in 2001 to restore the Children's Discovery Trail and Lost Creek Waterfall as well as protect the spring and riparian area. The spur trail also supports a wealth of cultural history and is the home to a rare desert spring and meadow. The major improvement was the construction of a wood walkway and deck costing over $23,000 funneling visitors away from the

Wildlife at Lost Creek

A volunteer in 2005 with trimmings from the restored riparian area

creek and off the easily damaged meadow. The boardwalk allows visitors to view both areas while protecting the fragile setting. The area is heavily used for elementary school educational purposes and is also popular with locals and tourists alike.

In addition to the walkway and viewing deck, Friends of Red Rock Canyon volunteers installed fencing around the Lost Creek parking lot and along the trail to block braided trails and protect a Native American rock shelter and rock art site.

IT TAKES A VILLAGE

Local support of FORRC and Red Rock continued to grow with increased attendance at volunteer work events, material donations, as well as direct financial support. The first Red Rock Day was held in 1999 with over 400 participants. Additional events, such as National Public Lands Day and Make a Difference Day, were added to the roster—the Las Vegas community was putting their money and talents where their hearts were: Red Rock Canyon. Locally based corporations such as REI, Southwest Airlines, Station Casinos and Pepsi to name a few, participated or sponsored volunteer events in partnership with FORRC and the BLM.

A local housing developer, William Bone of Sunrise Colony Homes, approached the BLM and FORRC in 1999 about making a donation to benefit Red Rock Canyon. The proposal was to donate $250 to FORRC for every building lot sold in their new planned community, Siena Sunrise. This generous act, ending with the build-out of Siena in 2004, resulted in adding over $260,000 to FORRC's ability to fund projects at Red Rock Canyon.

The Howard Hughes Corporation/Summerlin (Summerlin) was, and continues to be, a concerned neighbor of Red Rock Canyon: starting with the lands transfer (see chapter 19) that provided a critical buffer zone, Summerlin has funded trail signage and cosponsored many volunteer events.

FORRC gained another incredible community partner when REI opened their Las Vegas and Henderson stores: REI, FORRC and the BLM sponsored the first "Make a Difference Day" at Red Rock in 2005 with 85 volunteers working to restore wildfire damage. This event later grew to over 400 participants who restored boardwalks, rebuilt trails, painted bathrooms and removed invasive vegetation. REI has also awarded FORRC more than $85,000 in grant awards for area preservation and user outreach.

Knowing that the Sunrise Colony donations would, like all good things, come to an end, the FORRC board of directors began exploring other revenue sources to fund the increasing needs of Red Rock Canyon. Norman Wolin, a Friends member, volunteered to lead the efforts on obtaining a charitable license plate for FORRC. His efforts began in 2002 and in 2008 FORRC had a charitable license plate, believed to be the first associated with a BLM site. Through the volunteer efforts of Norman Wolin and the support of Nevada residents, the license plate sales have generated over $250,000 in funding to continue our goal of preserving and enriching Red Rock Canyon.

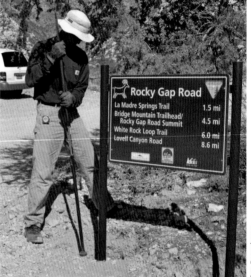

(top) Original Summerlin funded buff trail signage installed in 2000 (center) Mark Beauchamp, FORRC Volunteer, replacing trail signage in 2012 funded by Summerlin, REI and FORRC (bottom) Victorious Planters at Make A Difference Day 2005

AND IT TAKES FRIENDS

The original mission of Friends of Red Rock Canyon was to provide, fund, train and oversee a cadre of volunteers who could assist the BLM in the management and protection of Red Rock Canyon. Over the years, FORRC has funded trail signage, built boardwalks, worked on trails maintenance, removed graffiti, trained volunteers and BLM staff, cared for desert tortoises, sponsored community events and so much more.

The organization has more than lived up to the hopes and expectations defined at that first meeting in 1984. David Hunsaker, past BLM manager for the Red Rock Canyon Recreation Lands, wrote an article for the BLM about the value of Friends Groups in 2012:

Today, FORRC members continue their commitment to preserve, protect and enrich Red Rock Canyon National

(top) 2008 MADD registration (center) $10,000 grant check from REI presented to Friends of Red Rock Canyon in 2008 (bottom) License Plate with Norman Wolin in 2008

All Photos Friends Archives

Conservation Area. The organization now does all the things that the BLM could only dream about more than 25 years ago, including removing graffiti, picking up trash, maintaining trails and the visitor center grounds, leading hikes, staffing the information desk, monitoring cultural sites, sponsoring an annual art [and photo] show, and participating in community events. In addition, the organization provides more than $100,000 annually for program support, volunteer and staff training, and supplies and equipment. In a very real sense, the FORRC provided a roadmap for the BLM to work with others who desired personal involvement in managing public lands. The joint 1984 experiment would prove to be a role model for other groups across the nation including:

• Trail Tenders, Inc., in Baker City, Oregon (National Historic Oregon Trail Interpretive Center-Flagstaff Hill);

• Grand Staircase-Escalante Partners in Kanab, Utah (Grand Staircase-Escalante National Monument);

• Friends of the Desert Mountains in Palm Desert and the Coachella Valley, California (Santa Rosa and San Jacinto Mountains National Monument);

• Pompeys Pillar Historical Association in Billings, Montana (Pompeys Pillar National Monument);

• Friends of the Cascade-Siskiyou National Monument in Ashland, Oregon (Cascade-Siskiyou National Monument);

• Anza Trail Coalition in Tubac, Arizona (Juan Bautista de Anza National Historic Trail);

• El Camino Real de Tierra Adentro Trail Association in Las Cruces, New Mexico (El Camino Real de Tierra Adentro National Historic Trail);

• Snake River Raptors in Boise, Idaho (Morley Nelson Snake River Birds of Prey National Conservation Area) and many others (Hunsaker, 2012).

Authors note: This was a reasonably complete listing when Mr. Hunsaker wrote the article in 2012. The Friends Grassroots Network supporting our National Conservation Lands has since grown to over 55 organizations and is still increasing.

RECOGNITION OF OUR ACCOMPLISHMENTS

Volunteers are the backbone of Red Rock Canyon National Conservation Area: they donate their time, passion and talents towards the preservation of this remarkable place. The amazing thing about volunteers is that they generally do not expect or need awards to validate their efforts. However, it is worth noting that our members and the organization have been presented with some substantial awards through the years.

The Take Pride in America National Awards Program recognized the FORRC Natural Resource Committee in 1991 and the Public Lands Institute also honored the Committee in 2011 as the "Volunteer Group of the Year." The National Office of the BLM presented the "Making a Difference on the Public Lands" Award to FORRC volunteers in 2002, 2004 and 2010 and to the Cultural Resource Committee in 2010. Five FORRC volunteers have received the Presidential Call to Service Awards, recognizing their 4,000 hours of volunteer service. The Conservation Lands Foundation "Advocate of the Year" award for 2011 and the BLM "National Volunteers Milestone Award" for 2013 have also been presented to a FORRC volunteer.

However, the awards and recognition would not have been possible without…

THOSE WHO PAVED THE WAY

Red Rock Canyon's health and future is due to those who imagined what could be. Their goals of preservation, education and community ownership has been an inspiration for everyone who has worked to protect and preserve Red Rock Canyon National Conservation Area. Thank you to the following for providing the grassroots vision for Friends of Red Rock Canyon.

Anga Rebane (FORRC)	Joel Mur (BLM)	Frank Tepper (FORRC)
Bill Civish (BLM)	Howard Booth (FORRC)	Dave Hunsaker (BLM)
Chuck Ward (BLM)	Carol Ward (BLM)	Elaine Billets (FORRC)
Mike Sullens (FORRC)	Homer Morgan (FORRC)	Chris Miller (BLM)
Kathy Clinesmith (FORRC)	Barbara Wolin (FORRC)	Norman Wolin (FORRC)
Harley Decker (FORRC)	Jim Rathbun (FORRC)	Lois Rohay (FORRC)

It would be impossible to list everyone, both private citizens and dedicated BLM staff members, associated with the creation and perpetuation of Friends of Red Rock Canyon. The listing would be longer than this book. The thousands of heroes and volunteers of Red Rock Canyon know who they are. This chapter is just a small attempt at providing an overview of a vision that worked.

FORRC Milestones

- 1985 – First Volunteer Awards Banquet

- 1985 – *The Desert Trumpet*, Friends newsletter, begins publication

- 1986 – First annual Red Rock Clean-Up removing six tons of litter

- 1987 – First Volunteer Manual created and distributed

- 1988 – Red Rock Canyon Interpretive Association founded

- 1988 – Cooperative agreement regarding merchandise sales established with Red Rock Canyon Interpretive Association. This agreement ended in 2014

- 1988 – Visitor Center opens seven days a week, facilitated by volunteer staffing on the Information Desk

- 1991 – Red Rock Canyon National Conservation Area Dedication Ceremony

- 1994 – Funded and installed Moenkopi Trail interpretive panels

- 1995 – Tortoise Habitat is dedicated.

- 2000 – FORRC Volunteer Appreciation Program implemented

- 2000 – Secured funding from The Howard Hughes Corporation/Summerlin for trailhead signage

- 2000 – Cultural Resource Team Monitoring, Documentation and Protection reestablished in 2000; to date, archival documentation on 20 significant sites completed

- 2001 – Dedication Walkway established

- 2001 – First permanent memorial for 9/11 Attack dedicated at Red Rock Canyon

- 2001 – Friends funded the Lost Creek Boardwalk

- 2005 – Friends of Red Rock Canyon and REI co-sponsor the first Make a Difference Day at Red Rock Canyon with 85 participants

- 2007 – First part-time employee hired

- 2008 – New Visitor Center groundbreaking

- 2008 – Red Rock Canyon license plate became the first charitable plate associated with a BLM facility

- 2010 – Grand opening of the new Visitor Center

- 2010 – Inaugural issue of *The Rock* quarterly magazine published

- 2013 – Graffiti removal team re-established

- 2014 – Landscape Team re-established after a six year hiatus

CHAPTER 18

Red Rock Canyon Interpretive Association

By Crystalaura Jackson

The mission of the Red Rock Canyon Interpretive Association (RRCIA) is to enhance the recreational, educational and interpretive programs of the Bureau of Land Management (BLM) by providing materials and services that promote an understanding and appreciation of the natural history, cultural history and sciences of Red Rock Canyon National Conservation Area.

RRCIA was established in 1988. It was the first site-specific cooperating association for the Department of Interior, Bureau of Land Management (U.S. Department of the Interior, 2003). With the encouragement of two BLM employees, Interpretive Specialist Joel Mur and Area Manager Runore Wycoff, local publisher K.C. DenDooven was the driving force in getting the new organization started. The original Board of Directors consisted of Mr. DenDooven and two other local business leaders, Danny Riddle and Neil Slocum.

The Friends of Red Rock Canyon supported the start-up of RRCIA with the loan of $10,000 seed money (Danny Riddle, internal memo, February 2000).

EARLY HISTORY OF THE ORGANIZATION

The initial focus of the RRCIA was to operate the small, 400-square-foot retail operation in the bookstore at the area then called Red Rock Canyon Recreation Lands. RRCIA offered books and other sales items to the public to educate visitors about Red Rock Canyon and the surrounding areas. They also helped with printing brochures, developing exhibits and creating a reference library. In 1990, the same year Red Rock Canyon National Conservation Area was officially designated, the organization hired its first Executive Director, Denise Wiegand. The following year, RRCIA published its first two guides, *The Red Rock Canyon Trail Guide* and *The Red Rock Geological Map*.

The former Association store at Red Rock Canyon c. 2000

By 1992, RRCIA was offering Junior Ranger and other interpretive programs with a small staff. The organization's offices were housed in a small space adjacent to the gift store.

Some of the numerous awards and achievements attained by the Association include the National Association of Interpretation's Excellence in Interpretive Support Award (1994), BLM's Volunteer of the Year Award (1997), Nevada Governor's Tourism Development Award (1998), as well as a special Congressional Recognition from Senator Harry Reid for innovative contributions to the community and preservation of Nevada's Natural Resources (1997) (Internal document, 2001). In 2010 RRCIA received an Excellence Award from the Association of Partners for Public Lands for Education Programs, and in 2011 it received the Partnership of the Year Award from the BLM.

FEE COLLECTION

In 1996, the U.S. Congress passed the Recreational Fee Demonstration Program (RFDP) Act (National Park Service, 2002). Somewhat controversial at the time, under this Act an entrance fee of five dollars was charged for the first time at Red Rock Canyon NCA; it was implemented in 1997. RRCIA contracted with the BLM to operate the new fee station. Under the RFDP, 80 percent of the fees collected were returned to the region to assist the Department of Interior in the maintenance of the Red Rock Canyon Conservation Area (Department of the Interior, 2005).

The Fee Demonstration Program was originally a three-year experiment, later extended until 2005. As part of the 2005 Omnibus Appropriations Bill, a new authority under the Federal Lands Recreation Enhancement Act (FLREA) mandated that fees be charged only at federal sites that offer "a specified minimum level of development" (Dutton, 1997). Congress has continued to authorize fee collection on public lands under FLREA.

PROGRAMS

Executive Director Denise Wiegand left in 2001, and the organization was led by Pat Williams until 2002. RRCIA continued publishing original guides and collaborating with the BLM for interpretive projects, including *Plants of Red Rock Canyon* in 2001, the first field guide specific to the area. A Red Rock Canyon video was produced in 2001 and RRCIA worked with the BLM on an extensive Wayside Signage Project in 2001. *The Red Rock Canyon Trail Guide* was updated and reprinted in 2001. The organization also partnered with the BLM and Friends of Red Rock Canyon to train volunteers to lead programs and hikes in an effort to increase program availability to the public (Correspondence, May 2, 2001).

In 2000, RRCIA expanded operations to include a retail store at the historic Guard Station in the Spring Mountains National Recreation Area, near the town of Mt. Charleston. The organization also organized naturalist and volunteer-led hikes in the Spring Mountains. In 2003, a separate nonprofit organization

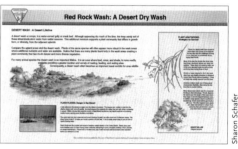

One of the signs placed as part of the Wayside Interpretive Project

was formed to take on operations outside of Red Rock Canyon NCA. This organization, originally called the Southern Nevada Interpretive Association, is now called the Southern Nevada Conservancy and still operates as a sister organization to Red Rock Canyon Interpretive Association.

ROLE IN PROJECT MANAGEMENT

A new Executive Director, Jackson Ramsey, Ph.D., was hired in 2002. At that time, the BLM began preliminary planning for a new expanded Red Rock Canyon Visitor Center, made possible by funding through the Southern Nevada Public Lands Management Act (SNPLMA). Due to the lengthy construction process for the new visitor center, the old visitor center was remodeled and

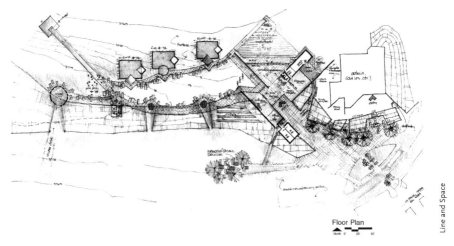

Floor Plan

Artist's rendering of the new Red Rock Canyon Visitor Center

enhanced interpretive displays were installed in 2006. This was the first major project RRCIA managed for the BLM.

Under Dr. Ramsey's leadership, RRCIA played a significant role in the interpretive planning and design of the new visitor center. RRCIA's involvement in the planning process marked an increased role and the growth of the organization's expertise in project management and interpretive planning. When Jackson Ramsey retired in 2008, then Associate Director Blaine Benedict was selected by the Board of Directors as the new Executive Director.

In October 2009, the new Red Rock Canyon Visitor Center opened, including the Elements Gift Shop operated by RRCIA. The increased retail space led to a robust increase in sales, allowing the organization to increase interpretive programming, community outreach and aid to BLM. The final phase of the new visitor center construction was the opening of the outdoor interpretive exhibits in April 2010.

RETAIL OPERATIONS AND INTERPRETATION

Proceeds from Elements Gift Shop are used to provide interpretive programming to enhance the visitor experience at Red Rock Canyon. Each year, RRCIA and the BLM work together to create an Annual Plan and establish priorities for interpretive programming. Together, the BLM and RRCIA's staff of certified Interpretive Naturalists offer frequent school field trips, guided hikes, tabletop exhibits and patio talks.

RRCIA has worked with a local high school developing a Biological Field Station program, offered programs at senior centers, and offered outdoor experiences for youth from diverse backgrounds and interests. This includes students from public and private schools, the juvenile justice system and underserved populations, as well as youth from leadership, achievement and special interest programs. RRCIA also plays a major role in the popular annual Las Vegas Science and Technology Festival as a planning affiliate and host venue.

RRCIA provides other assistance to the BLM as requested. Such projects have included visitor information publications, the restoration of Red Spring, maintenance of visitor center exhibits and graffiti removal from fragile rock art found in Red Rock Canyon.

OTHER PROGRAMS

The Mojave Max Education Program began under the umbrella of a conservation initiative to provide public information and education for the Clark County Desert Conservation Program. The first Mojave Max Emergence Contest took place in 2000. In 2003, the program was awarded first place for the Excellence in Interpretation and Environmental Education Award by the BLM. In 2005, the program expanded with a formal curriculum for assemblies and classroom presentations focused on desert tortoise education and the ecology of the Mojave Desert. Each year RRCIA staff and volunteers present programs to thousands of schoolchildren and also bring the Mojave Max program to the community through outreach.

Mojave Max is both a real desert tortoise living at the Red Rock Canyon Visitor Center tortoise habitat and a mascot who serves as a "spokes-tortoise" and outreach ambassador. As part of Clark County's Desert Conservation Program, RRCIA collaborates with the Clark County School District and the BLM to provide in-class presentations, teacher lesson plans, educational resources, Mojave Max school assemblies and the Mojave Max Emergence Contest. The program has also included art and poetry contests for children.

RRCIA has been a long-time supporter of the BLM's Wild Horse and Burro Program. Executive Director Blaine Benedict adopted Jackson the Red Rock Canyon Burro in 2012 through the Adoption Program. Other individuals who work closely with the organization adopted two wild mustangs, Carson Three Socks and Carson Blue. Education programs with Jackson and the mustangs have introduced thou-

Jackson the Red Rock Canyon Burro

Graham Wimbrow

*Artist Linda Campbell with visitors at an
Artist in Residence Workshop*

sands of adults and children to this unique BLM program.

In 2013, RRCIA partnered with the Bureau of Land Management and the U.S. Department of Immigration and Customs Enforcement to hold a naturalization ceremony in the beautiful natural setting of Red Rock Canyon. Friends of Red Rock Canyon assisted with the 2013 and 2014 ceremonies, assuming responsibility for overall coordination in 2015. In 2014, RRCIA began the Red Rock Canyon Artist in Residence program, the first of its kind in Southern Nevada. In the first year, three artists worked onsite at Red Rock Canyon and involved visitors in hands-on workshops. Linda V. Campbell, Maria Arango Diener and Myranda Bair were the first artists selected for residencies through the program. In 2015, the Artist in Residence program was expanded to allow artists using any medium, including music and poetry, to apply.

Looking forward, the staff and volunteer Board of Directors of RRCIA plan to explore opportunities to support enhanced interpretive programs aimed at connecting visitors to the natural beauty and resources of Red Rock Canyon. RRCIA networks with other Cooperating Associations and maintains a membership with the Association of Partners for Public Lands (APPL) to keep abreast of emerging trends and best practices for organizations working with federal partnering agencies for the benefit of public lands.

CHAPTER 19

Protecting the Land

By Chuck Williams

I think people are going nuts. Who needs rocks?
I say we need oil and if Red Rock has some, what are
we waiting for? Let's drill that oil.

Letter to the Editor (Lopez, 1979)

I hate to think we need oil so badly that we
would be willing to sacrifice the beauty and serenity of
Red Rock Canyon to obtain it.

Letter to the Editor (Duran, 1979)

I say drill for oil anywhere it might be found... When
the welfare of a human being is jeopardized by tiny
fish and a few red rocks, then we
humans become endangered species.

Letter to the Editor (Ten Eyck, 1979)

All the debate might have taken place during the oil embargo of 1967, or the first oil crisis in 1973. But there was one difference during the 1979 oil crisis. In 1977-1978 wildcatters had applied for leasing rights on almost all of Red Rock Canyon as well as 77 percent of the eligible land in Clark County

Red Rock Escarpment with sign reading "US Department of the Interior Fish and Wildlife Service – National Wildlife Refuge" c. 1962

(Oil and Gas Leasing in the Red Rock Canyon Recreation Lands: Final Assessment, 1980). The reason for the interest was a subsurface geologic feature called the "Overthrust Belt," thought to hide vast pools of oil. Part of this belt passed through southern Nevada and Mobil Oil was investing millions of dollars in a plan to drill a well up to 17,000 feet deep looking for oil at Mormon Mesa 65 miles north of Las Vegas (Kofol, 1979). The Bureau of Land Management released the draft version of the Red Rock Gas and Oil Environmental Assessment in November 1979 and asked for public comments. In a rare case of editorial agreement, both the *Las Vegas Review-Journal* and the *Las Vegas Sun* opposed drilling in Red Rock. This led Mr. Ten Eyck to comment in his Letter to the Editor, "Your editorial of Nov. 4, opposing drilling for oil in Red Rock Park is just another example of the stupidity of organizations like the Sierra Club and R-J."

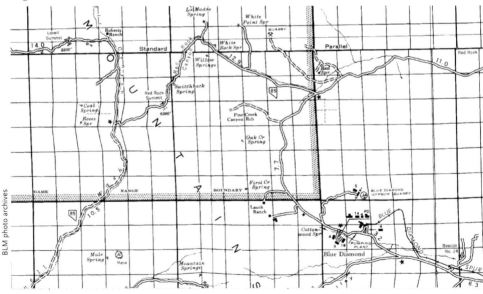

1952 Clark County Map showing part of Red Rock Canyon. Note map shows the border of the Game Range. Also notice that the Rocky Gap Road leading to Lovell Canyon is a designated State Highway number 85.

The debate to allow drilling and the Bureau of Land Management's ultimate decision was just one chapter in the story to protect Red Rock Canyon, sometimes from the government itself, a journey that began in 1936.

THE EARLY YEARS

Valley of Fire became Nevada's first State Park in 1935. The following year Boulder Dam Recreation Area and the Desert Game Range were created. The latter included parts of what is now Red Rock Canyon National Conservation Area.

The Great Depression and then World War Two consumed America's time and resources for the next ten years, but some positive things happened throughout southern Nevada because of the efforts of the Civilian Conservation Corps (1933-1942) whose crews built roads, trails, cattle and wildlife water guzzlers (spring-fed water tanks) as well as other improvements.

After the war, in 1946, the Bureau of Land Management (BLM) was formed by the merger of the General Land Office and the Grazing Service. Homesteading was still available in the Red Rock Canyon area as well as mining claims and grazing permits. In the late 1940s through the 1950s, several homesteading patents were issued for Mountain Springs and Calico Basin as the Las Vegas valley experienced population growth. The BLM would later remove Red Rock Canyon and the Spring Mountains from the Desert Game Range and designate the area as the Spring Mountain-Red Rock Recreation Complex.

THE 1960s

The National Park Service evaluated Red Rock Canyon for a possible inclusion into their system in 1961 but decided the area did not fit into the mission of the Park Service (Sub Committee Report: Spring Mountains Planning Unit, 1965.) That same year the State Park Advisory Commission asked that the BLM reclassify and protect portions of Red Rock Canyon (Vincent, 1967).

1964 became a watershed year for Red Rock Canyon as several activities occurred that spurred conservation activity. Congress enacted three laws that had a far-reaching impact on the management of public lands. The Public Land Law Review Commission Act provided for a review of the long-range needs and the ability of existing laws to meet those needs. The Classification and Multiple Use Act and Public Land Sale Act gave the Department of Interior management and sale authority to meet short-term needs pending the implementation of the Commission's recommendations (Harvey, n.d.). Utilizing the Multiple Use Act, the BLM withdrew 10,000 acres of Red Rock Canyon for protection.

Also in 1964, local organizations, ad hoc groups and private individuals began to advocate for Red Rock Canyon to have a protective designation. The Sierra Club, along with the Nevada Survey, presented a proposal for Red Rock Canyon to become a 64,000 acre National Monument to be managed by the BLM. The Red Rock Archaeological Association, an ad hoc group, petitioned state legislators for Red Rock Canyon to become part of the Nevada State Park System, stating, "We are concerned that the park will be taken over by private commercial interests unless it is set aside as a park as soon as possible" (Red Rock Survival Plan Here, 1964). Two years later the group would formally organize and later change the name to Archaeo-Nevada Society. The BLM asked interested persons and organizations to meet and discuss the future of Red Rock Canyon. At the meeting the group appointed a subcommittee to further study the area and make recommendations. The Bureau also asked the League of Women Voters to conduct a survey to determine the public interest and desired developments. Of the 6,500 questionnaires distributed, 3,500 were returned. The subcommittee report, along with the results of the survey, were published the following year. Almost 90 percent of the survey respondents indicated concern and felt a need for more outdoor recreation facilities. A surprising 66 percent indicated that they had used facilities in the Red Rock Canyon-Spring Mountain Complex (Subcommittee Report: Spring Mountain Planning Unit, 1965).

Type of Facilities Wanted:

84%	Picnic	42%	Nature Trails
50%	Museum	39%	Overnight Camping
49%	Hiking	26%	Horseback Trails

The Subcommittee's Report included thirty recommendations including:

- BLM should administer the resource.

- Domestic livestock grazing should be eliminated.

- Clark County should take the lead in trash removal and efforts to stop dumping.

- Mining should be excluded in the high value recreation lands.

- The Red Rock Canyon portion should be classified as a Recreation Area.

- The Red Rock Canyon Scenic Drive should be paved.

- The BLM should negotiate to acquire key land now in private ownership.

- Clark County should pave West Charleston Boulevard to the town of Blue Diamond.

- A master plan needs to be developed and implemented.

The BLM began site development at Willow Springs and other areas. In 1966 the BLM proposed that Red Rock Canyon become a National Recreation Area or, alternatively, that they manage the area jointly with the Nevada Division of State Parks.

BLM photo archives (all images)

(top right) Boy Scouts having
fun c. 1960s

(middle right) Shot-up abandoned vehicles being removed
along what is now State
Route 159 c. 1960s

(bottom right) Lunch served
courtesy of Jerry's Nugget
c. 1960s

(top left) Scouts and Volunteers near the town of Blue Diamond
c. 1960s (middle left) Junk vehicles being removed along what is
now Charleston Blvd/State Route 159. The Blue Diamond Hill is
in left background c. 1960s

(bottom left) Boy Scouts loading trash c. 1960s

SEEKERS, SAINTS & SCOUNDRELS 251

Secretary of the Interior Stewart Udall approved a designation of Red Rock Canyon Recreation Lands in 1967 with the 62,000 acres to be jointly managed by the BLM and Nevada Division of State Parks. That fall the BLM began to plan for a dedication ceremony by building a scenic overlook and installing an interpretive kiosk along west Charleston Boulevard (now State Route 159).

Over the years Red Rock Canyon had become a vast dumping ground. Abandoned vehicles and trash had accumulated and sharpshooters had used the vehicles, road signs, empty beer bottles, appliances, Indian rock art and just about everything else that didn't move for target practice.

In April 1967, as they had done the two previous years, youth groups along with adult volunteers joined together for "Clean up the Red Rocks Day." Over 750 volunteers joined Clark County employees and equipment to remove over 300 truckloads of litter and place six truckloads of native vegetation along the roadways. Jerry's Nugget Casino catered a free lunch for everyone who participated.

In November 1967 the Red Rock Cleanup Campaign was awarded the Keep America Beautiful Youth Award, "For its success in restoring public pride and interest in the Red Rock Canyon Recreation Lands." Explorer Scout Greg Kennedy of the Boulder Area Scout Council and Dennis Hess, Las Vegas District Manager for the BLM, traveled to New York City to receive the engraved bronze cup at the National Litter Prevention Organizations Annual Awards Luncheon (Red Rock Cleanup Gains Award, 1967).

DIGGING FOR BURIED TREASURE
IN THE
SANDSTONE QUARRY

In June 1967, Las Vegas District Manager Dennis Hess was heavily involved with the upcoming dedication of Red Rock Canyon Recreation Lands. Jean Ford, President of the League of Women Voters, called Mr. Hess on June 13 about another matter and casually asked what a bulldozer was doing in the vicinity of Sandstone Quarry. It had been reported to her by members of the Sierra Club.

Hess sent staff to investigate. They found a posted mining claim, soil stripped from the sandstone, a trench approximately 100 feet long, 10 feet wide and 10 feet deep plus two shafts, one over seven feet deep. The personnel working the claim said they were probing for an underground cavern said to contain buried treasure and that this location was chosen based on physical features in the area.

(top left) Bucket on end of string at bottom along with shovels c. 1967-1968

(bottom left) Large trench dug by Catepillar circled in background

(top right) Fifty pounds of dynamite and other supplies. "We lifted the lid and looked in. It is full of sticks, sitting out in the open. Anyone could have come up and played with it—no one there—work crew or supervisor," noted Jean Ford on the back of this photo.

(bottom right) Result of drilling with compressor (circled in background)

The BLM staff checked courthouse records and found that a claim had been recorded the past February by Terrestrial Monarch. The BLM staff determined that the claim was not valid and returned to the site delivering a notice that the company was operating without proper authority. The company agreed to fill in the cut and stopped all other operations except deepening one six-foot-square shaft. The men mentioned that the company had the support of the State Museum, the Governor's office, Sheriff Ralph Lamb and the Sheriff's brother, Darwin, a Clark County Commissioner.

Hess called Darwin Lamb who admitted to being an interested party to the venture that he considered important to southern Nevada. Mr. Lamb understood that the activity was fully authorized by law. He promised to check and call Hess back. Hess then called Sheriff Lamb and left a message. Neither Ralph nor Darwin Lamb returned the calls.

The next day, June 15, Archaeo-Nevada President Mary Kozlowski became involved and called State Senator Floyd Lamb who denied any knowledge or interest in the matter. That same day Eric Cronkhite, Director of the Nevada Division of State Parks, called Hess to inquire about the venture based on a call he had received from the Governor's Office, who in turn, had been contacted by Jean Ford.

Things began to move quickly over the next week with meetings and phone calls between all the interested parties with the State Museum and Governor's Office denying any knowledge or involvement. In the meantime, the board of directors of Archaeo-Nevada visited Sandstone Quarry and found an open box of dynamite and a can of gasoline near the remaining eight-foot deep shaft and wrote to Hess, concerned that excavation was continuing.

When Hess answered, his letter must have been a bit too condescending for President Kozlowski. In her rebuttal letter she ended by stating, "In the future Mr. Hess, please do not surmise to know what I am thinking!" Not quite finished, she added a postscript, "I find your attempts to describe my temperament throughout your memo interesting, amusing and highly irrelevant."

Hess met with Terrestrial Monarch on June 22 and was informed that he and the BLM could expect a restraining order from Terrestrial Monarch who intended to continue work on the claim. That evening the board of directors of Archaeo-Nevada held an emergency meeting where they authorized President Mary Kozlowski to contact legal counsel, notify the press and seek support of other conservation groups. The group had already sent overnight letters to Senators Bible and Cannon, Congressman Baring and Secretary of the Interior Stewart Udall.

The above, as you can imagine, resulted in a flurry of phone calls and letters between all parties involved and must have had Hess thinking about a career change. The only people smiling at this point were the attorneys.

In the end the claim was invalidated and the rest of the work site filled in.

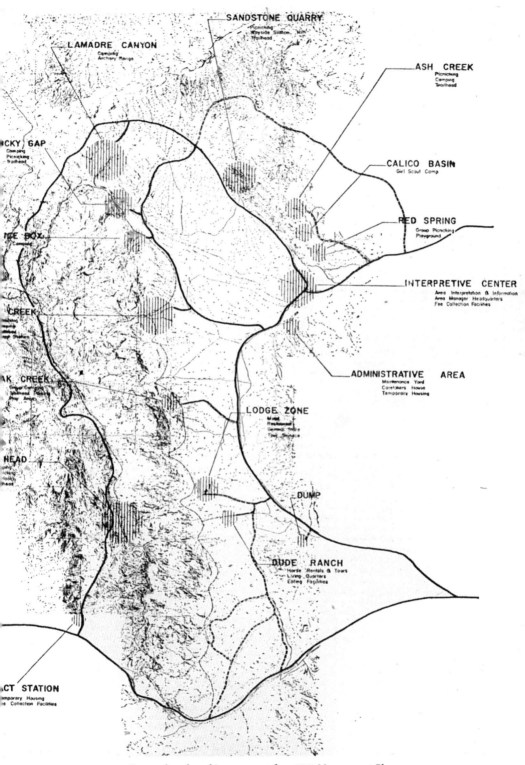

LAMADRE CANYON
Camping
Archery Range

SANDSTONE QUARRY
Picnicking
Wayside Station, Nat
Trailhead

ASH CREEK
Picnicking
Camping
Trailhead

CKY GAP
Camping
Picnicking
Trailhead

CALICO BASIN
Girl Scout Camp

ICE BOX

RED SPRING
Group Picnicking
Playground

CREEK

INTERPRETIVE CENTER
Area Interpretation & Information
Area Manager Headquarters
Fee Collection Facilities

AK CREEK

ADMINISTRATIVE AREA
Maintenance Yard
Caretakers House
Temporary Housing

LODGE ZONE
Motel
Restaurant
General Store
Tent Surface

HEAD

DUMP

DUDE RANCH
Horse Rentals & Tours
Living Quarters
Eating Facilities

CT STATION
mporary Housing
Collection Facilities

Proposed roads and improvement from 1968 Management Plan

The whole affair wound down as quickly as it materialized. The only questions that remain are why did Terrestrial Monarch think a hidden cavern was located in the quarry area and what was the treasure they sought (Kozlowski, June 27, 1967 & July 1, 1967 and Hess, 1967)?

THE DEDICATION AND 1968 MANAGEMENT PLAN

On Sunday, October 29, 1967, several hundred people arrived at the Charleston Boulevard Overlook by bus and car to witness the occasion. Featured speakers included Assistant Secretary of the Interior Harry Anderson and United States Senator Alan Bible of Nevada. The dedication plaque attached to the interpretative display stated:

RED ROCK CANYON

RECREATION LANDS

DEDICATED TO

THE USE AND ENJOYMENT

OF THIS AND FUTURE

GENERATIONS OF AMERICANS

In December, the BLM released the Recreation Management Plan for Red Rock Canyon and the Nevada Legislature approved funding for the development of Pine Creek as an interpretative center. The management plan was approved by the BLM Washington Office in early 1968 and officials there assigned it top priority. This would be the first recreation project attempted by the BLM.

It is apparent that the BLM wanted to make Red Rock Canyon a showcase, to be built in the manner of National Parks. The plan called for almost 40 miles of new paved roads, one of which would follow the Rocky Gap Road and then travel along the top of the escarpment to Mountain Springs. There would be 17 developed areas including a motel-resort operation, visitor center and dude ranch with restaurant. The developed areas would accommodate 620 family picnic units, two group picnic units (300 people total), 270 single / family camping units, 8 group camping areas (200 people maximum) and over 200 trailhead / overview parking spots. There would also be a maintained jeep road that snaked through Brownstone Canyon before joining the scenic loop north of Calico Hills. The plan called for homes or apartment-like dormitories to house the anticipated staff needed to administer the park.

The plan was developed with input from other federal organizations, the Sierra Club, the Nevada Division of State Parks and the Red Rocks Resource Committee which included private citizens. The private groups and individu-

(top) BLM State Director Nolan Keil addressing the crowd c. 1967

(middle left) Left to right; Senator Alan Bible, Assistant Secretary of Interior Henry Anderson and Chairman of the Clark County Commission James Ryan c. 1967

(bottom left) Senator Alan Bible with Boy Scouts at the dedication plaque c. 1967

(right) Participants and visitors are bused to the dedication site c. 1967

als voiced concern that the scope of the plan was too invasive, disruptive to wildlife and would spoil the remoteness of the area.

In 1969 the BLM and the Nevada Division of State Parks formally signed a cooperative agreement to manage the park.

THE 1970S

The public concerns about the 1968 Management Plan came to a head in 1972 after the BLM finished construction of Segment A of the Scenic Drive which ran from Charleston Boulevard to Willow Springs. Some felt construction of the roadway was too invasive and feared there would be future environmental impacts when construction on Segment B began. This second segment would begin at Willow Spring and pass Ice Box Canyon, Pine Creek and Oak Creek before rejoining Charleston Boulevard.

Red Rock Canyon was also experiencing increased vandalism and trash accumulation, caused in large part by a lack of BLM staff to protect the area.

A large limestone cave was discovered in Red Rock Canyon and made news in 1970 after it was discovered by Terry and Mike Lamuraglia who reported it to Gibson Jr. High Earth Science teacher L. F. Wilkinson. Wilkinson then alerted the BLM and State Parks about the find. The cave had been visited by others prior to 1970 but had been a well-kept secret. At least one earlier visitor was a pot

(top) Interior of the cave

(middle) Large formation inside the cave

(bottom) BLM District Manager Dennis Hess with Chief of Research Management Frank Bingham inspecting pot hunter excavation

BLM photo archives (all images) c. 1970

hunter looking for Indian artifacts as evidenced by a large hole dug in the floor.

The cave was still in exceptional condition with large stalagmites and stalactites, some of which had grown together to form pillars. Another smaller cave was located in the same area. The BLM twice installed a gate to seal the entrance and it was hoped that one day funds would be available to allow visitation and use as a science lab. Unfortunately knowledge of the cave led to its destruction. Within a few years vandals would remove both gates, once with explosives, and the cave became a party location. All stalagmites and stalactites were broken off. Visitors set fires which caused smoke damage and left their litter and graffiti behind (Vincent, 1970 & Red Rock Canyon reels under big visitor crush, 1991).

In May 1972, BLM District Manager Dennis Hess announced that the Sandstone Quarry would be closed until further notice. Hess reported that hundreds of cars and large numbers of young people were destroying the unique desert setting and leaving large amounts of trash, garbage and broken bottles. Even more damaging was the use of live desert plants for firewood (BLM Closing Quarry Site To Visitors, 1972).

In June 1972, President Mary Kozlowski and Vice President Howard Booth of the Nevada Open Spaces Council wrote to the BLM voicing their concerns. The BLM had already agreed to modify the 1968 plan by removing some of the unpopular features such as the "Crest Drive" that would have run along the top of the escarpment (Nevada Open Spaces, 1972). The BLM halted further implementation of the 1968 master plan until an Environmental Impact Statement could be prepared.

In January 1973, the Nevada Open Spaces Council Vice President Howard Booth submitted another statement, this one for the Clark County Legislative Delegation, requesting legislation calling for the State to purchase all 77,000 Red Rock Canyon acres from the federal government at $2.50 per acre, as covered by the Recreation and Public Purposes Act. They also requested the authorization of a contract between the State and BLM so the Division of State Parks could assume law enforcement and interpretative responsibility for Red Rock Canyon pending transfer of the lands to State ownership (Nevada Open Spaces, 1973).

Howard Booth was one of those individuals who, if you were going to war, you wanted on your side. Once he became involved with an issue, he was relentless in his pursuit, sometimes even wearing down members of his own organization. In February 1974, Dave Boroughf wrote a letter to Assemblywoman Jean Ford: "Dear Mrs. Ford, last Saturday evening at the Toiyabe Chapter of the Sierra Club Executive Committee Meeting we were discussing the Red Rocks Recreation Area. Howard Booth from Las Vegas was up, and for the umpteenth time he talked about the problems still troubling the area" (Boroughf, 1974).

As a result of the public concerns, the State Park Advisory Commission reactivated the Red Rock Advisory Committee and asked that they reevaluate the 1968 Master Plan.

In 1974 the BLM held public meetings on the Draft Environmental Impact Statement of the revised Recreational Management Plan. Major criticism originated from Assemblywoman Jean Ford, the Sierra Club and Friends of the Earth. Advisory Committee member Thalia Dondero stated: "The Committee agreed that alternative three which calls for full development below the escarpment with only primitive development above was acceptable. But most of all we'd like to see adequate supervision" (Conservationists want Red Rock left untouched, 1974).

There was another victory in 1974 for the protection of Red Rock Canyon. Businessmen Fletcher Jones and William Murphy had purchased the 523-acre Wilson Ranch (see Chapter 3) from the Howard Hughes Corporation in 1972. The following year Jones and Murphy applied for a zoning change that would allow their corporation to build an "Equestrian Orientated Development" that would feature 387 one-acre lots, 175 one-half-acre lots, 117 townhouses and 90 condominiums. Public reaction to the plan was immediate and the April Clark County Planning Commission meeting was packed with opponents who questioned how water, sewer, schools and other services would be provided. Those present asked that the state purchase the land to prevent the development (Vincent, 1973). Hours before the June Commission meeting, Jones and Murphy withdrew their application and announced that the ranch would be sold to the highest bidder at an August auction to be held in Los Angeles. In the meantime, both the state and federal government had allocated funds to purchase the ranch under a plan by Assemblywoman Jean Ford (Shone, 1973).

In January 1974, the state was successful in purchasing the 528-acre ranch as well as the 80-acre Pine Creek Ranch (see Chapter 5). The purchase costs for the ranches was jointly funded by the state and federal governments. Both the *Las Vegas Review-Journal* and *Las Vegas Sun* ran editorials approving both acquisitions and urged the state to purchase additional public land in the canyon (Red Rock bargain lost in giant mall's glare, 1974 & State Purchase Of Red Rock Land Welcome News, 1974).

The Nevada State Park System hired the architectural firm Royston, Hanamoto, Beck and Abey to develop a new master plan utilizing the Environment Impact Statement guidelines and working jointly with the BLM and State Park System. The plan was finished in 1976 and released to the public in 1977.

The revised master plan was much less invasive than the 1968 plan. The plan included Spring Mountain Ranch State Park, which would serve as the Administration and Service area for the southern part of the park. Another Administration and Service area including ranger residences was to be constructed about where the existing Cowboy Trail Rides are located. There would be six picnic areas with facilities. Rock climbing would be limited to Ice Box Canyon, Sandstone Quarry and the Mount Wilson area. The latter area would be restricted when the existing golden eagle and peregrine falcon nests were in use. Supervised group camping would be allowed at La Madre and Oak Creek. Seasonal camping, regulated by permit, would be allowed at La Madre, Red Summit and Brownstone. It was suggested that privately owned Oliver Ranch could be acquired and developed into a family camping site. The State did make attempts to purchase Oliver Ranch (see Chapter 7), but it remained in the Oliver family until the BLM purchased it in 1993. The plan also called for the creation of buffer zones to separate residential or commercial development from the park borders. Segment B of the Scenic Drive (starting at Willow Springs and connecting to State Route 159) was completed in 1978 and construction began on the Visitor Center in 1980. The building was designed as specified in the 1976 plan, "The building must be low and settled into the ground, not perched on top of the knoll. Ideally, one will enter at a low level with information and office functions cut into the hillside" (Master Plan Red Rock Canyon, 1976).

In the end, only a portion of the 1976 plan was ever completed. Funding was always an issue for both staff additions and capital construction projects. Rock climbing became extremely popular and routes were established all along the escarpment and Calico Hills. Golden eagle and peregrine falcon nests have not been seen on the escarpment for many years.

The other major development in 1977-1978, mentioned in the chapter introduction, was wildcat firms filing applications for gas and oil drilling within Red Rock Canyon. While the designation of Red Rock Canyon as a Recreation Area offered protection from surface development, it did not restrict mining and oil/gas drilling. Red Rock Canyon would receive full protection when Congress passed legislation to designate Red Rock Canyon a National Conservation Area thirteen years later.

The BLM released the Draft Environmental Assessment on Oil and Gas Leasing in 1979. The draft report pleased neither side of the argument as noted in the Letters to the Editor. Joanne Townsend of the *Las Vegas Review-Journal* wrote three articles about the report. The first report focused on the environment and summed up the effect that drilling would have on the area, "The only way to solve problems that may arise from oil and gas drilling in Red Rock Canyon would be not to drill there at all, according to a BLM environmental analysis" (Townsend, 1979, Nov 18). The second article provided information from both sides but noted that the general message residents were sending was, "Money-hungry corporations should not be allowed to deface one of the few natural scenic beauties in Southern Nevada" (Townsend, 1979, Nov 20). A few days later, her third article concentrated on the feelings of the oil interest, "In light of the energy problems this country is facing, it is 'utter nonsense and stupidity' to say the Red Rock Canyon area is too pristine for wildcat drilling, an oilman who wants to drill there said Friday." Dean Rowell, who had applied for oil and gas rights on about 40,000 acres of the park, said the report was, "totally geologically inadequate. The geology discussion is nothing but 'paint brush' work and cannot be taken seriously." Rowell went on to say, "At least 90 percent of the report deals with environmental matters and with protecting animals, flora and fauna that a drilling rig and its affiliated operations could not possibly harm" (Townsend, 1979, Nov 24).

During the thirty day comment period, the BLM received 2,300 responses from the public with 90 percent opposed to drilling at Red Rock Canyon (Red Rock drilling petition given to BLM, 1980).

THE 1980S

An ad hoc group of concerned individuals sponsored several protests at the park in early 1980 where they gathered 1,500 signatures opposing drilling. The petition was presented to the BLM in April and the group was assured it would be considered by the BLM staff while making the final decision. David Laurie, who led the group, said he received support from the Sierra Club, the Sagebrush Alliance and private citizens (Red Rock drilling petition given to BLM, 1980).

The BLM released the final assessment on August 6, granting tentative approval for 22 leases covering approximately 30 percent of the 62,000 acre park. Drilling was not allowed in the prime tourist area and the drilling equipment would have to be painted to blend with natural surroundings. There were other restrictions attached to the leases and the BLM specified a 30 day comment period. The decision came as a shock to all those who opposed drilling in Red Rock Canyon (Oil and Gas Leasing in the Red Rock Canyon Recreation Lands: Final Assessment 1970).

The next day the *Las Vegas Review-Journal* ran an editorial about the decision.

> First the Department of Defense laid claim to the area now called the Nevada Test Site, then the Air Force announced plans to take the central basin valleys of Eastern Nevada for the MX missile and now the Bureau of Land Management gives preliminary approval to oil drilling in the Red Rock Canyon Recreation Lands.
>
> When will it all end? How long must Nevada be the whittling stick for the federal government program and management?
>
> These questions must certainly be raised by many Southern Nevadans today. On Wednesday the BLM announced it would permit limited, restricted drilling in the Red Rock Canyon area. Outrage must be welling within the chests of the 2,222 citizens who told the BLM they opposed drilling in the canyon.
>
> And no wonder. The decision is an outrage.
>
> Given the great beauty of the area, it is almost inconceivable that the BLM would allow oil drilling anywhere near there. Even though the places marked for drilling are in areas that appear—we stress the word appear—to be at least somewhat away from the prime recreational area, this is the toehold that may eventually ruin one of our most precious sightseeing areas (Red Rock drilling approval an outrage, 1980).

On September 26, Ed Spang, State Director for the BLM, announced that an additional 520 acres of Red Rock Canyon was removed from oil and gas drilling; but the rest of the targeted area remained open for exploration. Spang reported that 19 formal complaints were received during the 30 day review period. While Spang said he was surprised by the low number of protests, he concluded, "Apparently the public must be satisfied with what we've proposed for the Red Rocks." The lease permits allowed the wildcat operators up to ten years to start exploration and 25 years to come up with oil (Manning, 1980).

The *Las Vegas Review-Journal* responded to the decision with one more editorial on October 1.

> ....You might think that in the face of the testimony of experts, the total failure of earlier drillers, the report by the BLM's own geologist, and the overwhelming opposition of the public, the request by the wildcatters to drill would be quickly dismissed.

You would be wrong. Las week, Ed Spang announced that 30 percent of the Red Rock Canyon Recreational Area would be open to drillers.

The decision makes no sense. It is not justified by the facts, and runs completely contrary to Spang's professed philosophy of a "joint team," where the input of the public is important (BLM's philosophy: Ignore the public, 1980).

After it was all said and done, the 1979 Oil Crisis abated. The price of gas dropped, as did the public's demand that the United States become self-sufficient in oil supplies. Drilling for oil in questionable areas moved to the back burner and no wells were drilled in Red Rock Canyon within the ten year time frame specified in the permit. In 1990 the issue of drilling completely fell off the table when Red Rock Canyon received additional protection as a National Conservation Area.

In 1981 a cooperative agreement was signed by the BLM and Nevada Department of Conservation and Natural Resources. Under the agreement the State would manage 17,000 acres in the southern half of the Recreation Area while BLM managed the remaining acreage. That same year BLM hired three visitor management personnel for Red Rock Canyon. One had already attended Federal Law Enforcement Training; the other two attended the training the following year (The Red Rock Experience, c. 1991).

The Red Rock Canyon Visitor Center was opened on a part-time basis on May 22, 1982. While the BLM had hired three law enforcement staff, they had yet to be granted law enforcement authority by the federal government. In order to provide on-site support, the BLM entered into a second cooperative agreement with the Nevada Division of State Parks for law enforcement assistance at Red Rock. The State opened two positions under the $44,000 contract; recruitment, however, proved difficult because of the uncertainly of BLM funding. The three BLM trained staff eventually transferred to law enforcement positions in other agencies (The Red Rock Experience, c. 1991).

Friends of Red Rock Canyon (FORRC), a volunteer organization, was formed in 1984 at the request of the Bureau of Land Management, becoming the first such organization to receive a cooperative agreement with the BLM (see Chapter 17).

Red Rock Canyon Interpretive Association (RRCIA) was formed in 1988 to sell interpretive materials in the visitor center book store and assist with interpretation programs. When an admission fee was approved for the park, RRCIA provided staffing for the fee booths (see Chapter 18).

In the late 1980s Las Vegas was enjoying a building boom with the town expanding westward towards Red Rock Canyon. The little town of Blue Diamond saw new homes built on the hill above the old town site and at Calico Basin a group of investors that had planned to develop 166 acres into a new subdivision were now trying to sell the property. The State Transportation Department was widening Blue Diamond Road for safety reasons and included a bike path on each shoulder. While most residents of Blue Diamond and Calico Basin opposed more growth in their area, they agreed the highway expansion was necessary. However Calico landowner George Heyer, who jokingly calls himself the "mayor of Calico Basin," still wishes his development dream had come true, "I wanted to build a western village out here" (Werner, c. 1987).

But with Howard Hughes Summa Corporation owning land that reached to the Red Rock boundary and Calico Basin, there was also concern from the general public that housing developments would someday reach into the canyon itself. In 1988 the BLM acquired 5,300 acres from the Hughes Corporation by a land transfer which provided a buffer area between the city and Red Rock Canyon. That same year the BLM was able to hire additional staff which allowed the visitor center to be open seven days a week (The Red Rock Experience, c. 1991).

THE 1990S

On November 16, 1990 President George H.W. Bush signed a bill, sponsored by U.S. Senators Harry Reid and Richard Bryan along with U.S. Representative James Bilbray, designating Red Rock Canyon as BLM's second National Conservation Area. The park's total acreage at that time was 83,100 and the new designation provided much more protection for the land and resources.

Maybe because of the new designation, or maybe just because Las Vegas was undergoing another population boom, visitation skyrocketed. In the 12-month period ending in September 1991, an estimated 800,000 people traveled the Scenic Loop, a 33 percent increase from the previous year (Red Rock Canyon reels under big visitor crush, 1991). People were loving it to death. Because Red Rock Canyon was now a Conservation Area, the BLM was charged with developing a new management plan. There were several politically sensitive issues that BLM would need to consider. For example, charging an entrance fee to deter vandals and prevent overcrowding. Another issue would be what to do about private lands within the boundaries of the conservation area; this included 600 acres of state land and 1,400 acres of private land. Although the 1990 law establishing the conservation area indicated that the federal government may have the right to condemn private land, the BLM did not envision the agency taking this route. Instead, the bureau was in the process of obtaining two private parcels of land totaling 100 acres by doing a land exchange for federal land in other areas of southern Nevada. Howard Booth, a member of the Sierra Club and charter member of Friends of Red Rock Canyon, explained why the BLM was not being more pro-active in private land acquisition, "One of the problems you have to realize is that the BLM is still underfunded and undermanned" (Red Rock Canyon reels under big visitor crush, 1991).

In the late 1980s the BLM obtained funding from the Land and Water Conservation Fund to purchase a 439-acre parcel of land from the Hughes Corporation that lay only 200 feet from the Visitor Center (Woyski, 1990). So far Clark County had been successful in stopping some of the projects. In the 1970s they denied a proposal by Al Levinson, owner of Bonnie Springs Ranch, to operate a casino on his property. In 1991 they denied another Levinson proposal to build a 200 space RV Park and miniature golf course. But even a conservationist like Howard Booth believed some development, such as more trails and picnic areas, were needed in order to protect the area, "If there aren't trails, people just wander all over the countryside destroying the vegetation," he said (Red Rock Canyon reels under big visitor crush, 1991).

In 1992 Stone of La Madre filed a claim to quarry building stone on a sandstone terrace that overlooks the Las Vegas Valley just east of the Red Rock boundary. It was feared that the company would develop homes on the property once ownership was established (see Chapter 13). Thanks to the efforts of Friends of Nevada Wilderness, the claim was invalidated by the BLM and the land later became part of the Conservation Area (Rogers, 1993).

In 1993 the BLM purchased Oliver Ranch, adding 320 acres to the park size; however, the biggest addition was made the next year when President Bill Clinton signed a bill which more than doubled the size of the conservation area to 196,000 acres.

The BLM published an Interim General Management Plan in June of 1995 that would serve as an operating guide while an Environmental Impact Study was completed and a final management plan was approved. This process would continue for the next ten years until BLM State Director Bob Abbey signed the Red Rock Canyon National Conservation Area Resource Management Plan in 2005 (Red Rock Canyon National Conservation Area Resource Management Plan, 2005).

An admission fee was instituted in 1997 which allowed Red Rock Canyon to retain all generated proceeds. This was another bonus for Red Rock Canyon as it provided ongoing funds for staff and maintenance expenses.

The BLM was able to find funding to purchase several parcels of private land in Calico Basin (see Chapter 9) during the decade; however, in 1998 Congress passed the Southern Nevada Public Lands Management Act (SNPLMA) which proved to be a financial boon for all of Southern Nevada in the early years of the new century.

The law, which was sponsored by U.S. Senators Harry Reid and Richard Bryan along with U.S. Congressman John Ensign, was an impressive feat by 1998 standards and would be next to impossible in today's political environment.

The Act allowed the BLM to auction off public land in the Las Vegas Valley with all proceeds used in Nevada as opposed to the funds being transferred to the United States Treasury Department. This "Nevada Only Funding" is something that Washington has attempted to reverse several times.

Under the terms of the Act, five percent of the funds would be paid directly to the State of Nevada for general education. Another ten percent would be paid directly to the Southern Nevada Water Authority. The remaining funds would be deposited into a special account in the Treasury of the United States for use: "pursuant to the provisions of paragraph (3). Amounts in the special account shall be available to the Secretary [of Interior] without further appropriation and shall remain available until expended."

Paragraph 3 defined the provisions as:

- The acquisition of environmentally sensitive land in the State of Nevada (with priority given to lands located within Clark County).
- Capital improvements in the four federal agencies in Southern Nevada.
- Development of multi-species habitats in Clark County, Nevada.
- Development of parks, trails and natural areas.
- Up to 10 percent of amounts available could be used for conservation initiatives.

The Act also added 1,002 acres to the National Conservation Area (Southern Nevada Public Lands Management Act, 1998).

Through 2013, SNPLMA projects have generated over $3 billion through the sale of 15,000 acres of land in the Las Vegas Valley (Reid Statement on House Efforts to Gut SNPLMA, 2014).

In Clark County, SNPLMA has funded over 700 projects including four new visitor centers: Red Rock Canyon, Clark County Wetlands Park, Desert National Wildlife Refuge and the Spring Mountains National Recreation Area. Other major projects funded include the Springs Preserve ($35 million), Lake Tahoe improvements ($300 million), Clark County Shooting Complex ($61 million) and Centennial Hills Park ($42 million). The school system has received over $151 million and the Southern Nevada Water Authority has received in excess of $300 million. However the largest share, $1.1 billion, has gone to local governments for parks, trails, open space land purchases and projects to prevent forest fires.

Because of the recession, income from the Act has fallen since 2004 when over 10,000 acres were sold for $884 million (Vogel, 2011). By comparison, the 2014 land auction sold 87.5 acres for $18 million (Land Sales Generate More Than $18 Million for Projects, 2014).

THE 2000S

In 2002 developer Laing Homes unveiled plans for a proposed 8,400-home, 3,000-acre Cielo Encantado ("Enchanted Sky" in Spanish) project on Blue Diamond Hill, just east of the Red Rock Canyon National Conservation Area. Laing had a tentative $50 million agreement with the James Hardie Gypsum Company, but the project hinged on the BLM agreeing to swap about 979 acres of federal land near the proposed development for 533 acres of private land. The Clark County Commission would also have to approve a zone change and the development plan before the project could proceed. Laing estimated that homes in the development were expected to sell for a low of about $250,000 and a high of between $5 million and $10 million (Geary, Aug 14, 2002).

At a meeting held in the town of Blue Diamond, residents and environmental groups were less than enthusiastic about the proposal. Opponents of the plan pointed to a conflict of interest after discovering that engineering firm G.C. Wallace, which was working for the Bureau of Land Management conducting a feasibility study of the proposed land swap, was also working with John Laing Homes on converting the mining property into a residential community. "There is a definite conflict of interest," said Ellen Anderson, a resident of the town of Blue Diamond. "If their feasibility study comes back positive, then they have really paved the way for themselves to make a lot of money on this project" (Geary, Aug 15, 2002).

Residents also questioned the availability of water, police and fire services, water drainage into the conservation area, the impact of thousands of cars on the area, the viability of the developer and lighting impairing a view of the stars at night.

State Senator Dina Titus attended the meeting because she was concerned about "leap frog" developments like Cielo Encantado. Several years earlier

Titus had proposed establishing a ring around the valley that would prevent development from taking root in outlying areas.

Others said the project didn't make sense because Red Rock Canyon was a precious resource that must be protected from development. "This many people next to a conservation area is asking for trouble," said Laura Glisman, a biology teacher. "In 10 years we won't believe what we have lost" (Geary, Aug 15, 2002).

Based on the overwhelming opposition to the plan, Laing dropped the proposal but any victory celebration by those who opposed the development was short-lived.

In March 2003 developer Jim Rhodes announced he had purchased the James Hardie mine for $50 million. Rhodes indicated that he had not decided what to do with the property as it was estimated there was twenty years of gypsum left to be mined, but he felt the land was better suited for residential use. Clark County Commissioner Mark James met with approximately 100 Blue Diamond area residents and urged that they try to work out a compromise with the new owner instead of just "locking horns." The suggestion did not go over well with the group as Commissioner James was already in trouble for blocking a proposal by the Clark County Commissioners to zone the area around Red Rock Canyon for one home on every two acres.

Meanwhile, influential lobbyist John Pappageorge and former Clark County Commissioner Erin Kenny testified against a bill sponsored by Senate Minority Leader Dina Titus that would lock in rural zoning standards near Red Rock and require a vote of county residents to change them (Geary, Mar 28, 2003).

Two days later the *Las Vegas Review-Journal* ran an editorial opposing the project.

> It should be a time of celebration at Red Rock.

> Recent rainstorms have coaxed a carpet of tender grass, and the newborn wildlife is beginning to emerge. The fleeting flowers of spring are coming.

> With the cool March air whipping across the face of the stunning sandstone escarpment that's 3,000 feet high and 13 miles long, the signs of the sweet season are everywhere. And the views are priceless.

> Or, do they have their price?

> That question hangs on the wind at the Red Rock National Conservation Area these days. It is the site of a development showdown with

nothing less than the future of the area at stake.

In this community, it's not news developers have a win-loss record that would make the Globetrotters envious. Expansion has paved the desert and created residential and commercial construction from Sunrise Mountain to the skirts of the Spring Mountains.

It's been great for the economy, but hard on the environment. And now it's come down to a line in the sandstone: Will we block further development inside the conservation area, or give in one last time and as good as write off this sacred place?

There's no room for compromise on this one.

Literally and metaphorically, this is a hill to die for…

If this community can't muster enough outrage to defeat a threat to the valley's last good place, then this is no community at all.

If priceless Red Rock isn't worth fighting for, what is? (Smith, 2003).

On April 30, 2003 Rhodes applied for the clearances to erect between 1,500 and 5,500 homes next to the scenic conservation area. In the meantime, Senators Ensign and Reid urged the county to use funds from the Southern Nevada Public Lands Management Act to purchase the land from Rhodes so it could be restored and added to the National Conservation Area (Geary, May 1, 2003).

In an effort to turn public opinion, Rhodes spent hundreds of thousands of dollars running newspaper and television ads to urging voters to write lawmakers to protest the proposed bill. Rhodes also provided free van tours of the site to interested members of the press and public (Packer, 2003).

On May 10, 2003 my wife and I, along with several other members of Friends of Red Rock Canyon, attended a special meeting of the Assembly Government Affairs Committee at the Sawyer Building to show support for a state bill that would enforce rural zoning on the Rhodes property. We almost didn't get a chance to attend as we found our way blocked by t-shirted Rhodes supporters. We happened to meet State Senator Dina Titus in the hallway and explained our problem. Senator Titus took charge and forced her way into the meeting room; my wife was able to follow her by crawling under a table. The rest of us were left to watch the proceedings via TV from another room. The next morning's *Las Vegas Review-Journal* described the meeting.

Hundreds of construction workers, real estate agents and others were part of a caravan developer Jim Rhodes organized Saturday in support of his development plans near scenic Red Rock Canyon.

They crowded onto six buses chartered by Rhodes, ate the breakfast he served in the parking lot, and put on T-shirts he handed out before they crammed into a legislative hearing on a proposal that would prevent Rhodes from building thousands of homes near Red Rock.

The special meeting of the Assembly Government Affairs Committee was so crowded that spectators filled three rooms at the state's Sawyer Building near downtown Las Vegas. The commotion delayed the start of the meeting for nearly an hour, and the Las Vegas Fire Department forced those standing to find a seat or leave the premises.

'This is a farce. A lot of money has been spent doing this,' Clark County Commissioner Myrna Williams said of Rhodes' effort to bring supporters to the hearing. 'This is an orchestrated event, but I am not sure how all these people were rounded up, with the T-shirts, the donuts and the coffee.' (Geary, May 11, 2003).

On May 19, 2003 legislation that limited development near Red Rock Canyon was signed into law by Governor Kenny Guinn. Senate Bill 358 passed unanimously in both houses of the legislature. Pat Van Betten, who represented the village of Blue Diamond on a committee that helped draft the ordinance for the county commission, said she was elated by Guinn's decision. "This has been a very, very long road for us" (Whaley, 2003).

The county passed the ordinance on May 21. An attorney for Jim Rhodes indicated that the developer may sue the county over the decision (Geary, May 22, 2003).

Rhodes would in fact sue, but development issues were placed on hold for the next few years with the crash of the housing market. In addition, Rhodes filed for bankruptcy protection under Chapter 11 and was in turn sued by the creditors who took over some of his business. The proceedings were not resolved until 2012 (O'Reiley, 2012).

In the meantime, Rhodes had submitted a conceptual plan to the Clark County Commission in August, 2011 to build approximately 4,700 homes on the property. The commissioners were on the defensive most of the day facing an overflow crowd who mostly opposed the plan. There were a few who supported Rhodes because they felt the proposal would create much needed jobs. The plans' critics, including many residents of the area, delivered hours of testimony and offered jeers and laugher towards those who favored Rhodes, including the commissioners themselves. It became a tense situation as the commissioners voted 5 to 2 to tentatively approve the plan. In truth, the commissioners were in a no-win situation as the Nevada Supreme Court was reviewing both the State and County laws that reduced the density to one home per two acres. Attorneys for both the county and Rhodes told commissioners they would be on shaky legal ground if they rejected the plan at this early stage. Rhodes' team would still have to determine site design, engineering and other construction issues before he could apply to have the area rezoned for higher density housing, a process that could last several years. One of the 26 conditions that the Commission placed on the plan was that Rhodes would need to build a new access road to connect the development with State Route 160.

Less than three months later Rhodes was back to the Clark County Commission asking for waivers on two of the 26 restrictions the Commission had placed on the project. The two restrictions specified that Rhodes could not use SR 159, which runs through the National Conservation Area, during construction and that Rhodes would have to secure a right of way to State Route 160 with the Bureau of Land Management. The following year Rhodes would drop both requests (Jourdan 2012; Morrison 2011; Wyland 2011).

In January 2013 the Clark County Commission voted to support a plan to swap Rhodes' property overlooking Red Rock Canyon with equal land elsewhere. Environmental groups, area land owners and Rhodes were all in favor of the idea. Commissioner Susan Brager, who was spearheading the effort, said the next step is to enlist the support of Nevada's congressional delegation and approach the Bureau of Land Management with the idea. Commissioner Chris Giunchigliani was the lone vote against the resolution. She said that although she is against developing the land, she could not support the swap because it "reinforces bad behavior." "I just haven't landed on a swap that in my mind just helps somebody out, and I think that was the agenda all along, to have land swapped," she said (Mower, Jan 23, 2013).

While Rhodes and the opponents were happy with the decision, in reality the Commission just threw the ball over the wall and into the BLM's lap.

And the BLM didn't want the property to begin with. They had said all along that the property does not fit into the National Conservation Area because all natural resources had been destroyed by strip mining. In addition, there was no funding available to restore the landscape, make it safe to use, create new facilities or provide for ongoing maintenance. The BLM suggested it would be much better suited as a city or county park than part of the Conservation Area.

Later in 2013, the Nevada Supreme Court ruled in favor of Rhodes' finding that the law restricting a zoning change violated a provision of the Nevada

Constitution that prohibits the Legislature from passing local laws that regulate county business (Mower, Feb 1, 2013). In July the state Board of Examiners agreed to pay $920,000 to settle a dispute over a 2003 law that sought to protect lands near Red Rock Canyon. The payment brought to a close the legal battle over Senate Bill 358 from the 2003 legislative session that sought to protect the area from development. The money would be used to pay attorney fees and costs to Gypsum Resources and developer Jim Rhodes. Failing to approve the proposed settlement could mean the state would end up having to pay even more, the board was told (Whaley, 2013).

While the ten year legal battle was going on, some good things were happening at Red Rock—the new Visitor Center opened in 2009 and the outside exhibit area opened in 2010. In 2014, the National Defense Authorization Act added 1,530 acres to the Conservation Area.

RED ROCK CANYON TODAY

Red Rock Canyon National Conservation Area has been described as the crown jewel of BLM's National Conservation Lands System. I'm sure this irritates all the other 878 federal areas included in the system, and rightly so as each area has its own charm and beauty and likely considers themselves the jewel of the system. I think the term is more of a recognition that Red Rock Canyon had the first BLM Visitor Center and Friends group. Being close to a metropolitan area, we have ready access to a large volunteer base and also experience a high visitation rate from both locals and tourists.

Protecting Red Rock Canyon's natural resources from all this visitation seems to become more difficult each year. Like most other natural areas, we see increased graffiti, trash accumulation, trail braiding (created when hikers use a shortcut instead of following the marked trail) and all the other issues associated with public visitation.

The question of a residential development on Blue Diamond Hill is still open as of this writing. Rhodes continues to mine gypsum at the site and truck the material to a processing plant. No land swaps are currently in the works, and Rhodes can apply for a zoning change or proceed with plans to develop two acre home sites if he so desires.

BLM's funding is a continuing concern, as almost yearly budget cuts erode staffing levels and maintenance dollars.

Visitation continues to increase, causing traffic congestion on weekends and weekdays in the spring and fall. There are currently 321 parking spaces along the Scenic Drive which quickly fill during peak visitation, forcing visitors to park alongside the road, adding to congestion and safety issues. At times the BLM has to shut down the Scenic Drive until more spaces become available. This is not a new issue as it was detailed in a 2001 transit study. Options include limiting access during peak visitation, increasing the size of parking lots or implementing a transit system. There is considerable expense and environmental issues associated with the last two options. A Scenic Drive repaving project is due to begin in 2015 which may provide some traffic and parking relief, but a longer term solution is still needed (Transit Feasibility Study, 2001).

Many people have opinions about what needs to be done to address maintenance issues and funding shortages. Some are quick to point out who is to blame: the President, Congress, BLM, etc.

But after emotion and rhetoric have been removed, we need only to look in the mirror to see who is responsible for Red Rock Canyon. This land belongs to all of us, and we each have our individual responsibility to protect the land for future generations. The cartoon strip Pogo (1947-1975) was set in the Okefenokee Swamp. One strip shows Pogo overlooking a trash and garbage-filled swamp. An oil derrick can be seen in the background. It is the caption that made it famous.

"We have met the enemy and he is us."

Treat the Earth well; it was not given to you by your parents, it was loaned to you by your children.
McCarthy, 2013

Acknowledgments

THE AUTHORS WOULD LIKE TO THANK the following for their invaluable help with the preparation of this book.

Blue Diamond History Committee and Pat Ven Betten

Debbie Boxton, Clark County Recorder's Office

Dustin Crowther, Clark County Surveyor's Office

Bill Durbin, Nevada Division of Minerals

Editors Elaine Holmes and Anne McConnell of Friends of Red Rock Canyon for finding and fixing commas, periods, semicolons, capitals, hyphens and the list goes on and on.

Lee Fosburgh, Caterpillar Corporate Archives

Roger Hembree, Friends Volunteer, Cover Photo

David Lowe, District Interpreter, Nevada Division of State Parks

Erik Martinet, Clark County Assessor's Office

James McClenahen, contact information for the Oliver family

Sam Monteleone, Water Application Research

Tom Moulin, Author of the "Red Rock Canyon Visitor Guide" for research help and support

Nevada State Museum, Cahlan Research Library – Crystal Van Dee and Paul Carson

Red Rock Canyon National Conservation Area, Bureau of Land Management Staff – Jim Cribbs, Kate Sorom and Kathy August

Reviewers Laverne Dickey and Kate Sorom of the Bureau of Land Management; Edwina LaBrecque and Linda McCollum of Friends of Red Rock Canyon; Crystalaura Jackson, Janis Kadlec and Robert Peloquin of the Red Rock Canyon Interpretive Association; and George Bogdanovich, Blue Diamond Town and Mine

Eric Schadeck, State of Nevada Division of Water Resources

University of Nevada, Las Vegas Special Collections – Delores Brownlee, Su Kim Chung, Kelli Lucks and Peter Michel

Pat Williams, Friends of Red Rock Canyon, book title, proofreading and research

Timeline

1829
Antonio Armijo and his party become the first known Europeans to visit Las Vegas

1844
John Frémont's expedition travels through Red Rock and the Las Vegas Valley

1850
The area now Clark County became part of the New Mexico Territory

1855
Mormons settle Las Vegas

1860
The Pah-Ute Campaign brings troops into Red Rock Canyon and Las Vegas

1861
Nevada becomes a territory (Clark County remains part of New Mexico)

1863
The area now Clark County becomes Pah-Ute County of the Arizona Territory

1864
Nevada becomes a state (what is now Clark County remains part of the Arizona Territory)

1865
Octavius Gass takes over the old Las Vegas Fort and begins to farm and ranch

1866
Pah-Ute County (Clark County) becomes part of Lincoln County in Nevada

1869
Lt. Wheeler conducts a military reconnaissance while camping at Red Rock Canyon

1876
James Wilson and George Anderson homestead Sandstone Ranch (Spring Mt. Ranch)

1901
Charles Stewart homesteads Cottonwood Spring (Town of Blue Diamond)

1905
The Town of Las Vegas is established and Sandstone Quarry opens at Red Rock Canyon

1909
Clark County is created from the south portion of Lincoln County

1915
Ella Mason homesteads what is now Calico Basin

1921
Orrin Taylor homesteads 40 acres at what will become part of Bonnie Springs Ranch

1922
Horace and Glenna Wilson homestead 80 acres at Pine Creek

1924
The Blue Diamond Corporation purchases mining rights from Buol and Matteucci

1927
William and Edith Morgan homestead 80 acres at what will become Bonnie Springs Ranch

1929
Reese Morgan homesteads 160 acres that will become Oliver Ranch

1934
William Wood homesteads 80 acres that will become Mountain Springs

1936
Red Rock Canyon (core area) becomes a part of the Desert Game Range

1938
Chauncey Oliver purchases 160 acre ranch from Reese Morgan

1941
The Blue Diamond Company begins building the company town of Blue Diamond

1946
The Bureau of Land Management (BLM) is formed by the merger of the General Land Office and the Grazing Service

1952
Bonnie Springs Ranch is established

1964
The company town of Blue Diamond is sold to Castella Corporation and two years later all the homes are sold to individuals

1967
Red Rock is dedicated as Red Rock Canyon Recreation Lands with 62,000 acres

1982
BLM opens the Visitor Center to the public

1984
Friends of Red Rock Canyon (FORRC) volunteer organization formed

1988
Red Rock Canyon Interpretive Association (RRCIA) formed

1990
Red Rock Canyon National Conservation Area is established

1993
Oliver Ranch is purchased by the BLM adding 320 acres to Red Rock Canyon NCA

1994
Red Rock Canyon expanded to 196,000 acres

1998
Red Rock Canyon expanded by 1,002 acres

2009
BLM purchases 80 acres at Pine Creek from the State of Nevada and the new Red Rock Canyon Visitor Center opens

2014
1,500 acres added to RRCNCA by Congress

References

Chapter 1

Background on the old Spanish National Historic Trail [Website], (n.d.) The Old Spanish Trail Association. Retrieved from *http://www.oldspanishtrail.org/*

Dale, H.C. (1991).*The Explorations of William H Ashley and Jedediah Smith – 1822-1829*. University of Nebraska Press.

Dominguez-Escalante Expedition [Website], (n.d.) Wikipedia. Retrieved from *http://en.wikipedia.org/wiki/Dominguez-Escalante_Expedition*

Fremont, J.C. (1845) *Report of the exploring expedition to the Rocky Mountains in the year 1842 and to Oregon and North California in the years 1843-44*. Washington, D.C.: Gales and Seaton, Printers).

History of the Grand Canyon [Website] (n.d.) Wikipedia. Retrieved from *http://en.wikipedia.org/wiki/History_of_the_Grand_Canyon_area*

Hopkins, A.D., & Evans, K.J. (1999) *The First 100 – Portraits of the Men and Women Who Shaped Las Vegas*. Las Vegas, NV Huntington Press.

Humans at the Grand Canyon. [Website]. (n.d.) Arizona State University. Retrieved from *http://grandcanyonhistory.clas.asu.edu/history_humansatgrandcanyon.html*

John C. Fremont [Website], (n.d.) Wikipedia. Retrieved from *http://en.wikipedia.org/wiki/John_C._Fr%C3%A9mont*

John Charles Fremont [Website], (n.d.) Digital-Desert: Mojave Desert. *Retrieved from http://mojavedesert.net/people/fremont.html*

Preuss, C. (1958) *Exploring with Fremont: the private diaries of Charles Preuss, Cartographer for John C. Fremont on his first, second, and fourth expeditions to the Far West*. E.G. Gudde, & E.K. Gudde (Trans.). University of Oklahoma Press.

Remley, D. (2011) *Kit Carson, the life of an American border man*. University of Oklahoma Press.

Steiner, H. (1999). *The Old Spanish Trail across the Mojave Desert: a history and guide*. Las Vegas, NV: Haldor Co.

Warren, E. (1974). Armijo's trace revisited: a new interpretation of the impact of the Antonio Armijo Route of 1829-1830 on the development of the Old Spanish trail. Unpublished master's thesis, University of Nevada, Las Vegas.

Other Reference Sources

University of Nevada Las Vegas: Lied Library Department of Special Collections: Las Vegas, NV.

Clark County Library District: Las Vegas, NV.

Chapter 2

Brewerton, G.D. (1930). *Overland with Kit Carson: a narrative of the Old Spanish*

Trail in '48. New York, New York: Coward-McCann, Inc.

Casebier, D. (1972). *Carleton's Pah-Ute Campaign*. Norco, CA: Casebier.

History of the Colorado: The Steamboat Era [Website]. (n.d.). The Lower Colorado River. Retrieved from *http:// www.socoloriver.com/id22.html*

Hopkins, A.D., & Evans, K.J. (1999). *The First 100 – Portraits of the Men and Women Who Shaped Las Vegas*. Las Vegas, NV: Huntington Press.

Joseph Christmas Ives [Website]. (2013). Wikipedia. Retrieved from *http:// en.wikipedia.org/wiki/Joseph_Christmas_ Ives*

Kenderdine, T. S. (1888). *A California Tramp and Later Footprints*; or, *Life on the plains and in the Golden state thirty years ago, with miscellaneous sketches in prose and verse*. Newton, PA: Philadelphia, Press of Globe Printing House.

Lyman, E.L. (2004). *The Overland Journey from Utah to California: wagon travel from the City of Saints to the City of Angels*. Reno, NV: University of Nevada Press.

Nevada State Parks. (n.d.) *Spring Mountain Ranch History – Docent Guide*. Spring Mountain State Park, NV: Nevada State Park.

Steiner, H. (1999). *The Old Spanish Trail across the Mojave Desert*: a history and guide. Las Vegas, NV: Haldor Co.

United States information: Nevada [Website]. (2010). Church News: The Church of Jesus Christ of Latter-day Saints. Retrieved from *http://www. ldschurchnews.com/articles/58714/United-States-information-Nevada.html*

Wheeler, G. M. (1870) Preliminary Report of General Features of the Military Reconnaissance through Southern Nevada / conducted under direction of Lieutenant George M. Wheeler assisted by Lieutenant D. W. Lockwood. Washington: Govt. Print. Off.

Wheeler, G. M. (1872) Preliminary Report Concerning Explorations and Surveys, Principally in Nevada and Arizona / prosecuted in accordance with paragraph 2, special orders no. 109, War Department, March 18, 1871, and letter of instructions of March 23, 1871, from Brigadier General A.A. Humphreys, Chief of Engineers. Washington: Govt. Print. Off.

William Sherley Williams [Website]. (n.d.) All Things William. Retrieved from *http://www.allthingswilliam.com/ willynilly/oldbill.html*

OTHER REFERENCE SOURCES

University of Nevada Las Vegas: Lied Library Department of Special Collections: Las Vegas, NV.

Clark County Library District: Las Vegas, NV.

CHAPTER 3

All Good Springs Awakened Early. (1920, July 10). *Goodsprings Gazette*, Goodsprings, NV: Vol. 5 #28, p. 1 Col.5.

Anderson (1974, November 9) Taped Interview. Nevada Division of State Parks File.

Auto Accident. (1916, December 9) *Las Vegas Age*, Las Vegas, NV.

Black Jack Mining Claim. (1932, January 27) *Las Vegas Age*, Las Vegas, NV.

Board Denies Parole Clark County Man, (1920, May 22). *Goodsprings Gazette*, Goodsprings, NV: p. 1 Column 6.

Book 1 Record of Chattel Mortgages, Book 2 of Mortgages, Clark Co. Nevada.

Boone Wilson Homestead Fight. (1972, April 9). *Las Vegas Review-Journal*, pp 3-5.

Certificate for Pension, 1899.

Confirm Hughes Ranch Sold for $1.5 Million. (1972, March 23). *Las Vegas Sun*. Las Vegas, NV: p. 1.

Connell, B. (1982, May 9). Yesterday's Headlines: The Great Krupp Diamond Caper. *Las Vegas Sun Magazine*. Las Vegas, NV: pp 10-13.

Dellenbaugh, F. S. (1902) *Romance of the Colorado*. New York, NY: G. P. Putnam's Sons.

Hafen, L. (1993) Old *Spanish Trail*. Lincoln, NE: University of Nebraska Press.

Hughes Purchase. (1972) *Las Vegas Review-Journal*, p. 1.

Indian Fights Sale of Krupp Ranch. (1973, March 23). *Las Vegas Review-Journal*, pp 1-2.

James Bernard Wilson. (1968). *The West*. (Vol. 9, #9, pp. 38-39, 64-66).

James Wilson settled Sandstone in 1867. (1972, April 9). *Las Vegas Review-Journal*, pp. 4-5.

Jones, G. (1973, March 25). Possible Rezoning Creates Conflict. *Las Vegas Review-Journal*, p.14.

Jones, G. (1973, June 5) Fletcher Jones Drops Red Rock Rezone Bid, *Las Vegas Review-Journal*, p. 1.

Kenderdine, T. (1888) A *California Tramp and Later Footprints*, Philadelphia, PA: Press of Globe Printing House.

Krupp Ranch Park Controversial. (1973, June 1) *Las Vegas Sun*. Las Vegas, NV: p. 1.

Krupp Ranch Sold. (1972, March 23) *Las Vegas Review-Journal*, p. 1.

Lake, A. (1975, March 27) Oral Interview, Las Vegas, NV: Nevada Division of State Parks File.

Lake-Eglington, O. (1975, March 27). Note Attached to Ada. Lake Oral Interview, Las Vegas NV: Nevada Division of State Parks File.

Lake, S. (1978, February 25). Oral Interview, Las Vegas, NV: *Nevada Division of State Parks File.*

Lauck, C. (1978, June 15) Taped Interview. Las Vegas, NV: Nevada Division of State Parks File.

Layton, A. (1982, October 15) Oral Interview, Blue Diamond, NV: Blue Diamond History Committee.

Lewis, G. (1972, April 9). Sandstone Ranch and the Indians. *Las Vegas Review-Journal*, p. 3.

Lincoln County Records Deeds Book A, p. 549.

Lum n Abner. (1982, December 12). *Las Vegas Sun Magazine*. Las Vegas, NV.

Military Service Records, Doc. #SC 880-088, National Archives, Washington D.C.

Notice of Application for Permission to Appropriate the Public Waters of the State of Nevada. Applications No. 3546, 3547 & 3548. (1915, December 11) *Las Vegas Age*, Las Vegas, NV: p. 2.

Real Estate Deeds, Lincoln Co. NV Book U.

Red Rock Rezoning Plan No Go. (1973, May 16). *Las Vegas Review-Journal*, p. 4, col.3.

Rogers, K. (2000, October 30) Archaeologist Charting Cabin's Significance. *Las Vegas Review-Journal*, p. 5B.

Sadovich, M. *(1966, April 19).* "Industrial Days" Section. *Henderson Home News Special*.

Sam Yount Purchases Old Wilson Ranch. (1925, February 7) *Las Vegas Age*, Las Vegas, NV: pp 1-2.

Scenic Land Plan Tabled for Further Study. (1973, March 28). *Las Vegas Review-Journal*, p. 4.

Sheriff Summoned to Ranch. (1935, June 13). *Las Vegas Evening Review Journal*, Las Vegas, NV.

Spring Mountain Ranch Corporation. (1981, June 7). *Las Vegas Review-Journal*.

Spring Mountain Ranch (SMR) Files: Deeds

Deeds Book A
  Pah-Ute County Records
  Wilsons
  George Anderson
  Willard George
  Chet Lauck
  Vera Krupp von Bohlen und Halbach
  Howard Hughes
Surveys Book B
  1871 (LV Springs with Howell)
  1875 (Sandstone Ranch)

Tax Assessment Rolls of Lincoln County, Nevada (1875)

Tax Assessment Rolls of Lincoln County, Nevada (1876)

Tax Assessment Rolls of Lincoln County, Nevada (1877)

Tax Assessment Rolls of Lincoln County, Nevada (1878)

Tax Assessment Rolls of Lincoln County, Nevada (1881)

UNLV Special Collections. Wilson File. Las Vegas, NV.

Warner, P. (1975, September 9) personal interview.

Warren, L. (1974, November 9). Comment on Anderson interview by Warren. Nevada Division of State Parks (NDSP).

Warren, L. (1979, April) *Red Rock Docent Training Manual* compiled by L. McCollum from personal research of former NDSP District Interpreter's historical files, lectures and training material.

Warren, L. (1985, September 9). Blue Diamond History Presentation at the Blue Diamond Library. Blue Diamond, NV.

Wheeler, Lt. George (1875) *Preliminary Report Upon a Reconnaissance Through Southern and South-eastern Nevada Made in 1869.* Washington: Government Printing Office.

Wheeler, Lt. George (Rep 1970) *Preliminary Report Concerning Explorations and Surveys Principally in Nevada and Arizona 1872.* Freeport, New York: Books for Libraries Press.

Whitaker, F. (1972, March 22). Hughes Land Sale Talks: Lips Sealed. *Las Vegas Sun.* Las Vegas, NV: p. 4 col 6.

CHAPTER 4

Blue Diamond Buys Buol Gypsum Deposit. (1924, November 22). *Las Vegas Age.* Las Vegas, NV: p. 1.

Blythin, E. (2010). *Vanishing Village: The Struggle for Community in the New West.* Las Vegas, NV: Stephens Press.

Chesson, R. (1970, June 7) Blue Diamond's Mystery House. *The Nevadan,* Las Vegas, NV: p. 4.

Fremont, J. (1970) *The Expeditions of John Charles Fremont. Volume I Travels from 1838-1844 and Map Portfolio.* University of Illinois Press. Chicago, Ill.

Hafen, L. & Armijo, A. (1947, November). Armijo's Journal.

Huntington Library Quarterly. Vol. II, No.1. University of California Press. pp. 87-101.

Hopkins, A. (1999, February 7). Part I: The Early Years. John C. Fremont. Putting Las Vegas on the Map. *Las Vegas Review-Journal.* Las Vegas, NV.

Hurtado, M. (2003, December 2) Oral History interview. Blue Diamond History Committee. Blue Diamond, NV.

J. R. Hunter Promoted. (1908, July 11). *Las Vegas Age.* Las Vegas, NV: p. 1.

Lake, O. & Lake, A. (1975, March 25 & 1977, April 17) Oral History interviews. SMR Files.

Las Vegas. (1906, March 3). *Las Vegas Age,* Las Vegas, NV: p. 1.

Lincoln County. (1903) Deeds Book "U," p. 350.

Local Notes. (1910, June 11). *Las Vegas Age,* Las Vegas, NV: p 5.

Nevada Division of State Parks (NDSP) Files.

Phelps, D (n.d.) Oral History interview. Blue Diamond History Committee. Blue Diamond, NV.

Railroad Letters, Blue Diamond History Committee Files, Blue Diamond, Nevada.

Ritenour, D. (1975) *Blue Diamond Adobe.* Las Vegas, NV: University of Nevada, Department of History.

Steiner, H. (1987, August 1) The Old Spanish Trail: 1829-1850. *Southern Nevada Times.* Volume 1, No. 11. p. 3.

Stultz, J. (n.d.) Calendar by Historical Society. Las Vegas.

Warren, E. (April 1979), *Red Rock Docent Training Manual*, compiled by McCollum, L. from personal research of Warren's historical files. Blue Diamond, NV, Xerox.

Wheeler, G. (1872, Ref. 1970), *Preliminary Report Concerning Explorations and Surveys Principally in Nevada and Arizona 1872*. Freeport, N.Y.

CHAPTER 5

Las Vegas Sun Timeline (Website). Retrieved from *http://www.lasvegassun.com/history*

Rankin, R. (2012). Interview by C. Williams [Audio file]. Friends of Red Rock Canyon Cultural Resource Committee Archives. Red Rock Canyon NCA, NV.

Vincent, Bill (1967, September 27). Homesteading on Pine Creek. *The Nevadan*, pp. 4-5.

Vincent, Bill (1974, June 30). Pine Creek, a pearl in the park system. *The Nevadan*, pp. 30-31.

CHAPTER 6

Bill Morgan Feted on 70th Birthday. (1939, Apr 10). *Las Vegas Review-Journal*. p. 6.

Born: Bentley. (1914, Jul 7). *Las Vegas Sun*, p. 3.

Card Games Cause Fracases on Xmas. (1930, Dec 26), *Las Vegas Review-Journal*. p 2.

Death Bed Vows Unite Divorced 2. (1935, May 14), *Las Vegas Review-Journal*. p. 2.

Death Calls Vegas Matron Last Night. (1936, Mar 27), *Las Vegas Review-Journal* p. 1.

Department of the Interior U. S. Land Office. (1922, Oct 21), *Las Vegas Age*. p. 5.

Free Bureau for Jobless. (1931, Sep 5). *Las Vegas Age*, p. 8.

Hurtado, M. (2006), Interview by P. VanBetten [Audio file]. Blue Diamond History Committee, Archives. Blue Diamond, NV.

Notice for Publication Department of the Interior. (1932, Oct 26). *Las Vegas Age*, p. 3.

Notice for Publication Department of the Interior. (1937, May 26). *Las Vegas Review-Journal*, p. 7.

Notice of Application. (1915, Jan 2). *Las Vegas Sun*, p. 4.

Notice of Application for Permission to Appropriate the Public Waters of Nevada. (1937, Jan 1). *Las Vegas Age*, p. 11.

Old Timers. (1948, Aug 3). *Las Vegas Review-Journal*, p. 16.

One of Six Caught in Federal Dry Raid out on Bail. (1928, Jun 8). *Las Vegas Age*, p. 1.

Pioneer Las Vegans Ride in Parade Here (1942, May 30). *Las Vegas Review-Journal*, p. 3.

Reese Morgan is Accidentally Shot. (1934, Jan 29). *Las Vegas Review-Journal*, p. 1.

Reese T. Morgan Pioneer Vegan, Dies Saturday Eve. (1941, Dec 22). *Las Vegas Review-Journal*, p. 3.

Re-Enact Scene of 10 Years Ago. (1936, Apr 17). *Las Vegas Review-Journal*, p. 8.

Shipping Ore. (1911, Apr 8). *Las Vegas Age*. p. 4.

Sunday Morning Fire Damages Morgan Home. (1925, Dec 19). *Las Vegas Age*, p. 3.

The Public Waters of the State of Nevada. (1918, May 18). *Las Vegas Age*, p. 2.

To Ranch. (1930, Aug 11). *Las Vegas Review-Journal*, p. 2.

Unloaded Gun Claims Victim. (1912, Oct 5). *Las Vegas Age*, p.3.

Water Hearing. (1937, May 7). *Las Vegas Age*, p. 3.

W. C. "Bill" Morgan, Vegas Pioneer, Dies After Illness in California. (1948, Aug 2). *Las Vegas Review-Journal*, p. 1.

Westside House Razed by Flame. (1928, Jun 2). *Las Vegas Age*, p. 1.

OTHER REFERENCE SOURCES

United States Census Bureau Records [Website]. (n.d.). Retrieved from *http://home.ancestry.com/*

U. S. Department of the Interior: Bureau of Land Management: General Land Office Records [Website]. (n.d.). Retrieved from *http://www.glorecords.blm.gov/search/default.aspx*

U. S Department of the Interior: Bureau of Land Management: Nevada Land Records [Website]. (n.d.). Retrieved from *http://www.nv.blm.gov/LandRecords/index.php*

Clark County Nevada GIS Records [Website]. (n.d.). Retrieved from *http://gisgate.co.clark.nv.us/openweb/*

Clark County Recorder Office Records: Las Vegas, NV.

Clark County Assessor Office Records: Las Vegas, NV.

Las Vegas-Clark County Library District Database for *Las Vegas Sun* and *Las Vegas Review-Journal* archives.

University of Nevada Las Vegas: Lied Library: Department of Special Collections: Las Vegas, NV.

Nevada State Museum: Las Vegas: Cahlan Research Library: Las Vegas, NV.

State of Nevada: Division of Water Resources [Website]. (n.d.) Retrieved from: *http://water.nv.gov/waterrights/ Morgan Application* Permits: 3116, 5070 and 10054. Gilcrease Application Permit: 7306.

LEGAL DESCRIPTION
OF THE MORGAN RANCHES

Bill and Edith's 7 acre ranch located north of the present down town Las Vegas: Located in South half of SE ¼ of Section 22, Township 19 S, Range 61 E

Bill and Edith's 160 acre Henderson homestead located at Coyote Run and Hemsdale: SW ¼ of Section 9, Township 22 S, Range 62 E

Bill and Edith's 80 acre ranch located at Grand Teton Drive and North Buffalo: SE ¼ of SW ¼ and SW ¼ of SE ¼ of Section 9, Township 19 S, Range 60 E

Reese's 80 acre homestead located at Grand Teton Drive and North Buffalo: North half SW ¼ of Section 9, Township 19 S, Range 60 E

Edith's 40 acre homestead at Centennial Parkway and Grand Montecito Way: NW ¼ of NW ¼ of Section 28, Township 19 S, Range 60 E

Bill and Edith's 80 acre Red Rock ranch now part of Oliver Ranch (ownership was not valid – seller did not own the land): The east ½ of the SW ¼ of Section 1, Township 22 S, Range 58 E

Bill and Edith's 80 acre homestead now part of Bonnie Springs: SE ¼ of SW ¼ and SW ¼ of SE ¼ of Section 2, Township 22 S, Range 58 E. And additional 40 acres was added to the ranch in 1939: SW ¼ of SW ¼ of Section 2, Township 22 S, Range 58 E

Reese's 160 acre homestead which is now Oliver Ranch: SW ¼ of Section 1, Township 22 S Range 58 E

CHAPTER 7

Bracken, W. (1938, March). Letter about water rights. Friends of Red Rock Canyon: Cultural Resource Committee Archives. Red Rock Canyon NCA, NV.

Clinesmith, K. (2012). Interview by C. Williams [Notes]. Friends of Red Rock Canyon: Cultural Resource Committee Archives. Red Rock Canyon NCA, NV.

Clinesmith, K. (2013, January). Last Ride. Story of the last horse ride at Oliver Ranch. Friends of Red Rock Canyon: Cultural Resource Committee Archives. Red Rock Canyon NCA, NV.

Clinesmith, L. (2012). Interview by C. Williams [Notes]. Friends of Red Rock Canyon: Cultural Resource Committee Archives. Red Rock Canyon NCA, NV.

Denman, N. (2012). Interview by S. Kolar [Notes]. Friends of Red Rock Canyon: Cultural Resource Committee Archives. Red Rock Canyon NCA, NV.

Edner, A. (1996). Interview by C. Miller [Audio file]. Friends of Red Rock Canyon: Cultural Resource Committee Archives. Red Rock Canyon NCA, NV.

Frejlach, K. (2015). Interview by C. Williams [Audio file and Email]. Friends of Red Rock Canyon: Cultural Resource Committee Archives. Red Rock Canyon NCA, NV.

Hinricksen, L. (2013). Interview by C. Williams [Audio file]. Friends of Red Rock Canyon: Cultural Resource Committee Archives. Red Rock Canyon NCA, NV.

Hurtado A. (2013). Interview by C. Williams [Audio file]. Friends of Red Rock Canyon: Cultural Resource Committee Archives. Red Rock Canyon NCA, NV.

Hurtado, M. (2006). Interview by P. Van Betten [Audio file]. Blue Diamond

History Committee Archives. Blue Diamond, NV.

Logan – Denman, N. (2012). Interview by C. Williams [Notes]. Friends of Red Rock Canyon: Cultural Resource Committee Archives. Red Rock Canyon NCA, NV.

Logan – Smith, S. (2012-2013). Interview by C. Williams [Notes and Email Messages]. Friends of Red Rock Canyon: Cultural Resource Committee Archives. Red Rock Canyon NCA, NV.

Nevada State Parks. (n.d.) *Spring Mountain Ranch History – Docent Guide*. Spring Mountain State Park, NV: Nevada State Park

Oliver, E. (1967). *Miss Anna*. Oak Park, IL: Broland Publishing

Oliver, R. (1993). Interview by S. Wolf [Notes]. Friends of Red Rock Canyon: Cultural Resource Committee Archives. Red Rock Canyon NCA, NV.

One of Six Caught in Federal Dry Raid out on Bail. (1928, Jun 8). *Las Vegas Age*. p. 1.

Price, E. (2012). Interview by C. Williams [Audio file with Email follow-up]. Friends of Red Rock Canyon: Cultural Resource Committee Archives. Red Rock Canyon NCA, NV.

Rankin, B. (2012). Interview by C. Williams [Audio file]. Friends of Red Rock Canyon: Cultural Resource Committee Archives. Red Rock Canyon NCA, NV.

Rankin, R. (2012). Interview by C. Williams [Audio file]. Friends of Red

Rock Canyon: Cultural Resource Committee Archives. Red Rock Canyon NCA, NV.

Richardson, G. (2013). Interview by C. Williams [Audio file]. Friends of Red Rock Canyon: Cultural Resource Committee Archives. Red Rock Canyon NCA, NV.

Richardson, V. (2013). Interview by C. Williams [Audio file]. Friends of Red Rock Canyon: Cultural Resource Committee Archives. Red Rock Canyon NCA, NV.

Smith, S. (2012). Interview by S. Kolar [Notes]. Friends of Red Rock Canyon: Cultural Resource Committee Archives. Red Rock Canyon NCA, NV.

Wedding, J., & Winslow, D., & Joye, A., & Smith, A. (Eds.), Riddle, J. (2008). *Oliver Ranch Project Final Report*. Las Vegas, NV. Cultural Resources Division of the Harry Reid Center for Environmental Studies.

OTHER REFERENCE SOURCES

United States Census Bureau Records [Website]. (n.d.). Retrieved from *http://home.ancestry.com/*

U. S. Department of the Interior: Bureau of Land Management: General Land Office Records [Website]. (n.d.). Retrieved from *http://www.glorecords.blm.gov/search/default.aspx*

U. S. Department of the Interior: Bureau of Land Management: Nevada Land Records [Website]. (n.d.). Retrieved from *http://www.nv.blm.gov/LandRecords/index.php*

Clark County Nevada GIS Records [Website]. (n.d.). Retrieved from *http://gisgate.co.clark.nv.us/openweb/*

Clark County Recorder Office Records: Las Vegas, NV.

Clark County Assessor Office Records: Las Vegas, NV.

Nevada Division of Minerals Records: Carson City, NV.

Las Vegas-Clark County Library District Database for *Las Vegas Sun* and *Las Vegas Review-Journal* archives.

Nevada State Museum: Las Vegas: Cahlan Research Library: Las Vegas, NV.

State of Nevada: Division of Water Resources [Website]. (n.d.) Retrieved from: *http://water.nv.gov/waterrights/ C Oliver Application 7987 Certificate 2418*

LEGAL DESCRIPTION OF THE OLIVER RANCH

Core area of Oliver Ranch (Reese Morgan homestead): SW ¼ of Section 1, Township 22 S Range 58 E

Land transfer with BLM in 1947 adding 160 acres to the ranch:

SW ¼ of SE ¼ of Section 1 Township 22 S Range 58 E

East 1/2 of SE ¼ of Section 2 Township 22 S Range 58 E

NW ¼ of NW ¼ of Section 12 Township 22 S Range 58 E

Land in the Spring Mountains west of Lee Canyon Road given up in the transfer:

SW ¼ of SW ¼ of Section 12 Township 18 S Range 56 E

N ½ of NW ¼ of Section 13 Township 18 S Range 56 E

NE ½ of NE ¼ of Section 14 Township 18 S Range 56 E

CHAPTER 8

BLM Records at: U.S. Department of the Interior: Bureau of Land Management: General Land Office Records [Website]. n.d. Retrieved from: *http://www.glorecords.blm.gov/search/default.aspx*

Boles, John. Retrieved from *http://www.goldensilents.com/stars/johnboles.html*

Bought Ranch. (1917, Mar 24). *Las Vegas Age*, p. 2.

Internet Movie Database, Retrieved from IMDb.com.

Levinson, B. (2004) Interview by G. Schroeder [Audio file]. Blue Diamond History Committee Archives. Blue Diamond, Nevada.

One of Six Caught in Federal Dry Raid out on Bail. (1928, Jun 8). *Las Vegas Age*, p. 1.

Recreational Vehicle Park (1978, May 17 and June 7). *Las Vegas Review-Journal,* p. 7B and p. 10D.

Trafzer, Gilbert, Sisquoc (Eds.). 2012. *The Indian School on Magnolia Avenue*: Oregon State University Press.

Wilson Shearer, Gloria (2010). Interview produced by Robert D. McCracken. Nye County Town History Projects. Tonopah, Nevada.

Chapter 9

Levin, P (1966, November 27). Calico Day Camp for Happy Girl Scouts. *The Nevadan*. p 24-25.

Local Notes. (1909, November 13). *Las Vegas Age*. p 5.

Local Notes. (1915, June 17). *Las Vegas Age*. p 3.

Notice of Application. (1915, January 30). *Las Vegas Age*. P 4.

Notice of Publication. (1921, November 19). *Las Vegas Age*. p 2.

Red Rock Canyon reels under big visitor crush. (1991, Nov 3). *Las Vegas Review-Journal*. p 1B, 10B-11B.

Red Rock Survival Plan Here. (1964, Jan 12). *Las Vegas Review-Journal*, p. 4.

Triolo. (2013). Interview by C. Williams [Audio file]. Friends of Red Rock Canyon: Cultural Resource Committee Archives. Red Rock Canyon NCA, NV.

Other Reference Sources

Clark County Nevada GIS Records [Website]. (n.d.). Retrieved from *http:// gisgate.co.clark.nv.us/openweb/*

Clark County Recorders Office. Las Vegas, NV.

Las Vegas-Clark County Library District Database for *Las Vegas Sun* and *Las Vegas Review-Journal* archives.

Nevada State Museum: Las Vegas: Cahlan Research Library: Las Vegas, NV.

State of Nevada Division of Water Resources: [Website]. (n.d.). Retrieved from *http://water.nv.gov/index.cfm* Wilson Water Application Permits: 1048, 1049, 1051 and 1052 Mason Water Application Permits: 3245 and 3246

United States Census Bureau Records [Website]. (n.d.). Retrieved from *http:// home.ancestry.com/*

U. S. Department of the Interior: Bureau of Land Management: General Land Office Records [Website]. (n.d.). Retrieved from *http://www.glorecords. blm.gov/search/default.aspx*

U. S. Department of the Interior: Bureau of Land Management: Nevada Land Records [Website]. (n.d.). Retrieved from *http://www.nv.blm.gov/ LandRecords/index.php*

Warner, L (c 1987). Growth at park's edge. *Las Vegas Review-Journal*. Newspaper clipping from UNLV Special Collections – Red Rock Collection. MS98-03. Box 1 of 1.

LEGAL DESCRIPTION OF THE
1922 ELLA MASON'S HOMESTEAD

Lot 1 or NE ¼ of NE ¼ of Section 1, Township 21 S, Range 58 E

Lot 4 or NW ¼ of NW ¼ of Section 6, Township 20 S, Range 58 E

Lot 5 or SW ¼ of NW ¼ of Section 6, Township 20 S, Range 58 E

Lot 6 or NW ¼ of SW ¼ of Section 6, Township 20 S, Range 58 E

LEGAL DESCRIPTION OF THE 1966 GIRL SCOUT HOMESTEAD

NE ¼ of NE ¼ of SE ¼ of Section 1, Township 21 S, Range 58 E

E ½ of SE ¼ of NE ¼ of Section 1, Township 21 S, Range 58 E

CHAPTER 10

Casebier, D. (1972). *Carleton's Pah-Ute Campaign*. Norco, CA: Casebier

Fremont, J.C. (1845) *Report of the exploring expedition to the Rocky Mountains in the year 1842 and to Oregon and North California in the years 1843-44.* Washington, D.C.: Gales and Seaton, Printers)

Notice for Publication Department of the Interior. (1937, January 6). *Las Vegas Review-Journal*, p. 5.

Preuss, C. (1958) *Exploring with Fremont: the private diaries of Charles Preuss, Cartographer for John C. Fremont on his first, second, and fourth expeditions to the Far West*. E.G. Gudde, & E.K. Gudde (Trans.). University of Oklahoma Press

Trousdale R. (2012). Interview by C. Williams [Audio file]. Friends of Red Rock Canyon: Cultural Resource Committee Archives. Red Rock Canyon NCA, NV.

Trousdale R. (2014). Telephone interview by C. Williams [Added to transcribed audio file]. Friends of Red Rock Canyon: Cultural Resource Committee Archives. Red Rock Canyon NCA, NV.

Wheeler, G. M. (1872) Preliminary Report Concerning Explorations and Surveys, Principally in Nevada and Arizona / prosecuted in accordance with paragraph 2, special orders no. 109, War Department, March 18, 1871, and letter of instructions of March 23, 1871, from Brigadier General A.A. Humphreys, Chief of Engineers. Washington: Govt. Print. Off.

OTHER REFERENCE SOURCES

United States Census Bureau Records [Website]. (n.d.). Retrieved from *http://home.ancestry.com/*

U. S. Department of the Interior: Bureau of Land Management: General Land Office Records [Website]. (n.d.). Retrieved from *http://www.glorecords. blm.gov/search/default.aspx*

U. S. Department of the Interior: Bureau of Land Management: Nevada Land Records [Website]. (n.d.). Retrieved from *http://www.nv.blm.gov/ LandRecords/index.php*

Clark County Nevada GIS Records [Website]. (n.d.). Retrieved from *http://gisgate.co.clark.nv.us/openweb/*

Clark County Recorder Office Records: Las Vegas, NV.

Las Vegas-Clark County Library District Database for *Las Vegas Sun* and *Las Vegas Review-Journal* archives.

Nevada State Museum: Las Vegas: Cahlan Research Library: Las Vegas, NV.

Bureau of Land Management: Land and Mineral Legacy: *http://www.blm.gov/lr2000/*

LEGAL DESCRIPTION OF
WILLIAM WOOD HOMESTEADS
AND TWO MINE CLAIMS

William Wood Homestead

NE ¼ of SE ¼ of Section 19, Township 22 S, Range 58 E

NW ¼ of SW ¼ of Section 20, Township 22 S, Range 58 E

Copper Hill 1943 Mine Claim

NE ¼ of Section 19, Township 22 S, Range 58 E

Findlay Copper Chief Mine 1911 Homestead

West Half of Section 19, Township 22 S, Range 58 E

CHAPTER 11

Big Bug. (1910, May 28). *Las Vegas Age.* p 1.

Big Devil Wagon. (1905, May 20). *Las Vegas Age.* p 6.

Caterpillar. (1910, May 7). *Las Vegas Age.* p 4.

Commissioners. (1910, Jun 11). *Las Vegas Age.* p 1.

Company History [Website], (n.d.) Holtca. Retrieved from *http://www.holtca.com/company/company-history*

Excelsior Stone Quarry. (1905, Apr 7). *Las Vegas Age.* p 1.

Harriman Jealous. (1906, July 14). *Las Vegas Age.* p 3.

Hopkins, A.D., & Evans, K.J. (1999) *The First 100 – Portraits of the Men and Women Who Shaped Las Vegas*. Las Vegas, NV Huntington Press.

Las Vegas and Tonopah Railroad [Website], (n.d.) Wikipedia. Retrieved from *http://en.wikipedia.org/wiki/Las_Vegas_and_Tonopah_Railroad*

Las Vegas Brevities. (1905, May 20). *Las Vegas Age.* p 6.

Las Vegas Oil Report Hoax. (1924, Apr 5). *Las Vegas Age.* p 2.

Local Notes. (1910, Apr 2). *Las Vegas Age.* p 5.

Local Notes. (1910, Apr 9). *Las Vegas Age.* p 5.

Local Notes. (1910, Apr 30). *Las Vegas Age.* p 5.

Local Notes. (1910, July 16). *Las Vegas Age.* p 5.

Local Notes. (1910, Aug 13). *Las Vegas Age.* p 5.

Local Notes. (1911, Jan 6). *Las Vegas Age.* p 5.

McWilliams Townsite [Website]. (2008) Online Nevada Encyclopedia. Retrieved from *http://www.onlinenevada.org/articles/mcwilliams-townsite*

Nevada Auto Route. (1905, Aug 26). *Las Vegas Age.* p 2.

Railroad Situation. (1910, Jan 8). *Las Vegas Age.* p 1.

Sandstone. (1909, Jan 9). *Las Vegas Age.* p 1.

Sandstone Quarry. (1910, Mar 12). *Las Vegas Age.* p 1, 4.

Squires, C.P. (1912). Clark County. In Sam P. Davis (Ed.), *History of Nevada* Vol. II (pp. 795-805) Reno, NV-Los Angeles, CA: The Elms Publishing Co.

Stone Quarry. (1905, Aug 26). Las Vegas Age. p 1.

Stone Quarry. (1906, Dec 29). *Las Vegas Age.* p 1.

Summons. (1906, Oct 20). *Las Vegas Age.* p 6.

Taken Away. (1906, Oct 13). *Las Vegas Age.* p 4.

Tonopah and Tidewater Railroad. [Website]. (n.d.) Wikipedia. Retrieved from *http://en.wikipedia.org/wiki/Tonopah_and_Tidewater_Railroad*

Traction Engine. (1906, Nov 24). *Las Vegas Age.* p 1.

Triolo. (2013). Interview by C. Williams [Audio file]. Friends of Red Rock Canyon: Cultural Resource Committee Archives. Red Rock Canyon NCA, NV.

Untitled ad. (1905, May 6). *Las Vegas Age.* p 4.

Vegas's First Baby. (1905, Aug 26). *Las Vegas Age.* p 4.

OTHER REFERENCE SOURCES

Caterpillar Corporate Archives: Peoria, IL.

Las Vegas-Clark County Library District Database for *Las Vegas Sun* archives.

Nevada State Museum: Las Vegas: Cahlan Research Library: Las Vegas, NV.

University of Nevada Las Vegas: Lied Library: Department of Special Collections: Las Vegas, NV.

CHAPTER 12

Bureau of Land Management [BLM]. (n.d.). Las Vegas, Nevada.

Personal Interviews with T.P.'s daughter Faye (with input from her sisters Pam and Joy). 2010.

Special Collections. (n.d.). University of Nevada Las Vegas (UNLV). Las Vegas, Nevada.

CHAPTER 13

Rogers, K. (1993, January 19), Group attempts to derail mining plan. *Las Vegas Review-Journal*, p. B1.

OTHER REFERENCE SOURCES

Personal Email from Friends of Nevada Wilderness.

Las Vegas-Clark County Library District Database for *Las Vegas Review-Journal* archives.

Clark County Department of Public Works, Survey Division.

CHAPTER 14

Appledorn, J. (2007, January 30) Oral History Interview. Blue Diamond History Committee, Blue Diamond, Nevada.

Blue Diamond Mine Information Sheets (n.d.).

Bogdanovich, G. (2009, September 8) Oral History Interview by Gretchen Schorder. Blue Diamond History Committee, Blue Diamond, Nevada.

Bradley, W. G. (1932, September). Methods and Costs of Mining and Crushing Gypsum at the Mine of the Blue Diamond Corporation (Ltd), Arden, Nevada. University of Michigan. Information Circular, Department of Commerce, Bureau of Mines.

Delong, A. (2008, September 23) Oral History Interview by Pat van Betten. Blue Diamond History Committee, Blue Diamond, Nevada.

Hurtado, A. (2003, December 2) Oral History Interview by Shirley Leavitt. Blue Diamond History Committee, Blue Diamond, Nevada.

Hurtado, M. (2003, December 2) Oral History Interview by Shirley Leavitt. Blue Diamond History Committee, Blue Diamond, Nevada.

Leavitt, R. (2011, November 16) Oral History Interview. Blue Diamond History Committee, Blue Diamond, Nevada.

Mower, L. (2013, January 31). "Rhodes wins Red Rock ruling; land swap move continues." *Las Vegas Review Journal.* Retrieved from reviewjournal.com.

Phelps, R. (1978, November 2) Oral History Interview by Kim Geary. Blue Diamond History Committee, Blue Diamond, Nevada.

Phelps, Stella (n.d.) Oral History Interview. Blue Diamond History Committee, Blue Diamond, Nevada.

Rogers, B. (2005, April) Interview with Works Manager.

Wolters, N. (2009, March 9) Oral History Interview by Pat van Betten. Blue Diamond History Committee, Blue Diamond, Nevada.

CHAPTER 15

LaMadra. (1907, July 13). The Las Vegas Age, p. 1.

Lucky Strike. (1907, April 20). *Beatty Bullfrog Miner.* Reprinted in *Southern Nevada Times,* February, 1989, p. 92.

Midnight Group. (1911, April 18). *Las Vegas Age,* p. 4.

Morrison, Jane Ann (2012, September 13). With land swaps curtailed, owners try fears of Mining. *Las Vegas Review-Journal* (NV). Retrieved from hnfoweb. newsbank.com.ilsweb.lvccld.org

Nevada West Naval Facilities Engineering Command, Civil Defense Dept. (1969). National Fallout Shelter Updating Survey. Retrieved from http://www.forgottennevada.org/sites/fallout.html

Ore Shipped. (1907, March 2). *Las Vegas Age*, p. 1.

Rich Ore. (1907, January 19). *Las Vegas Age*, p. l.

State of Nevada, Department of Business and Industry (Jan.-Dec., 2012). Directory of Nevada Mine Operations, Retrieved from http://dirweb.state.nv.us/msts/minedirectory.pdf

Sunday's Killing. (1905, October 7). *Las Vegas Age*, p. 1.

U.S. Geological Survey Bulletin 1730-A. (1986). *Mineral Resources of the La Madra Mountains Wilderness Study Area, Clark County Nevada*. Washington, DC: U.S. Government Printing Office.

Vanderburg, W.O. (1989). *Mines of Clark County*. Las Vegas, Nevada: Nevada Publications.

CHAPTER 16

Kolvet, R. & Ford, V. (2006). *The Civilian Conservation Corps in Nevada: From boys to men*. (2006). Reno, NV. University of Nevada Press.

One of Six Caught in Federal Dry Raid out on Bail. (1928, Jun 8). *Las Vegas Age*, p. 1.

White, W. (2003). *The Civilian Conservation Corps in Clark County,*

Nevada: an historic overview and context. UNLV Special Collections (F847.C5).

OTHER REFERENCE SOURCES

Clark County Nevada GIS Records [Website]. (n.d.). Retrieved from *http://gisgate.co.clark.nv.us/openweb/*

Clark County Recorder Office Records: Las Vegas, NV.

Las Vegas-Clark County Library District Database for *Las Vegas Sun* and *Las Vegas Review-Journal* archives.

Nevada State Museum: Las Vegas: Cahlan Research Library: Las Vegas, NV.

University of Nevada Las Vegas: Lied Library Department of Special Collections: Las Vegas, NV.

U. S. Department of the Interior: Bureau of Land Management: General Land Office Records [Website]. (n.d.). Retrieved from *http://www.glorecords.blm.gov/search/default.aspx*

U. S. Department of the Interior: Bureau of Land Management: Nevada Land Records [Website]. (n.d.). Retrieved from *http://www.nv.blm.gov/LandRecords/index.php*

LEGAL DESCRIPTION OF THE NAYLOR PROPERTY

SW ¼ of SW ¼ of Section 2 Township 22 S Range 58 E

LEGAL DESCRIPTION OF THE COLEMAN-NOON PROPERTY

E ½ of SE ¼ of Section 29 Township 20 S Range 58 E

NE ¼ of NE ¼ of Section 32 Township 20 S Range 58 E

LEGAL DESCRIPTION OF THE BEAM PROPERTY—CCC CAMP 122

NW ¼ of NE ¼ of Section 8 Township 22 S Range 61 E

N ½ of NW ¼ of Section 8 Township 22 S Range 61 E

CHAPTER 17

Fleming, P. (1984, Oct). Friends of Red Rock Canyon Board Meeting Minutes.

Hunsaker, D. (2012). "Leading by Example: Volunteers and Friends Groups." Bureau of Land Management Library. Retrieved from *http://www.blm. gov/wo/st/en/info/history/sidebars/social_ resources/leading_by_example.html*.

OTHER REFERENCE SOURCES

Friends of Red Rock Canyon Volunteer Training Manual – April 1987. Lisa Heithmar, Chris Miller, Joel Mur, Carol Ward

Friends of Red Rock Canyon organizational history and photo archives

Friends of Red Rock Canyon – *The Desert Trumpet* (1997–2010)

Friends of Red Rock Canyon – *The Rock* magazine (2010–2015)

CHAPTER 18

U.S. Department of the Interior, Bureau of Land Management (2003), Publication H-8362-1, *Working with Cooperating Associations*, p. II-I.

Fee Demo Program Beneficial, But Could Be More Effective (2002) Report No. 2002-I-0045. Retrieved from *http:// www.nps.gov/pub_aff/feedemo/reports/ oig%20report.pdf*

Frequently Asked Questions Federal Lands Recreation Enhancement Act (FLREA) (2005, January 25) Retrieved from *http://www.doi.gov/initiatives/ ImplementationFAQ.pdf*

Dutton, Elizabeth (1997, November 13) Red Rock Visitors Find Fee, Not Free. *Las Vegas Sun*. Retrieved from *http:// www.lasvegassun.com*.

(1999, January 22) Entrance Fees Beginning to Provide Big Dividends. *Las Vegas Sun*. Retrieved from *http://www. lasvegassun.com*

CHAPTER 19

A Recreation Management Plan for Red Rock Recreation Lands (1969). [Website]. (n.d.) Bureau of Land Management Library. Retrieved from *https://archive. org/details/recreationmanage7287unit*

BLM Closing Quarry Site To Visitors. (1972, May). *Las Vegas Review-Journal.*

BLM's philosophy: Ignore the public. (1980, Oct 1). *Las Vegas Review-Journal.* p. 2B.

Boroughf, D. (1974, Feb 4). Letter from Dave Boroughf to Jean Ford. UNLV Special Collections, Jean Ford Archives.

Conservationists want Red Rock left untouched. (1974, Apr 17). *Las Vegas Review-Journal*. p. 3.

Duran, M. (1979, Nov 22). Incensed over proposed drilling. *Las Vegas Review-Journal*. p. 2B.

Geary, F. (2002, Aug14). Residents fear plan final blow to area's rural beauty, quiet. *Las Vegas Review-Journal*. p. 1A.

Geary, F. (2002, Aug15). Resident's blast proposed housing project. *Las Vegas Review-Journal*. p. 1A.

Geary, F. (2003, Mar 28). LAND NEAR RED ROCK: Development opposed. *Las Vegas Review-Journal*. p. 1B.

Geary, F. (2003, May 1). Builder applies for clearances. *Las Vegas Review-Journal*. p. 1A.

Geary, F. (2003, May 11). Hearing brings Red Rock combatants together. *Las Vegas Review-Journal*. p. 7B.

Geary, F. (2003, May 22). County OKs Red Rock restrictions. *Las Vegas Review-Journal*. p. 2B.

Harvey, D. (n.d.) Public Land Management Under The Classification And Multiple Use Act [Website], (n.d.) Hein Online. Retrieved from *http://heinonline.org/HOL/LandingPage?handle=hein.journals/narl2&div=31&id=&page=*

Hess. D. (1967, June 29). Letter from Dennis Hess to Nolan Keil. Mary Kozlowski files. Friends of Red Rock Canyon Archives.

Jourdan, K. (2012, Feb 9). Developer backs off access via Route 159. *Las Vegas Review-Journal*. p. 5B.

Kofol, A. (1979, Nov 25). Is There 'Black Gold' in 'Them Thar' Red Rocks? *The Nevadan*. p. 8-9.

Kozlowski, M. (1967, Jun 27). Letter to Dennis Hess. Mary Kozlowski files. Friends of Red Rock Canyon Archives.

Kozlowski, M. (1967, Jul 1). Letter to Dennis Hess. Mary Kozlowski files. Friends of Red Rock Canyon Archives.

Land Sales Generate More Than $18 Million for Projects. [Website], (n.d.). Retrieved from *http://www.blm.gov/nv/st/en/info/newsroom/2014/may/southern_nevada__1.html*

Lopez, G. (1979, Dec 16). Let's drill that oil. *Las Vegas Review-Journal*. p. 3B.

Manning, M. (1980, Sep 29). Drillers Booted Off More Acres At Red Rock. *Las Vegas Sun*. p. 13.

Master Plan Red Rock Canyon. (1976). Royston Hanamoto Beck & Abey. Ram Graphics. San Rafael, California.

McCarthy, P. (2013). *Friends of the Earth: A History of American Environmentalism.* Chicago, IL: Chicago Review Press, Incorporated.

Morrison, J. (2011, Oct 31). Let games begin with Rhodes' Blue Diamond waiver request. *Las Vegas Review-Journal*. p. 1B.

Mower, L. (2013, Jan23). Clark County, Rhodes in accord on land swap plan. *w.* p. 1B.

Mower, L. (2013, Feb 1). Nevada Supreme Court backs developer. *Las Vegas Review-Journal*. p. 3B.

Nevada Open Spaces. (1972, Jun 1). Letter from Nevada Open Space to Dennis Hess, BLM District Manager. UNLV Special Collections, Jean Ford Archives. MS25 Box 19.

Nevada Open Spaces. (1973, Jan 5). Letter from Nevada Open Space to Clark County Legislative Delegation. UNLV Special Collections, Jean Ford Archives. MS25 Box 19.

Oil and Gas Leasing in the Red Rock Canyon Recreation Lands: Final Assessment (1980). [Website]. (n.d.) Bureau of Land Management Library. Retrieved from *https://ia601604.us.archive.org/23/items/oilgasleasinginrunit/oilgasleasinginrunit.pdf*

O'Reiley, T. (2012, May 15). Creditors group sues Rhodes. *Las Vegas Review-Journal*. p. 1D.

Packer, A. (2003, May 7). Tours change some minds about development. *Las Vegas Review-Journal*. p. 1B.

Red Rock Canyon National Conservation Area Resource Management Plan (2005) [website] (n.d.). Retrieved from *https://ia601604.us.archive.org/23/items/oilgasleasinginrunit/oilgasleasinginrunit.pdf*

Red Rock bargain lost in giant mall's glare. (1974, Jan 28). *Las Vegas Review-Journal*. p. 26.

Red Rock Canyon reels under big visitor crush. (1991, Nov 3). *Las Vegas Review-Journal*. p. 1B, 10B, 11B.

Red Rock Cleanup Gains Award. (1967, Nov 11). *Las Vegas Review-Journal*. p. 20.

Red Rock drilling approval an outrage. (1980, Aug 7). *Las Vegas Review-Journal*. p. 2B.

Red Rock drilling petition given to BLM. (1980, Apr 24). *Las Vegas Review-Journal*. p. 10.

Red Rock Survival Plan Here. (1964, Jan 12). *Las Vegas Review-Journal*. p. 4.

Reid Statement on House Efforts to Gut SNPLMA. [Website]. (n.d.). Retrieved from *http://www.reid.senate.gov/press_releases/2014-02-26-reid-statement-on-house-efforts-to-gut-snplma#.U_op7fldU1I*

Rogers, K. (1993, January 19), Group attempts to derail mining plan. *Las Vegas Review-Journal*, p. B1.

Royston, Hanamoto, Beck & Abey. (1976). Master Plan Red Rock Canyon. Copy located in Friends of Red Rock Canyon Archives.

Shone, R. (1973, Jun 24). Red Rock ranch land debate hot. *Las Vegas Review-Journal*. p. A19.

Smith, J. (2003, Mar 30). It's time to draw line in the sandstone to block Red Rock developers. *Las Vegas Review-Journal*. p. 1B.

Southern Nevada Public Lands Management Act (1998). [Website]. (n.d.). Retrieved from *http://www.blm.gov/pgdata/content/nv/en/snplma.html*

State Purchase Of Red Rock Land Welcome News. (1974, Jan 30). *Las Vegas Sun*. p. 2.

Sub Committee Report: Spring Mountains Planning Unit. (1965, Mar 1). UNLV Special Collections, Jean Ford Archives. F847.C5 S82

Ten Eyck, C. (1979, Nov 28). I say drill for oil anywhere. *Las Vegas Review-Journal*. p. 3B.

The Red Rock Experience. (c 1991). BLM Las Vegas District Office / BLM Nevada State Office.

Townsend, J. (1979, Nov 18). Red Rock drilling won't work. *Las Vegas Review-Journal*. p. 10.

Townsend, J. (1979, Nov 20). Red Rock drilling opposed. *Las Vegas Review-Journal*. p. 11 &13.

Townsend, J. (1979, Nov 24). Red Rock oil report rapped. *Las Vegas Review-Journal*. p. 10.

Transit Feasibility Study. (2001, Dec 1). Robert Peccia and Associates.

Vincent, B. (1967, Dec 31). Master Plan for Red Rocks. *The Nevadan*. p. 26-27.

Vincent, B. (1970, Sep 27). Desert Limestone Cave Discovered. *The Nevadan*. p. 30-31.

Vincent, B. (1973, Apr 29). Shootout at the Bar Nothing. *The Nevadan*. p. 26-27.

Vogel, E. (2011, Oct 3). Park Money Drying Up. *Las Vegas Review-Journal*. p. 1B.

Werner, L (c 1987). Growth at park's edge. *Las Vegas Review-Journal*. Newspaper clipping from UNLV Special Collections—Red Rock Collection. MS98-03. Box 1 of 1.

Whaley, S. (2003, May 20). RED ROCK LEGISLATION: Guinn signs development limit into law. *Las Vegas Review-Journal*. p. 2B.

Whaley, S. (2013, Jul 10). Settlement set in dispute about Red Rock zoning. *Las Vegas Review-Journal*. p. 2B.

Woyski, W. (1990, Sep 16). Las Vegas devouring rural land. *The Nevadan*. p. 9-10.

Wyland, S. (2011, Aug 18). Red Rock area project OK'd. *Las Vegas Review-Journal*. p. 1A.

OTHER REFERENCE SOURCES

Las Vegas-Clark County Library District Database for *Las Vegas Review-Journal*. archives.

Nevada State Museum: Las Vegas: Cahlan Research Library: Las Vegas, NV.

University of Nevada Las Vegas: Lied Library: Department of Special Collections: Las Vegas, NV.

About the Authors

THE CULTURAL RESOURCE COMMITTEE has recorded 20 rock art sites within the Red Rock Canyon National Conservation Area requiring over 10,000 volunteer hours. The documentation includes drawings for 509 panels of rock art detailing 8,700 individual motifs on 1,022 pages of archival paper. In 2010, the committee received the National Making a Difference on Public Lands Award from the Bureau of Land Management in Washington, D.C.

CAM CAMBURN has been a member of Friends of Red Rock Canyon since 1999. Cam volunteers at the Information Desk, in the Tortoise Habitat, and with the trash clean-up crew. Currently she serves on the editorial team for *The Rock* magazine and is the Historian for Friends. Cam has a Bachelor of Science Degree in Nursing from the University of Iowa, her Masters in Nursing from Wayne State University and a certificate in Gerontology from Portland State University. ANCC Certified in Gerontological Nursing, Cam has her own business as a nurse in geriatric case management.

CRYSTALAURA JACKSON is currently the Board Liaison for the Red Rock Canyon Interpretive Association. Originally from Northern California, Crystalaura has a Bachelor of Arts Degree in Public Administration with a Nonprofit Emphasis from the University of San Francisco. She has worked in nonprofit administration since 2002.

NORM KRESGE has been hiking at Red Rock Canyon since the fall of 2001 and volunteering with Friends' since 2002 working at the Information Desk in the Visitor Center, with the Tortoise Team and with Cultural Resources. Norm has co-edited the Friends newsletter and now writes a column about Red Rock Canyon hikes for *The Rock* magazine. As a volunteer for the National Park Service, he spent a year and a half working on an abandoned mines identification project. He has a Bachelor of Arts Degree in Economics and a Certificate of Advance Study for New York State Public School Administration. Norm served as a teacher and principal in Whitney Point, New York for 33 years.

LINDA MCCOLLUM has lived in Blue Diamond since 1977 and has been involved in historical projects beginning with the docent program at Spring Mountain Ranch. In 2008 she joined the Friends of Red Rock Canyon Cultural

Resources Team and is glad to be able to share all the historical information she has gathered about the area. Linda received her Bachelor of Arts Degree at the University of California, Berkeley and her Masters Degree in Theatre from Humboldt State College. While she served as Professional Staff at the University of Nevada, Las Vegas, she edited *The Flight Master Journal* and coordinated the National Stage Combat Workshop for the Society of American Flight Directors for twenty years.

SHARON SCHAAF has been an active member of Friends of Red Rock Canyon since 2009 serving with the Tortoise Habitat, Landscape and Canyon Clean-Up Teams. She is on the editorial team for *The Rock* magazine and serves as its articles editor and columnist. A Michigan native, she has a Bachelor of Arts Degree in Elementary Education from the University of Michigan, Dearborn. Sharon taught in Las Vegas for eleven years before retiring and enjoyed sharing her love for reading and writing with second and third grade students.

CHUCK WILLIAMS began volunteering at Red Rock Canyon in 1999 and has served on its board as Secretary and three terms as President. He has chaired the Cultural Resource, Red Rock Canyon Ambassador and Dedication Walkway Committees, in addition to serving on the Natural Resource and Tortoise Habitat Teams. An Indiana native, Chuck has a degree in Management from Indiana Wesleyan University. After serving in the Army, he worked for 32 years in Information Systems and Field Operations for Sprint before retiring in 1999.

DAN WRAY, a United Kingdom native, has been volunteering at Red Rock Canyon with his wife Vera since 1995, when his first day at the Visitor Center Information Desk was March 25. They were among the first Tortoise Monitors when the original Tortoise Habitat was built. Dan and Vera are longtime Cultural Resource Team members and have hiked many of the canyon trails. Dan's Bachelor and Master of Arts Degrees are from the University of Leeds. He has had a rewarding and fascinating work career in education administration in England and Scotland.

INFORMATION ABOUT JOINING
FRIENDS OF RED ROCK CANYON

We are working today... to protect tomorrow.

In 1984 a group of enthusiastic people formed Friends of Red Rock Canyon. The original mission was to provide volunteers for Red Rock Canyon National Conservation Area.

Friends of Red Rock Canyon, Las Vegas, Nevada, has since expanded our mission to provide not only critically needed volunteer assistance, but substantial financial support for education and environmental programs. During the past fiscal year Friends members donated over 21,000 volunteer hours and over $100,000 in direct support.

All members receive the following:

Monthly emailed updates and the quarterly newsmagazine, *The Rock*, to stay informed of Red Rock Canyon related news, programs and issues

A discount on purchases made at Elements, the Red Rock Canyon Interpretive Association Gift Store

Invitations to special members-only functions

Members volunteering more than 40 hours annually are also eligible for complimentary tickets to the Annual Volunteer Appreciation and Awards Banquet and recognition awards from Friends of Red Rock Canyon as well as a free Annual Red Rock Canyon Support Pass from the BLM and the satisfaction of knowing you are assisting in addressing the challenges facing Red Rock Canyon National Conservation Area.

FRIENDS OF RED ROCK CANYON

P.O. Box 97

Blue Diamond, NV 89004

702-515-5360